The Ten Keys to
Successful Change Management

The Ten Keys to Successful Change Management

John Pendlebury
Benoît Grouard
Francis Meston

JOHN WILEY & SONS

Chichester • New York • Weinheim • Brisbane • Singapore • Toronto

Original translation by Joe Laredo, Daphne Williams and Naomi Laredo for SMALL PRINT.
Subsequently updated and expanded by the authors.

English language Copyright © 1998 by John Wiley & Sons Ltd,
Baffins Lane, Chichester,
West Sussex PO19 1UD, England
National   01243 779777
International   (+44) 1243 779777

e-mail (for orders and customer service enquiries):
cs-books@wiley.co.uk
Visit our Home Page on http://www.wiley.co.uk
or http://www.wiley.com

Previously published 1995 by Dunod, Paris under the title "L'entreprise en mouvement"

Other Wiley Editorial Offices

John Wiley & Sons Inc., 605 Third Avenue,
New York, NY 10158-0012, USA

WILEY-VCH Verlag GmbH, Pappelallee 3,
D-69469 Weinheim, Germany

Jacaranda Wiley Ltd, 33 Park Road, Milton,
Queensland 4064, Australia

John Wiley & Sons (Asia) Pte Ltd, 2 Clementi Loop #02-01,
Jin Xing Distripark, Singapore 129809

John Wiley & Sons (Canada) Ltd, 22 Worcester Road,
Rexdale, Ontario M9W 1L1, Canada

Library of Congress Cataloging-in-Publication Data

Pendlebury, John.
  [Entreprise en mouvement.   English]
  The ten keys to successful change management / John Pendlebury,
Benoit Grouard, Francis Meston.
    p.   cm.
  Translated from the french.
  Includes bibliographical references and index.
  ISBN 0-471-97930-9 (hardcover)
  1. Organizational change.   2. Industrial management.
  3. Industrial organizations.   4. Strategic planning.   I. Grouard,
Benoit.   II. Meston, Francis.   III. Title.
  HD58.8.P4513   1998
  658.4'06—dc21   97–46626
                                                      CIP

British Library Cataloguing in Publication Data

A catalogue record for this book is available from the British Library

ISBN 0-471-97930-9

Typeset in 11/13pt Palatino by Footnote Graphics, Warminster, Wiltshire
Printed and bound in Great Britain by Biddles Ltd, Guildford and Kings Lynn.

This book is printed on acid-free paper responsibly manufactured from sustainable forestation,
for which at least two trees are planted for each one used for paper production.

Contents

Foreword

We have all been witness to the massive changes which have taken place in the way in which we conduct our business and social affairs. I have experienced these changes in terms of the revolution in the aero-engine business which we at Rolls-Royce have lived with over the past three decades. Equally, dramatic changes have become the way of life in practically every major field of organisational endeavour. Today, our ability to manage change itself is arguably the most important barrier to progress.

The Ten Keys to Succcessful Change Management focuses on this very point, enabling organisations to speed up and intensify their efforts to exploit new developments in the world at large.

We cannot stay put. We must change and adapt as our customers and markets change and as our competitors evolve. In my view leadership is the essence of successful change. As the authors point out, leadership begins with *Defining the Vision* as a basis for rallying the organisation around a sense of purpose.

Perhaps more difficult than creating the vision is to be selective in making the right choices and having the ability to implement them rapidly and effectively for best results in terms of value, cost and time. This is essentially what the authors describe under the headings of *Mobilising, Catalysing, Steering* and *Delivering*.

These are the programme management dimensions of change: planning, organising, resourcing and controlling. There is no organisation, no matter how effectively it implements change, which does not aspire to do still better along these dimensions.

However, without a doubt, the most taxing aspects of major organisational change are the people and culture dimensions. Change programmes of any significant scale are simply threatening to most people in most organisations. Such programmes foster anxieties of many kinds related to one's future job stability, ability to perform, compensation, position and stature, and working relationships, to name but a few. These are anxieties that the average executive is not well-prepared to manage effectively, or indeed even to understand adequately because they do not arise in the course of normal 'business-as-is' operations. I personally found the authors to be particularly helpful in laying out the keys to the effective management of the human and cultural dimensions of change. These insights are relevant not only to the management of internal organisational resources, but also to suppliers and customers to the extent than they are important participants in the change process.

At Rolls-Royce we operate in a demanding competitive environment, requiring us to react with great speed to changes in customer demand, customer expectations, and customer business economics, while striving to be at the very forefront of new developments in design, manufacturing, and materials technologies.

The business is also subjected to cyclical fluctuations in the way our ultimate customers invest in new equipment (i.e., in our products) which complicates our planning activities. At the same time our next-in-line customers, the major airframe builders on the civil aerospace side, are producing an item of which our products are only a (substantial) part. We need to respect their schedules at very high levels of conformity if we are to retain our preferred status with them, as they strive to exceed their own customers' rising expectations.

Over the last few years we have increasingly had to recognise that the only way to confront these issues is to be ready for change, radical as it may be, and to become resilient to it. All areas of our business have been affected, whether we've been making hard decisions on decreasing or increasing our capacity, investing heavily in new products and new manufacturing or testing facilities, adjusting our supplier network, or setting out our manufacturing strategy concerning for example what should be made where within our extended industrial structure.

None of these issues requires a once-and-for-all decision for resolution, more a continuum of choices which are each made at a cost in order to optimise our performance with respect to the market situation we face at the time, while not losing sight of our longer-term strategy or objectives.

This need for flexibility and continuous learning is fundamentally a question of agility, requiring openness to change at all levels of the company, including our global network of external suppliers who incidentally may often supply our competitors, or even be our competitors in another situation.

In our 'better performance faster' initiatives which constitute our major change programme, we have been making many changes in the way we conduct our affairs, at a pace which is certainly fast enough for our ability to accommodate change to become the factor which limits our possibilities.

I am only too aware of the demands these initiatives make on our people, to adapt constantly to both new technologies and new ways of working. In addition we have been living in recent times with rapid rates of growth in our business and this too places other demands on the shoulders of our people. We have always been aware that to maintain and enhance our position in the industry we must change and adapt as our competitors seek to enhance their offerings to our customers and to their own. This has required that our leaders bring to the organisation not only a vision, but also a sense of reality, unquestioned ethics, customer orientation, a strong sense of responsibility, courage, sustained initiative-taking, and strong attention to teamworking at all levels in the organisation.

In this book, by referring to the Case Study material featuring our company, the reader will gain some understanding of how we have been able to define a new vision for our company and also secure the participation of our staff in creating the organisation to implement the vision and create the offerings which we believe are most appropriate to the needs of our markets. The changes we have been making are substantial and represent an enormous effort for all of us in terms of the new thinking entailed and the magnitude of the changes we are all expected to undergo.

It is all too easy when confronted with change to react adversely, or suggest it is for some one else to undertake, or simply to go into denial, to offer passive resistance or not respond, waiting for the management fad or flavour of the month to pass one by. In this book the causes for such reactions are analysed and explained to be a natural consequence of unfamiliarity with, or lack of guidance in, the change process. People demonstrating these characteristics often have simply not been involved with change often enough or successfully enough to appreciate the new company and personal dynamics that are created by radical and successful processes of change.

There is however a group of people who have lived through change often enough and successfully enough to be experienced in applying the process. Such people have very different characteristics. They welcome change, they are stimulated by, and respond to it. Such people are not a figment of the imagination, they are real and can be found throughout our company.

It is from among this group that will come the leaders of tomorrow, those best adapted to meet the needs of the next millennium. It is to their requirements that this book is particularly addressed.

Colin Green
Director – Operations
Rolls-Royce plc

Preface

'The leading businesses of the 80s were the winners in the productivity and quality wars. Today the winners are those which are most fluid, in other words capable of anticipating change and of adapting and developing, not only continuously but more rapidly than their competitors, in order to strengthen their position still further.'

Two years after writing these words in the introduction to the first French edition of our book (Benoit Grouard and Francis Meston (1995), *L'Entreprise en Mouvement*, Nouvelle Edition, Dunod), we are even more aware of how right we were. The need for fluidity and change is evident in every sphere, whether economic, political or social. There is a general realisation that to remain static and to duplicate existing models of behaviour is neither viable nor safe in a profoundly changing environment. Moreover, there is a striking contrast between the achievements of companies like General Electric, Hewlett-Packard, Peugeot, Renault and British Airways, all of which have been on the move for several years and have a policy of constant reassessment and change, and those of companies which are only just embarking on the necessary changes (or have not even started yet).

In a changing world, the ability to achieve objectives rapidly is just as important as defining the right objectives in the first place. Without this, a business will forever be 'fighting the last war'. Besides, achieving an objective is more difficult than establishing it. The managers of every business, authority and society want their organisation to put the customer or user of services first, to react to changes in the environment, to offer near-perfect quality, and so on. But despite their best efforts, they often find it difficult to realise these objectives quickly and cost effectively, in financial and in human terms. In fact, in most of these organisations, the skills needed for managing change and increasing speed of response are poorly developed. The recent flurry of publications and conferences on re-engineering, exploiting new technologies and increasing employee accountability are of little use. While often they help in defining relevant and worthwhile objectives, they give no advice as to how to achieve them.

The aim of this book—and perhaps a reason for its success in the earlier French and Spanish editions—is to establish a practical method for change management and business transformation; in other words, a set of tools and guidelines drawing on a wealth of actual case histories. We shall deal with the process of change itself, i.e., how to:

- draw up a process for change;
- direct and guide such a process;
- win the support and participation of the whole workforce;
- combine change with normal activities;
- ensure the durability of the changes introduced;
- speed up the process of change and minimise its financial and human cost;
- maintain continuous improvement afterwards.

We shall discuss the theoretical background as well as giving practical advice on managing change and transforming a business, since effective management requires a command of both underlying theory and practice. The former provides the general framework for understanding and assessing any given situation, while the latter enables the changes to be put into effect on the ground.

Throughout, we shall focus primarily on the needs of the individual, since people are a business's most precious asset—all the more so now that the Taylorian model is being re-evaluated and individual initiative is at a premium. Businesses not only need their employees to be skilled and experienced; they also need them to be motivated, involved and proactive. This is what underpins our method, which seeks to create the right conditions for employee development and contribution to business success.

The main changes for this English language edition are revised chapters dealing with delivering change and on training and coaching. The chapters have been completely rewritten and expanded to incorporate the lessons of our own recent experience as well as the latest findings of leading theoreticians on these subjects. We have also included new case study material drawn from major corporations with whose change programmes we are familiar. We have used these examples to illustrate aspects of our method, although they are not all using the method *per se*. Together we believe they make an important contribution to the reader's appreciation of our subject.

Throughout this book we shall use the term 'business' to mean any organisation, whether it is a private company, public body, partnership, cooperative or whatever. We are aware that there are differences between these different types of organisation, but we suggest that our observations are applicable to all of them, provided that allowance is made in certain specific cases for differences such as managerial titles and functions. This means that we can use the term 'organisation' to refer to the way in which all these 'businesses' are organised.

THE TEN KEYS TO SUCCESSFUL CHANGE MANAGEMENT

Key 1: *Defining the vision*: establishing the overall objective of change and outlining the way in which it will be implemented.

Key 2: *Mobilising*: creating a dynamic for change among employees, evaluating the issues raised by the vision and specifying the main directions for improvement as a consequence.

Key 3: *Catalysing*: defining the project structure and how it will work in supporting, facilitating and accelerating change.

Key 4: *Steering*: defining and carrying out the set of actions which will guide the process of change and keep it on course.

Key 5: *Delivering*: implementing the changes by realising the vision in terms of the day-to-day operation of the business, in other words altering structures, methods, attitudes and culture in order to produce the anticipated quantitative and qualitative results.

Key 6: *Obtaining participation*: ensuring that all employees affected by change participate, in order both to enhance the vision and to ease its implementation.

Key 7: *Handling the emotional dimension*: overcoming resistance and mental blockages, so that change can be delivered.

Key 8: *Handling the power issues*: redirecting power relations to bring them into line with the vision so that they contribute positively to the process of change.

Key 9: *Training and coaching*: providing training in both technical and interpersonal skills, to help employees maximise their contribution to the process of change and subsequently incorporate the vision into their everyday working life.

Key 10: *Communicating actively*: initiating and coordinating a communication explosion, to encourage universal participation and involvement and hence promote change.

Chapter 1

Business and Change

THE NEED FOR CHANGE

Businesses are increasingly concerned with change and, more and more, change is all-pervasive. There is constant talk of restructuring, reorganisation, reorientation and re-engineering, of implementing new technologies and new distribution methods, of mergers and acquisitions and of changing ways of thinking. What was once the exception is now the rule. No business can escape the need for change as it evolves in the context of a more rapidly changing environment. It can either instigate or submit to change, but one way or the other it must change.

The evolution, or rather the revolution, of the business environment is beyond the control of individual business entities. Whole sectors such as automobile manufacturing and information technology are being compelled to undergo constant changes, with new products, new technologies and new organisations being needed, even though many players might prefer to see a slowing down of the rate of change, since the goal no longer seems clear. Technologies quickly become obsolete, products have shorter and shorter shelf-lives and competition leads to more and more innovation. Businesses in the private sector are not the only victims; public bodies, partnerships and cooperatives, for example, are equally affected by change. The rate and frequency of change may be different, as may the forces that drive it, but change they must. A monopoly situation is no longer a guarantee of stability. Change is universal and all-embracing.

Change means no longer being the same, but being in a state of evolution or flux. Change encompasses a wide variety of phenomena, differing in both degree and extent. Some changes constitute complete upheavals, where the entire business is profoundly transformed. This is what happens when change takes the form of significant alterations to strategy, structures, systems, human resources, and business culture.

In other cases change may be profound but limited to one part of the business. This is what happened in the seventies, for example, when Saab revolutionised its production methods by changing over from production lines to team working and was soon imitated by other car manufacturers. At the other extreme are changes of limited degree and extent such as adjustments to procedures or the re-design of a process and introduction of IT. These are widely differing phenomena, but all these types of change can be managed by applying the same fundamental techniques.

The status of change itself has changed. Once regarded as quite foreign or incidental to business organisation, it was simply a means of getting from the state the business was in to the state it wanted to be in. It was a necessary evil, a transitional stage to be kept as short as possible. Nowadays, change is an integral part of business life, of the way businesses function. The pursuit of stability has been superseded by the pursuit of fluidity.

We all know that nothing is fixed, that everything is soon overtaken. New technologies are quickly replaced, new organisations modified. The shelf-life of a product or system varies between a few months and several years, but from the very beginning it is recognised as being temporary and subject to change. This situation presents many problems. The feeling of being continuously in an interim stage can easily lead to dissatisfaction and to lower standards of skill, quality and effectiveness. Any imperfection or dysfunction is more readily accepted if the situation it derives from is regarded as temporary.

Change, then, becomes the perfect alibi for a failure to give total commitment to the current state of affairs. This is a common phenomenon among businesses which change their systems every time there is a change in fashion. Never mind the weaknesses of the current system; the latest restructuring plan will change the ground-rules and nullify any efforts which might have been made to improve the way things are currently organised. Similarly, there is a danger that technical staff will become less competent, since to achieve full competence in this new world requires a considerable amount of effort over a shorter space of time. The pressure to acquire knowledge quickly is offset by the realisation that everything will soon have to be relearned in order to keep up with technological developments. Nothing is acquired for good. Everything is continually called into question.

At the same time businesses aim for ever-higher levels of performance in all areas: quality of products and services, frequency of new product launches, speed of response to customer demand, productivity, and so on. Awareness of an enhanced need for change varies from business to business and from individual to individual. Change is still often regarded as an inferior condition, merely a means of attaining stability. In most businesses frequent change is generally considered to be the result of managerial error, a reflection of indecision and lack of control over external forces (which is sometimes the case). It is still rare to find businesses like 3M which have successfully institutionalised change.

Change is not a 'natural' condition in business. Businesses are designed to work, not to change. Their *raison d'être* is to produce, to sell, to satisfy their customers and to reward their shareholders. Even today, working and change are not synonymous. On the contrary, businesses are busy fighting against internal disorder and dis-organisation, while change presupposes disorder, imbalance and instability. Businesses are equipped to act, not to change. Existing systems are geared towards making the business work as it is by laying down procedures, defining tasks and roles, imposing analysis and planning systems. Everything conspires to reinforce the *status quo*.

Businesses which have most fully perfected their organisation and systems generally have the greatest difficulty in changing. Their very perfection makes them rigid. Everything is organised, ordered, predicted and controlled, but they are almost unable to react or adapt to unexpected external stimuli. They can easily make any adjustments which may be necessary to carry out their activities, but cannot implement profound evolutionary or revolutionary changes. While modifications to budgetary procedures, to the sales and marketing set-up or to information systems might be comfortably assimilated, the introduction of a new concept of customer relations or new channels of communication, both of which require profound changes at all levels, including new ways of thinking and acting, will be much more difficult. Powerful companies like General Motors, IBM, Philips and Air France are experiencing, or have already experienced, great difficulty in adapting to a new environment. Finding themselves victims of what in the past made them successful and enabled them to achieve high levels of performance, they are all making great efforts to reintroduce an element of fluidity which will allow them to make vital changes to their culture, management systems, structure and way of operating. British Airways, who began taking action almost ten years ago, have spent tens of millions of pounds on changing their *modus operandi* at every level of the business. The training and con-sciousness-raising campaign introduced by management has affected every single employee.

Whatever form it takes, change necessitates destabilisation of the existing state. The more stable this is, the more difficult it will be to effect change. Being perfectly adapted to a given environment can suddenly become a major handicap when the environment changes. The business will have mustered all its resources to make the most of a situation and, when the situation changes, it will have difficulty in reacting. In today's more and more rapidly shifting environment the capacity to evolve quickly is a much more valuable asset than perfect organisation. The growing importance of speed in achieving com-petitive advantage is also relevant to change. And since the ability to change quickly is now essential to business survival, change needs to become a *natural* function of business.

Change can be voluntary or involuntary. No business can avoid the need to change, but its managers can either force themselves or be forced to undergo it. This is not simply a play on words. It involves a considerable difference in the way change is managed, voluntary change being much more comfortable and often more efficient. The difference between the two types of change depends essentially upon when the decision to adopt change is taken. Voluntary change is embarked upon while the business is still performing well and there is no apparent need for reorganisation: market share and profitability are on target, customer satisfaction is high, systems are operating satisfactorily, and the technology in use is working efficiently. The decision to change is made either to improve the present situation or to anticipate a possible deterioration in that situation. We shall be looking at the forces that drive change in the next chapter, but whatever these may be, the managers of the business will have plenty of room for manoeuvre in implementing the process of change. They will not be hemmed in by severe constraints on their freedom of action which may force them to rush into dramatic courses of action like halting production or making large-scale redundancies. These latter actions are the characteristics of involuntary change, change which has been adopted too late and has therefore become a prerequisite for the survival of the business or of whichever part of it is affected.

There are several possible causes of delay in implementing change, one of the most common being inaccurate forecasting, or indeed lack of foresight, on the part of management. They do not believe their business is threatened and think that only minor adjustments are needed, whereas in fact significant changes are necessary. American automobile manufacturers, who believed themselves to be immune to foreign, particularly Japanese, competition are a good example of organisations making such an error of judgement. When they realised their mistake in the 1980s, they were forced to make sudden and far-reaching changes under difficult circumstances and with dramatic social consequences. But despite this drastic reaction, they have found it difficult to regain their former level of performance.

Procrastination is another common cause of involuntary change. Managers are aware of the need for change, but fail to take the necessary actions, either because they are reluctant to run the risks associated with any kind of change, or because they refuse to accept the consequences, even though they know them to be inevitable, such as large-scale redundancies or a temporary drop in margins or profitability.

The third factor which leads to involuntary change is the inability to put ideas into practice. In this case management is aware that the business needs to evolve and has even decided to set changes in motion, but although the decision has been made, nothing actually changes. The action taken fails to achieve the intended results, and the required changes simply do not take effect. So the business fails to change at a time when circumstances would have allowed it to do so voluntarily, and ends up having to do so in conditions which have by now become problematic. This is probably the most widespread cause of involuntary change and reflects the fact that many businesses still find change an 'unnatural' attitude to adopt. While they have learned how to function effectively and how to predict developments in their environment, they are not yet able to change quickly.

To change successfully demands a particular set of skills which are not often found in today's businesses. Change is a management issue, just like customer relations, financial control, the use of technology and the acquisition of skills. As businesses become aware of the increasing importance of controlling change, they are beginning to set up 'development groups' or 'innovation units' or 'transition teams'. When marketing became essential to their success, they set up new marketing departments. When image and identity became important, PR specialists appeared, just as 'quality directors' were introduced when quality became paramount. Since managers had always been concerned with marketing, image-building and quality, the creation of special departments was merely a way of expressing the increasing importance of these factors and the need for improving skills and concentrating effort on them. It is the same with change. Businesses have always been involved with it and have always had to make profound changes, but it is the acceleration in the rate of change and its leading role in business success which are now forcing businesses into devoting significant resources to it and into developing the necessary skills for managing change.

THE DRIVING FORCES FOR CHANGE

Change affects all businesses but, just as it manifests itself in various ways, there are very diverse motives for bringing it about. Change is the result of a decision-making process which may be either formal or informal, implicit or explicit, and which integrates the need to adapt with internal imperatives. Because every business has different needs and imperatives, every instance of change is unique. Nevertheless, the motivating factors can be seen to have a number of common characteristics, and the forces for change can be divided into two categories: external and internal.

- *External forces* for change are factors arising outside the entity which is to be changed. This generally means elements of the business environment such as customers, competitors, technological innovations or developments in lifestyle, although elements which are internal to the business but external to the part of the business affected can also engender a similar effect. The company post room, for example, might need to be reorganised because it no longer meets the needs of other parts of the business (its internal customers) in terms of speed and reliability. The force for change is therefore external to the post room, but internal to the business as a whole.

- *Internal forces* for change, on the other hand, come into play where changes are initiated by the business itself, essentially as a result of a desire to evolve and a new management vision.

External forces are by far the more common. We said earlier that businesses are designed to work and not to change. The force for change is therefore rarely to be found within the business itself. It is usually the external environment which generates the driving forces for change. Developments in its overall frame of reference oblige the business to change in order to survive or to achieve its objectives. It often happens, for example, that changes in customer requirements force a business to rethink its structure, systems and culture in order to focus exclusively on customer satisfaction, whereas previously it had given precedence to its own internal procedures and technical requirements. Such changes are essential if the business is to retain its market share and achieve satisfactory performance levels. The failure to change would, in time, lead to its extinction, or at least to a considerable weakening of its position. Circumstances therefore impose change on businesses, regardless of all the difficulties, traumas and doubts which change brings.

The sensitivity of a business to changes in its environment depends on its position in the marketplace. If it enjoys a dominant or even monopolistic position, it will be less susceptible than others to external environmental factors. It will in fact attempt to influence its environment in order to maintain or reinforce its position. Vast businesses like Microsoft, Intel, Air Liquide and Coca-Cola are examples of such leaders in their markets. Nowadays, though, such dominance is more difficult to sustain and is increasingly vulnerable. The advent of the global economy has increased competition. All markets are world markets and the key players are active in all areas. Unless it has a monopoly, every business is threatened. Even dominant businesses must constantly beware of being overtaken by more mobile competitors which attempt to move the goalposts, as

Canon succeeded in doing in the copier market to the detriment of Xerox or as the Japanese motorcycle manufacturers did at the expense of companies like Harley Davidson, Triumph and Norton.

Change never has a single cause. Change is always driven to varying degrees by a number of external and internal factors. In some cases there may be one predominant driving force, such as competition, technology or a management vision. But in other cases there is a combination of several equally strong forces. The principal forces for change are now described in turn.

External Forces

The market (i.e. actual and potential customers, be they individuals, companies or public bodies) has a powerful influence on businesses. They must respond to the needs and expectations of the market or find their customers turning away from them (unless they have a monopoly or something unique to offer, which in any case will not last long). Changes in the marketplace, whether they affect the products or services on offer, their price or their means of distribution, oblige businesses to adapt. The market for some products and service contracts may even disappear altogether (e.g., black and white televisions, typewriters, nuclear power station equipment), while the market for others expands strongly (e.g., pharmaceuticals, compact discs, computers).

Such changes in demand mean profound changes in businesses. Significant developments take place even in mature and stable markets. These have more to do with particular characteristics of products or services, especially their quality (including their reliability and durability). Consumers are becoming increasingly demanding and expect the products they buy to be of higher and higher quality, which can only be achieved through significant changes in the businesses that produce them. Car buyers no longer expect their vehicles to break down, and purchasers of electronic components insist on absolute reliability. These developments can also affect the way products and services are made available. The increasing variety of consumer demand has led to greater diversity in distribution methods as well as levels of service and warranty cover. The introduction of revolutionary new industrial management techniques such as just in time (JIT) and Kanban has meant that businesses are rethinking or have rethought their entire manufacturing and logistics processes. Market development is clearly one of the major causes of change.

Competitive action is another factor which frequently causes businesses to change. The actions of competitors can challenge their position. The launch of a new product, a change of distributor, an improvement in production methods, the introduction of new technology or a new price structure can cause other businesses to react if they think that these changes will strengthen their competitors' position and consequently weaken their own. Businesses respond to perceived threats, real or imaginary. Instant reaction is sometimes essential to parry the attack. There are no absolute criteria of good performance of products or quality: everything is relative. The action of one competitor may alter the benchmark so that what was considered good is now only mediocre. Businesses are always vulnerable to such threats and can try to anticipate them by continually striving to improve their position and/or react as quickly as possible whenever they appear. Japanese car manufacturers have forced their European and American counterparts to reduce the time they take to develop new models. Five to seven years, which used to be the norm, is no longer acceptable. With the Japanese bringing out a new model within three or even two years, manufacturers in the West have had to embark on major change processes to attain what has become the new industry standard.

Technological innovation is an increasingly significant force for change (and is of course an internal force in the case of the business which introduces it). Indeed, both the rate and the number of innovations are constantly increasing. They may not always be as significant as the invention of the steam engine or electricity or the transistor, but innovation makes possible new ways of making things and of making them work which simply did not exist before. Innovation leads to improvements which render existing products and methods obsolete. Innovations both large and small are compelling businesses to change.

These changes may affect a business's core activity, as in the case of instrument manufacturers who have had to switch from mechanics to electronics, or a business's procedures, or even its strategy. Advances in robotics have led to constant retooling and updating of production methods in many industries, which in turn have meant significant changes in organisation and working practices. Similarly, office work has been revolutionised by developments in personal computing.

Legislative and regulatory developments can also cause businesses to introduce changes, either by affecting the business environment or by altering the constraints imposed on business. In the former case, legislation and regulation have an impact on the market (for example by creating or removing tax advantages for consumers) and/or on the competitive environment (as for example with the creation of the European Common Market, which made it easier for other European businesses to access neighbouring markets, or through the adjustment of import quotas on textile products). In the latter case, new regulations impinge directly on businesses by forcing them to comply with new rules or react to the annulment of existing rules. European legislation requiring industry to use recyclable packaging is one example. Another is the introduction by various governments of a maximum working week. The increase in lobbying activity by business is an indication of the potential impact of this sort of legislation.

A change of shareholders is a less common force for change, but one which can nevertheless result in radical changes when, for example, a business and its management are set new objectives, especially financial targets. The demand for greater profitability usually causes considerable disruption. The many takeover bids of the eighties showed just how far-reaching the effects of a change of shareholders can be. A different kind of transformation can occur when a change of shareholders is accompanied by merger with another business or integration into a new group of businesses.

Businesses are also subject to changes in social behaviour, lifestyle and attitudes. They cannot afford to be out of step with the society of which they are part, but must evolve along with it. Here we are dealing with gradual, yet sweeping and profound changes. After all, employees are also people, consumers and individuals in their own right, and businesses have had to assimilate a new value structure which prizes autonomy, independence and personal development, in order to avoid the internal conflicts and recruitment problems which could afflict what are perceived as the more old-fashioned businesses. It is social changes which are largely responsible for breaking down formal hierarchical structures and for increasing individual responsibility.

Internal Forces

Business development and growth can cause significant change. A rise in productivity creates new problems which cannot be solved effectively simply by duplicating existing methods. An increase in output above a certain level generally necessitates a rethink of production methods and internal logistics as well as quality control procedures and supply policy. A change of outlets or distributors entails the reorganisation of sales and marketing. Winning new customers or breaking into new market areas also means making big changes. In all these situations, communications need rethinking. What might have worked when the business had a hundred employees no longer works when it has a thousand. Similarly, what were effective solutions when it had a thousand customers are no longer adequate now that it supplies ten thousand. Growth therefore forces businesses to rethink and reorganise everything, not just to streamline what already exists.

Management vision is one of the major driving forces for change in that it often sparks off similar changes in other businesses. In attempting to change the existing situation to the advantage of their own business, managers inevitably alter the competitive stakes. They might decide they need to launch new products, improve quality, acquire new skills or perhaps move away from certain activities. So the business is forced into changing of its own accord by the sheer willpower of managers who want to make it more productive. This was what happened with Danone, for example, which completely switched its operations from packaging to agricultural foodstuffs when research conducted by its President, Antoine Riboud, revealed greater opportunities for growth in that sector. In some businesses, like General Electric and Motorola, this turns into a whole culture of change—constant reassessment and transformation in a continuous drive to increase the strength of the business.

Change has no fixed pattern, its course being determined by the characteristics of each business. Businesses operating in the same sector can react differently to the same external forces. Even when their reactions are similar, the results can be very different. The various forces for change must therefore be studied very carefully if we are to understand what has made a business change or what ought to make it change. The causes we have just described determine the directions our investigations will take.

THE DIFFERENT TYPES OF CHANGE

Just as there are various forces driving change, so there are widely different types of change. In some cases change can be quite limited and brief, in others extensive and prolonged, and in others still, quick and violent. It can be introduced by consensus or imposed by management. For example, if the staff in the legal department of a business decide on a new way of allocating their tasks that makes better use of their computer equipment, so that they can cope with an increase in the number of files they have to deal with, and they achieve it over a period of six months, that constitutes a change. If management decides to introduce flexitime, that is also a change, as is a merger of two businesses which takes several years to accomplish. The different types of change can be categorised in terms of three main variables:

1. depth of change
2. speed of change
3. how change is implemented.

These three variables, which are of course closely interrelated, are discussed in more detail below.

Depth of Change

Depth of change is the degree to which it affects the nature of the business which may be altered profoundly or superficially, or to an infinite variety of degrees in between.

Superficial changes, which play an essential role in business, must never be regarded as secondary changes or changes of lesser importance. These changes (which might affect any aspect of the business—strategy, structure, culture, management style, etc.— although they more usually concern systems) are the perfect solution for businesses which need to develop continuously in order to respond to a fluid environment. In Japan these constant small changes are called 'kaisen'.

The increasing globalisation of markets exposes businesses to more and more frequent competitive attack from every quarter. A business which is not a clear leader in its market must continually respond to its competitors' assaults by developing its products, improving its logistics, reducing delivery times or revising prices. These changes, which must be made as quickly as possible, are essential to its survival, and yet they are only superficial (even though achieving them may require great effort). It might, for example, involve reducing delivery times to distributors from 72 hours to 48 hours, or visiting customers every month instead of every two months, or launching a new product within four months instead of six. Again, it is the Japanese who are past masters at gaining competitive advantage by the accumulation of small changes. Instead of looking for *the* solution, they constantly improve their strategies, their systems and the quality of their products and services, often by organising a campaign around each area in turn.

One of the characteristics of superficial changes is that the decision to implement them is usually easily taken, because the consequences are not serious and the costs not high if they fail. There may in fact be so many superficial changes that collectively they end up making a profound change to the business. They are an essential weapon in business strategy.

At the other extreme are the profound changes—those which completely transform the nature of a business. These are also necessary, but must not happen too often because they are so costly. Not only can they require direct investment (in new machinery, new premises, the acquisition of patents or companies, etc.), but they also demand the expenditure of vast amounts of energy. This sort of change becomes necessary when 'superficial' changes prove inadequate or when the competitive stakes need to be raised. 'Profound' changes therefore affect mainly the strategy, organisational structure and culture of a business. In more recent years, large groups like IBM, Schneider and Siemens have completely revised their organisational structures in order to improve efficiency. Companies like British Airways and Usinor have totally changed their business culture, among other reasons, to become market-led and more focused on external competition. Profound changes always come as a big shock to employees, whether positive or negative. Unlike those of superficial changes, their consequences have a deep and lasting impact. They generate high expectations when they are introduced and, if successful, have positive effects which are often felt outside the area where the changes actually take place. But if they fail, they frequently have truly devastating results.

The depth of change varies between these two extremes and, depending on the position of the business, the level at which it takes place can be a matter of choice or accident. If a business is in difficulty, it will often be obliged to make profound changes, even though it may not wish to. Similarly, some of the forces for change, such as technological innovation, necessitate profound reactions.

Speed of Change

Speed of change is a measure of the combination of depth and duration of change. It is more significant than just duration, which has little meaning in isolation and has to be related to the depth of change and the adaptability of the business in question. How can one compare a change which took a month with one which required a year? Nevertheless, all things being equal, any change should take as little time as possible, for two main reasons:

- First, because of the need to allocate business resources during the change process to tasks other than those they were originally intended for. The purpose of a sales manager is to sell as many products at the highest profit for as long as possible, not to participate in introducing a new style of customer relations. Similarly, a production engineer's job is supposed to be to meet production targets while ensuring low costs and high quality, rather than to alter his production plant to make it more flexible. But these incidental tasks are necessary for the business, even though they may, at least temporarily, affect its performance by reducing quality or by increasing costs or delivery times. This is why it is important for change to take as short a time as possible.
- Second, on account of the capacity of individuals to become involved in the change process. It is noticeable that they become decreasingly motivated and increasingly sceptical when change takes too long. If it goes on for more than a year or eighteen months, the process simply runs out of steam and it becomes unlikely that the changes will be fully implemented. We shall describe this effect in more detail later in the book.

Speed of change is a measure of the amount of time a business needs to make a given change and is a factor of increasing importance given the constant requirement to reassess a business's competitive position. Changing is not enough; it must be done quickly in order to maintain or improve the position. Speed of reaction and implementation have become crucial to businesses, which must continually adapt, innovate and counter-attack, not just in one area, but in all areas: range of products and services, distribution networks, market position, logistics, R&D, production, accounting, human resources, training and so on. The determining factor in business survival is the ability to make many different types of change simultaneously as well as rapidly. Being under constantly increasing pressure, businesses are forced to tackle several changes at once, whereas previously they would have taken them on one at a time. The contrast in behaviour between businesses which face intense competition and those which do not, particularly if they enjoy a monopoly position, shows clearly the extent to which the speed of change is governed by environmental factors. While the former give the impression of being in a state of perpetual flux and unable to find their balance, the latter present an image of calm and stability.

Speed of change varies considerably, not only from one business to another, but also within the same business, according to the changes which need to be made. It is at its greatest when change is dictated by circumstances, when managers are aware of the need for it and when the business itself is well adapted to it. If all these conditions are met, even profound changes can be made in a very short space of time. The war between Honda and Yamaha in the eighties is a well-known example of such a situation, as well as of the crucial importance of the ability to change quickly in order to maintain or even strengthen a business's position. Honda was able to resist aggression from Yamaha, which sought to gain the lead in the motorcycle market, because of its ability to redirect resources towards motorcycle design and manufacture in the space of a few months, at a time when the business was busy expanding its automobile interests, and also because of its ability to completely alter its research methods, launch procedure and production processes in order to bring out more than a hundred new models in less than two years. Thus Honda completely frustrated Yamaha's ambitions and strengthened its own position in the process.

The more accustomed a business is to changing, the quicker it becomes at doing so. If change is experienced only occasionally and is regarded as a major ordeal, it will take a great deal of time to over-come resistance and motivate people to support the effort and implement the necessary changes. If, on the other hand, every employee has already assimilated the experience of change by having been through similar processes before, the business will be able to react quickly and change rapidly. Market leaders like Benetton, L'Oréal and Sony, which have had to face extremely fluid and competitive business environments for several years, now have a highly developed aptitude for continuous and rapid change. It is this capacity which keeps them out in front by allowing them constantly to improve their position and to respond immediately and effectively to competitive attacks. We can see the same thing happening now with change as happened in the sixties and seventies with costs. The results of that experience (i.e. the 'learning curve') had a significant effect on future business strategy. The experience of change seems to be having a similar effect in the late nineties, in that it appears to lead to quicker and less costly changes, just as increases in volume led to lower unit costs. Detailed study should enable us to evaluate more precisely the impact of this experience of change. Businesses which are able to make constant changes both quickly and effectively will greatly strengthen their competitive position relative to less mobile and flexible businesses.

In most cases, change is still carried out slowly. It may only appear that way in retrospect ('we could have done it more quickly') or it may seem like it at the time and cause frustration among employees who can see the need for action and change. This 'slowness' can inadvertently be introduced at various stages: when the need for change is first realised, when the decision to change is taken, or during the process of change itself. Or it could happen at any two stages, or even at all three. Depending on the type of change to be made, the length of time between realisation and accomplishment can be as much as several years.

How Change is Implemented

The way in which change is instigated can vary greatly: it may be forcibly imposed or it may be the result of a total consensus. Since, as we have seen, change is 'unnatural', it is almost always imposed to a greater or lesser extent, even today. Nevertheless, in some cases, a manager wanting to make changes will try to convince those concerned of the validity of the idea and win their support, even though it means abandoning the idea if he fails. In other cases, however, change is instigated without any prior consultation. Since 'imposed' change results from management authority, it generally takes place in businesses with a strong hierarchy, where authority is accepted. But it also happens in businesses which are more oriented towards dialogue when the urgency of a situation forces them to act quickly or a new manager takes over and wants to break with tradition.

Change can also be imposed in situations where there are opposing interests and common ground cannot be found, as for example when a business effects a takeover against the wishes of the company it is acquiring. The Schneider Group, for example, imposed change on Télémécanique by bringing off a takeover despite strong opposition from Télémécanique's management and staff, who launched an aggressive press campaign in an attempt to preserve their independence. In the UK a similar situation occurred with the takeover of Trust House Forte by Granada. Change can also be said to be imposed in many cases where it leads to a reduction in staff or a worsening of working conditions. Nevertheless, it is extremely unusual for the entire change process to be imposed, since its success actually depends on the cooperation of those involved. In the case of the Schneider Group, change could not be considered effective unless the acquisition led to improved performance from the new group, which presupposes that the workforce at least partially supported and collaborated in the process of change. So even when change is 'imposed', it must subsequently achieve a certain level of consensus in order to be successful, and one of the principal objectives of managers, as soon as they instigate change, should be to obtain consensus, at least among a critical sub-group of managers.

Change 'by consensus', on the other hand, is characterised from the outset by the complete support of all concerned. Although it can be difficult to obtain such support, the aim is to improve the chances of success by a high initial level of motivation and participation. The effort needed to achieve consensus and the compromises which have to be made are justified by the increased likelihood of success and of the process going smoothly. Change 'by consensus' suits the culture of businesses in which motivation takes precedence over authoritarianism. It is also well-suited to certain types of innovation, such as those relating to working hours or pay, which require employees' strong support from the start if serious conflicts are to be avoided. Trades unions are therefore often an important party to the way changes are implemented.

The choice between the different types of change, just like change itself, can be voluntary or involuntary. It is no good choosing to start

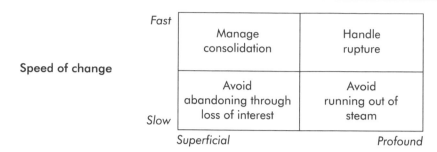

Figure 1.1   Key Actions in the Speed—Depth Dimensions

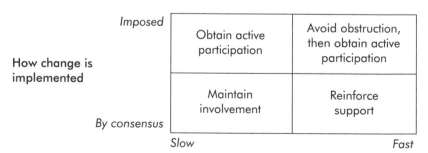

Figure 1.2   Key Actions in the Change Style—Depth Dimensions

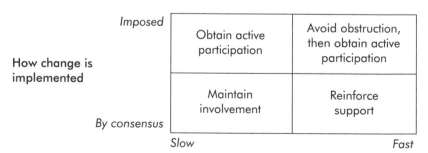

Figure 1.3   Key Actions in the Change Style—Speed Dimensions

with a series of superficial changes with a consensual style if either the business environment or the business itself is unsuited to it. Good planning makes it easier to proceed by means of many small changes. Firm control of the environment creates more time and enables the business to choose the best moment and the optimum speed for the changes it wants to make. If the business is highly flexible, it will be able to progress more rapidly and more frequently, without jeopardising consensus. Managers are rarely completely at liberty to choose what type of change to initiate, since the choice depends partly on their own intentions and partly on opportunities and constraints which exist both inside and outside the business.

Figures 1.1 to 1.3 summarise the various factors affecting change in the various different circumstances likely to be encountered. They serve to provide clarity, but perhaps at the risk of over-simplification.

Chapter 2

The Domain of Change

In the previous chapter we built the case for change, discussed the variety of motives that can generate the need and described the different forms change can take. Before setting out our recommended approach to this kind of business transformation, we would like to spend a little time describing the object to which it is applied: the business itself. The intention is not to give a detailed description of the complexity of businesses, but to show how the business environment can influence the management of change by creating special opportunities and constraints.

THE COMPLEXITY OF BUSINESSES AND CHANGE

Few would deny that the modern business is a complex entity. At first sight it might appear to be quite simple, since any business is the product of three easily identified and clearly defined elements: human resources, tangible assets (buildings, machinery, land, etc.) and negotiable assets (patents, trade marks, brand names, expertise, etc.). However, the constituents of these elements and the relationships and interactions between them are sufficiently diverse to create a highly complex whole. The efficiency of a business depends on the ability of its managers to make every constituent element function properly and in accordance with the objectives of that business. In other words, it is a matter of managing diversity and handling relationships and interactions within the business as effectively as possible.

'Managing diversity' can be defined as achieving a satisfactory balance between consistency and inconsistency and between uniformity and disparity. Any business must possess these four characteristics, although in varying proportions, if it is to function properly.

Consistency

Consistency is what makes all the resources of the business work together to achieve the same objectives and ensures that correct decisions are reached on major issues (growth, profitability, capitalisation, long- and short-term objectives and so on). It is in pursuit of consistency, for example, that before investing in new machinery a business will check whether it is in line with overall policy, can be operated easily by production personnel and meets the needs of the salesforce. The aim of consistency is to ensure that business activities do not contradict one another and serve the agreed objectives.

Ambiguity

In spite of its negative connotations, ambiguity is equally necessary for a business to be effective, in so far as it creates imbalance, which in turn encourages the business to change and develop. Ambiguity creates unstable situations and sometimes conflicts which have to be resolved, and this often stimulates the business to rethink. As long as it is kept within acceptable limits, ambiguity helps to prevent the business from stagnating. There can be such conditions in any part of a business, but how they are perceived will depend on the point of view from which the situation is analysed. The desire to minimise costs and at the same time improve quality, or managing a contract from head office when the business is organised into regional divisions, are two examples of inconsistencies which can have a positive long-term effect on a business. The wish to tackle costs and quality simultaneously totally unbalances the *status quo* and forces a complete operational reassessment, which frequently results, as experience shows, in lower costs and higher quality. The apparent ambiguity disappears as the problem is redefined and resolved. In a similar way taking over direct management of a contract in a decentralised business can reintroduce an element of flexibility *vis-à-vis* the customer and lead to an improvement in the way the business operates.

Uniformity

Uniformity facilitates communication and consequently reduces re-action time. It means that the information disseminated can be easily understood. As there is only one language and signals are easily interpreted, no one is surprised by decisions or actions taken. Conformity takes precedence over individuality, so that the cost of control can be kept to a minimum. Uniformity tends to increase consistency by reducing the discrepancies which can develop between different divisions, functions, offices and levels of management. It can manifest itself in the way people behave, the way they think or function, the way they resolve conflicts, even in the way they dress. Multinational businesses like IBM, Procter & Gamble and Siemens have developed uniformity to an exceptional degree.

Disparity

Disparity is one of the most precious of business assets. A business is made up of initially disparate elements, which it then attempts to render more or less uniform. But since all individuals are different, as are skills, machines and geographical locations, a business can unleash vital forces by using these disparate elements effectively. This can create an explosion of ideas and initiatives for exploiting opportunities, solving problems and improving the state of the business. The pooling of different types of expertise, experience and thinking can produce results which would not have been achieved by each of them in isolation. Not only can disparity have a very positive impact on the performance of a business, it is often essential for the business to adapt to new environments. Sales techniques are not the same in London or Milan as they are in New York or Toronto; human resources are managed in a different way in the UK, Germany, the United States and Japan. In the interest of efficiency, differences of this kind must be allowed for and approaches developed specifically in response to them.

Managing Diversity

One of the key issues in the change process will be, therefore, how to make the best use of the opportunities which the diverse elements comprising the business offer in terms of finding and implementing solutions to the problems that are encountered. This means finding the best balance between the four characteristics of diversity in order to enhance, facilitate and accelerate the process of change. Our method takes account of this issue by providing for the active participation of all employees in a process which allows them to help to make decisions and to take action.

By managing the relationships and interactions we shall be able to coordinate the activities of the various parts of the business. Each part of the business relates to all others and its existence can only be justified in terms of those relationships. Because they are dependent on each other in the way that they communicate and function, close links and interactions develop between them. An action which affects one element or one component (e.g. an individual, a machine or a brand), will also affect others, which will in turn react on other elements, often including the element originally affected. So there is not simply a one-dimensional, circumscribed cause-and-effect re-lationship, but a much more complex phenomenon involving a succession of causes and effects, side-effects and sometimes extensive repercussions, which therefore cannot be fully predicted or perfectly controlled. An individual might act on or be acted upon by another individual or by a machine, the machine by the skill brought to bear on it, an operating agreement by yet another individual, and so on. It is therefore necessary to have a global view of a business in order to transform it, which is why we suggest that 'globality', in which we view the business as a an interconnected set of elements or 'system', should be one of the fundamental principles.

The growing recognition that it is impossible to control all the complexities of a business and the realisation that this is nevertheless a source of opportunity are having a major influence on business management and business transformation. The traditional pyramid model, in which almost all movement is up and down, is tending to give way to less centralised, more interactive models. At the same time, the role of management is changing profoundly. It is no longer a matter of managing a business, but much more of leading it; that is, directing it and guiding it. The effects of these developments are shown clearly by writers such as Warren Bennis and Bert Nanus who, in their book *Leaders: Strategies for Taking Charge*, define the gulf that exists between managers and leaders: 'Managers do things right, leaders do the right things.' The control function is undergoing a similarly radical transformation. Increasing autonomy and account-ability means that many elements of a business are no longer so centrally controlled, while others, such as skills, are being monitored more and more closely. So the whole perception of businesses and what is important to them is being transformed.

Successful change in this new world is not easy. Those in charge may only partially understand and control their existing business, let alone change and development, which throw the interrelated elements which constitute the business into a state of flux. Successful change implies making everything move in the required direction by exploiting the rich diversity of these constituent elements. As absolute control and perfect anticipation are impossible, the process of change must embrace diversity rather than attempt to suppress or restrict it by artificially limiting the domain of change. This cannot be confined to a single part of the business, whether in the physical sense, the functional sense or in the sense of its values or systems. Making changes to the way research and development is managed, for ex-ample, inevitably has an effect on production, sales and human resources. Similarly, a change in organisational structure will affect operational procedures, information systems and even individual behaviour. These unavoidable side effects make it particularly risky to forecast the precise impact of business changes. Managers have to anticipate possible effects without knowing exactly what form they will take or where they will occur. They must identify these effects as quickly as possible if they are to make the best possible job of controlling them. Our method relates to this situation by taking the unpredictable nature of change as another of its fundamental principles: the principle of indeterminacy.

THE FIVE DIMENSIONS OF CHANGE

Like human beings, businesses can be thought of as having a body and a soul with the physical components being the body, and the psychological components the soul.

The physical components of a business make up its structure. They are visible and tangible, like markets, products, organisational structures, information systems, procedures and control systems. They are generally part of the strategies, structures and systems of the business.

The psychological components of a business are what makes the business function. They are invisible elements, such as shared values, relationships, and ways of thinking and behaving. The psychological components, then, essentially relate to the culture and management style of the business.

These components can be grouped together in several ways. The framework we shall use here groups the components into five main areas, which help to define and explain the nature of businesses: strategy, structure, systems, culture and management style. They are all closely intertwined, and are all affected by change, but each alters in a different way and has a different role to play in the process of change. We shall now describe each of them briefly, highlighting their particular characteristics as they relate to bringing about change.

Strategy

Strategy is what determines the activities of the business, its objectives and the methods it employs to achieve those objectives. Strategy directs the business's efforts and is central in determining the relationship between what is external to the business (i.e. customers, competitors, government authorities, suppliers, technological innovations, etc.) and the business itself. Strategy therefore plays a crucial role in change, since in most cases it is strategy which initiates or provokes it. The forces that drive change always come either directly or indirectly from questions of strategy. A merger with another business, the development of a new technology, cost reductions, improvements in customer service or quality are all examples of changes instigated by strategic concerns, with the aim of enabling the business to achieve the objectives it has set itself. Strategy, which influences each of the other four areas and is formulated by taking them all into account, is the product of the confrontation between market forces (i.e. the opportunities and threats represented by the market) and the business, with its strengths and weaknesses. Strategy is heavily dependent on the ability of the business to move forward, to evolve and transform itself; in short, to change. The choice of strategy enables the business to adapt in order to retain its strength, but without exceeding its capacity for change, or else the strategy would be rejected or become disruptive.

The traditional method of formulating strategy runs just such risks, as it is carried out by experts (strategists) who set the goals and the means to be committed to attaining them, and specify the actions to be taken after evaluating their feasibility. This top-down method effectively foists a strategy on the business and establishes a framework which limits the other components' scope for action and therefore their contribution.

Another method, as yet little used by Western businesses, does not refer specifically to strategy, but to strategic alterations guided by the business's 'strategic intent' (C.K. Prahalad and G. Hamel (1990), *Harvard Business Review*, June, and Gary Hamel and C.K. Prahalad (1994), *Competing for the Future*, Harvard Business School Press). The strategic intent of a business relates to its medium- to long-term global objective: to be No. 1 in the car market by the year 2000 or to produce the best civil engineering materials in the world, for example. The business then sets up internal competitions in order to achieve competitive advantages which will enable it to meet its objective. Everyone competes in putting forward suggestions for improvements which, if valid, are adopted as strategic modifications.

In this way strategy is also created from the bottom up by an effective upward flow of information and ideas. This does not involve grand strategic designs, but a continuous accumulation of attempts to strengthen the position of the business by improving the amalgam of elements of which it is composed, by using its skills to acquire new markets and by moving the goalposts to unsettle the opposition. Japanese businesses were the first to develop their strategy along these lines (even though they hardly used the word strategy). Their conquest of the American automobile market is a perfect example. None of the Japanese manufacturers had a market entry strategy such as is understood by Western businesses or business schools. Initial attempts by Toyota, Datsun and Mazda were a failure and it was only by dint of constantly introducing tiny improvements (such as adapting their products to the demands of American consumers, improving their relationships with dealers and their standards of service, etc.) that they finally succeeded.

This concept of strategy obviously has a strong influence on the question of change. It envisages a business which is continually transforming itself by rapid and superficial changes that are usually agreed upon from the outset because management has adopted a 'bottom-up' approach. Our own method, which we shall be developing in the course of this book, accords with and accommodates this concept of change.

Structure

Structure can be defined as the way in which the resources of a business are organised by segmenting the business into branches, divisions, departments or services and for locating each of these entities. Structure defines the pigeon-holing of resources (staff, machinery, brands, etc.), the function of each pigeon-hole and the relationships between them. Structure tells employees where they stand in the business, what their role is, who their superiors and subordinates are, what authority they have and how they relate to other members of staff and to the business environment as a whole. The structure of a business is determined by its managers in relation to its responsibilities towards its customers and the requirements of internal communication. Structure is an area which, particularly in terms of business performance, is at once both important and unimportant.

It is important because the structure of a business is the framework within which each individual works on a day-to-day basis. Therefore, depending on how it is set up, it can either make that individual's activity simpler and more efficient or, on the contrary, complicate it and become a source of inefficiency. Structure actually dissects a business and divides it into separate parts, and most of the difficulties arise not within each part, but in the relationships or interfaces between them. These relational problems are particularly severe between the major business functions (sales, production, research, administration, etc.), which normally form one of the main components of a definition of structure. The idea of transforming the way a business is organised from a function-based structure to one based on core processes, which is gaining popularity as a way of overcoming the intrinsic weaknesses of a functional structure, shows just how important the influence of structure is on the operation and performance of a business. From the point of view of change, the structural framework is often something that needs to be broken, because its boundaries seldom coincide with the solutions which need to be implemented.

Structure is at the same time unimportant because the efficient and effective operation of a business is only partly dependent upon its structure. Experience, social relationships, the ability to establish social relationships between 'pigeon-holes' and getting to know the people you deal with, both internally and externally, are all more important than being able to describe your position, your level in the hierarchy or your membership of a particular department. The structure of a business can and sometimes must change, but its impact on the performance of the business should not be overestimated. Restructuring and other forms of reorganisation should not be carried out too often, because they destabilise the business by upsetting the social relationships which are essential to its operation and by creating the illusion that the new organisation will solve the problems of the current one, whereas in fact it will probably only move them around. Structural changes should be made in order to allow the business to function more easily and to create consistency with the business's strategy, culture and management methods. They should not be made because managers want to make their mark or follow the latest trend.

Depending on the objective in mind, our approach allows business structure either to be changed by managing the power issues which inevitably arise whenever restructuring takes place, or to be sidelined in order to focus on the problems which really need addressing.

Systems

Systems control the flow of everything within the structure: information, raw materials, finished products, money, human resources and so on. How, and especially how quickly, a business reacts is largely determined by its systems, which have a direct influence on decision-making and on the flexibility of the business and its ability to mobilise. Systems are involved in most business activity. A business will expend a great deal of energy on making systems work, and they have a significant effect on its level of performance.

Systems concerned with the circulation of information and with decision making are particularly influential. The ability of a business to seize opportunities and to react to aggression depends largely on these systems (as well as on its culture, as we shall see). It is obviously not only the formal and explicit aspects of systems that matter. The informal and implicit aspects are just as important, if not more so. Communication and exchange of information other than through official channels or between individuals who 'have no need to talk to each other' are an integral part of communication and information systems. Such informal systems of communication are vital to the smooth running of a business. Indeed, dysfunctions are often recognised and resolved by unplanned and informal discussion. We know that Japanese businesses place great importance on informal systems of communication, which they believe are as much a part of the business as formal systems. Although Western businesses' informal systems are valued far less highly, they are no less prevalent and acknowledging them can assist in running the business. Some analysts, like Henry Mintzberg for example, even claim that 'the organisation can be seen as a collection of constellations of work activity, which are simply quasi-independent cliques of individuals working on questions that concern them, at their level of the hierarchy' (Mintzberg, Henry (1979), *Structuring of Organisations: A Synthesis of the Research*, Englewood Cliffs: Prentice Hall).

Systems are always central to change, whether because a change directly affects a system (such as management control, production, promotion, etc.), or because it has implications which affect systems. The multiplicity and diversity of systems and the interactions between them make changing them a complex matter, in spite of their relative flexibility and adaptability. Our method takes the nature of systems, both formal and informal, into account and emphasises the importance of transforming them. Systems undoubtedly play an influential role in task alignment, which according to our method is fundamental to delivering change.

Culture

The culture of a business is the set of lasting values shared by its entire staff, who express them through their behaviour, their habits and their rituals. Culture is heterogeneous, but comprises the fundamental values of the business, in other words those which give its activities meaning (beyond that of meeting economic targets), establish the framework of business activity and thereby set the limits to that activity. Culture also encompasses, for example, the ways in which members of staff socialise, the status of customers and how they are treated, and the importance given to the different functions of the business. Attitudes towards work in general, interpersonal relationships and even people's degree of involvement in the business can equally be seen as aspects of culture. Culture therefore has a very strong influence on the way in which a business carries out its activities. Speed of reaction, which was discussed in relation to systems, depends just as much on culture. The business will be able to respond more quickly to customers' requests or to competitors' changes of strategy if the employees who first notice them feel involved and motivated to pass on the information immediately so that the business can react. By encouraging a positive attitude among employees and creating the necessary conditions for their initiatives to be acted upon, culture can play an essential part in the ability of a business to react and consequently in its performance.

In their study of more than 200 big business managers, John P. Kotter and James L. Heskett show that there is a positive relationship between the strength of a business's culture and its performance, without however actually proving that a strong culture causes better results (Kotter, John P. and James L. Heskett (1992), *Corporate Culture and Performance*, New York: The Free Press). They also conclude that a business's performance depends more on how well its culture is adapted to the business environment than on how strong it is. A well-adapted culture does generate much better performance. All this begs the question of how to change culture, when it is supposedly permanent. The answer given by these writers is that businesses like British Airways, Xerox and General Electric apparently prove that it is possible to change culture and adapt it better to the environment. It seems that several conditions need to be met in order to achieve this, including a very strong belief that innovation, change and learning are absolutely central to the business and need to be taking place all the time, at every level of business activity.

One thing is certain: the ability to change culture is problematic but crucial. Since culture influences and is influenced by every other area of change, any alteration of these can necessitate a cultural trans-formation. Little by little, the physical components of the business inevitably leave their mark on its culture, as a result of the working practices they promote. In fact, culture changes much more under the influence of everyday actions than as a result of training initiatives or management decisions. Because it develops slowly, culture is by far the most stable and inflexible of the five areas of change. But one way of using culture to facilitate and accelerate the changes that are needed is to make change itself a shared business value. Culture can then play its part as a unifier, stabiliser and guide, while also helping the business to follow the developments in its environment.

Our method transforms business culture by bringing it into line with the new business objectives. It must be borne in mind, however, that culture changes slowly and cannot be transformed 'to order'. Profound changes in culture may take several years, so it is essential to take this time constraint into account from the outset and make the first steps in that direction part of the initial phase of change.

Management Style

Management style, or the way in which managers run a business, is one of the important components of the 'soul' of the business, and for two reasons. Unlike culture, management style is closely linked to the personality of the managers themselves, who are after all responsible for imposing change on the business. Their concerns and the way in which they deal with them therefore have a strong influence on the way the business behaves and develops. Managers who give priority to financial considerations and to their relationship with shareholders will act in a different way and guide the business differently from those whose priorities lie with sales and relationships with customers. The entire business will feel the effects of their particular sympathies and inclinations.

Another reason why management style is such an important component is that managers set an example to their employees. Everyone in the business watches the manager or managers—how they behave, what they do and how they think. Their management style, which tends to be duplicated all the way down through the structure, is therefore a lever for change in the business. In theory, that lever should be easy to actuate, being in principle easily aligned with the objectives of change, and managers, who are usually the initiators of change, should understand the need to adapt their style to their intended goals. But this is not always so, as can be seen in the case of changes which aim to reduce costs or to redirect the business towards its customers, for example. So management style has a crucial role to play in making a success of change.

Our method takes management style into account and places the responsibility for successful change squarely with managers, thereby making it easier for management style to be transformed and redirected towards the principal objectives of the business.

Chapter 3

The Ten Keys to Change

The ability to change is essential to any business and will become increasingly so in a world where competitive strategies alter more and more frequently and with greater speed. The successful businesses of today and tomorrow are and will continue to be those which are increasingly in a state of continuous flux, and the management of change will become just as much part of business activity as the management of customer relations, cash flow or resources. But since, as we have seen, the management of change is far-reaching and all-embracing, it must be supported by certain methods, techniques and tools.

The object of this book is to set out a method which we know to be effective, as a set of ten keys, together with the techniques and tools on which it is based, to help businesses to accomplish more easily and more quickly the changes they want to make. This method is intended to be both modest and ambitious. It is modest because modesty is called for in the face of the chaotic phenomenon of change, which is so difficult to grasp and control. When confronted by change, we must renounce all pretensions to omnipotence and be prepared to listen, observe, question and adapt. Pragmatism is the order of the day. It is an ambitious method because its aim is *to succeed in changing*. It describes the conditions which must be met in order to succeed, the resources required and the approach to be adopted.

Our method consists of ten keys (the keys to change) derived from four main underlying principles.

THE BASIC PRINCIPLES

For a method to be practical and effective, it must be based on sound and clearly formulated principles. These principles are the platform on which the method is constructed, and they must be both appropriate to it and capable of supporting it. Moreover, the major decisions which reflect our vision of change and of the way businesses can be transformed are taken at the level of these principles. They dictate the entire method, which will translate them into concrete actions. It is therefore essential to begin by specifying them so that the logic and consistency of the method can be fully understood and so that it can be followed effectively. Those who follow it will of course frequently be confronted by particular situations when they will have to decide on the best way of using the method. They will only be able to make the correct decisions if they can relate the techniques and tools at their disposal to an underlying purpose and appreciation. It is the four principles which meet this need.

Our vision of change and business transformation has been formulated from the results of studies in various fields including mathematics, systems, and the natural and social sciences, for example the work of researchers such as Michel Foucault, Claude Lévi-Strauss, Jacques Monod, Ilya Prigogine, René Thom and Paul Watzlawick, underpinned by our own knowledge of how businesses work. This has led us to stress the complexity of business organisms, the random nature of evolution and the importance of individual accountability within such an environment. The four basic principles are discussed in turn below.

Globality

Change necessarily affects both the body and the soul of a business. Thus the desire to change a business (or any part of it) means acting upon the physical components (strategy, structure, systems, etc.) as well as the psychological components (shared values, culture, style), taking account of the way these two groups of components influence and interact with one another, since they are so intimately connected. (For more details see Chapter 2 under The Five Areas of Change. The 'body' of a business consists mainly of its strategy, structure and systems, while its 'soul' relates to its culture and management.) The process of change must incorporate this fusion of body and soul, whereas traditional methods usually separate them and deal with them individually. This is why it is essential to have a global view of the business, even when change only appears to affect one part of it (a single site, function or system, for example). Considering the business in relation to its core processes, such as launching new products, meeting customer demands and so on, favours such a global view. Our own method forges links not only between the two different types of component, but also between the different components of each type. Depending on the kind of change taking place and the objectives to be met, the measures that need to be taken may of course affect one type of component more than another, but under no circumstances can either of them be ignored. So revising an organisational structure or production methods, which involves acting on the physical components of the business, cannot be done properly if the process of change does not also address the intrinsic emotional and political problems, for example, or the way individuals think and act.

When the objective is to make profound changes to the business, as in the case of revitalisation, restructuring or transformation, the two types of component must be accorded equal importance if the changes are to be valid and lasting. This rarely happens today. British Airways is a striking exception in that its successful recovery is the outcome of a revitalisation process lasting several years which assigned equal importance to the physical and the psychological aspects of the business. Yet it would seem obvious that an attempt to transform a product-led business into a customer-led business by making changes solely to its structure and systems or solely to its culture and management style would not be very successful. The best organisational structure or information system in the world is of little use if customer service and constant attentiveness to customers' needs are not values shared by all staff, including management, and reflected in their behaviour. The reverse is also true. This is why our method concentrates equally on changing both the physical and the psychological components of businesses.

Dislocation

The process of change involves destabilising the *status quo* and maintaining instability throughout the process.

This second principle, which might seem obvious to a physicist, has important implications for the management of change, which requires a dislocation to take place in relation to the current situation. The actual severity of this dislocation, as well as its perceived severity to members of staff, varies according to the changes which are to be made and the adaptability of the business. In some cases dislocation consists of nothing more than a simple adjustment which is readily accepted, while in others it can cause major traumas, as it did when the European steel, French textile and American automobile industries were completely restructured, putting tens of thousands of people out of work.

Change is uncomfortable. It creates worries, tensions and irritations. As soon as the ultimate aim of change has been established, its first objective should be to create dislocation. This will not be easy to accomplish, but is nevertheless essential. Considerable resources need to be mobilised to ensure that the existing situation is destabilised in a planned and controlled manner. Partial instability will jeopardise the whole process of change, with some people remaining as they were and others participating only half-heartedly or else the whole process slowing to a crawl, so that the overall vision (i.e. the desired outcome) will not be satisfactorily implemented.

Once the initial dislocation has been created, change can only take place if a high degree of instability is maintained. As soon as the situation restabilises, the process of change ceases. The change programme must therefore preserve the condition of instability and deal with the opportunities and risks it inevitably creates. Employees must experience instability as a positive condition, or else they will make every effort to regain stability. Maintaining a positive sense of instability is one of the key issues in the process of change. This is not too difficult for businesses in which change is part of the culture and therefore a shared value, but much more so for the vast majority of businesses in which change is still regarded as something out of the ordinary and potentially dangerous.

Universality

Change requires the participation of every employee. The entire workforce must be involved in and committed to the process of change if it is to be successful and lasting. Universal participation and commitment is only possible if everyone can and does play an active part in the process, which means that the workforce cannot be split into two groups: a small minority who decide what action is to be taken and how it is to be carried out, and the rest who simply implement what has been decided by the first group. The principle of universality demands that *all* employees make suggestions and decisions and take responsibility for their actions according to their position within the business.

The greater the involvement of the workforce in a 'bottom-up' process of developing ideas and making decisions, the more easily people will be able to participate in carrying out actions and commit to achieving results, which is essential for change to succeed. So the principle of universality, which is important in making the process of change more efficient in terms of both speed and results, requires a communication system and a decision-making structure which operate both downwards and upwards. This allows those employees who have the best access to information on which decisions must be based, actually to influence those decisions. In many cases they will be out in the field, a long way from the places where decisions are made. It will be seen that our method assigns particular importance to universal participation and to ensuring that all decisions have maximum relevance to the workforce.

Indeterminacy

Change can be guided, but not completely controlled. Any sort of change is a leap in the dark. As we have seen, change is chaotic and does not conform to the law of cause and effect. As a result, the fact that it is complex and impossible to control completely must be accepted and allowed for. Change is not *un*controllable, as we know from experience, but it is only *partially* controllable, so managing change is a matter of guiding, directing and steering it. The method adopted must leave room for flexibility and responsiveness, while also providing close supervision and guidance. The business vision must therefore be precise enough to give clear direction and at the same time general enough to persist in spite of the pitfalls it may encounter and to allow individuals to enhance the process along the way.

The complexity of change and the difficulty of controlling it completely must be countered by making all members of staff account-able. No single person or group of people can maintain control of it, anticipating every development and making all the right decisions. So it is imperative to have confidence in everyone involved and to trust in their abilities. This is not a question of blind faith, but of developing each person's decision-making capacity, so that the multitude of decisions that have to be made every day in so many different areas can be taken as needed.

Guidance therefore has a decisive role to play, firstly in evaluating the relevance of the decisions taken and their effectiveness in implementing the vision, and secondly in adjusting and redirecting them where necessary. Our method makes allowance for the complex and chaotic nature of change and consequently assigns considerable importance to guidance, which is what makes it possible to monitor and direct change.

THE TEN KEYS TO CHANGE

The method set out in this book comprises ten keys. We consider these ten keys to be essential for accelerating change and maximising its chances of success. Each key makes possible the accomplishment of a task (e.g., consolidating change, motivating employees, handling the emotional dimension and so on) which is necessary for successful change. Each key comprises a procedure, a series of actions and a set of tools for implementing change. In this chapter we shall introduce these keys, explain how they help to realise the four fundamental principles, and describe how they should be applied to the different types of change. In the remainder of the book we shall describe them in greater detail.

Each of the ten keys has the characteristics of necessity, continuity, flexibility and interdependency.

Necessity

All the keys are necessary for change to progress efficiently and quickly. Each fulfils a different function but each is essential to business transformation. Omitting any one of them would create additional problems and reduce the chance of change being successful, while omitting several of them would, in the case of major change, cause the whole process to fail. If the managers of a business which is about to embark on a process of change believe that they are not in a position to implement all ten keys simultaneously, it is better for them to wait until the conditions are right. The resources allocated to implementing each key should obviously be in proportion to the extent of the changes to take place.

Continuity

These ten keys must be applied not only simultaneously but continuously throughout the change process. Some keys play a more active part than others during certain phases, but none applies to only a single part of the process. They all have an important role to play throughout. Our method concentrates particularly on applying and sequencing the tools and measures within each key and across different keys during the change process. Key 1: *Defining the Vision*, must obviously be applied first, but it will continue to be relevant throughout the process. The only slight exception to the continuity of application is, as we shall see, Key 5: *Delivering*, which cannot be applied until Key 2: *Mobilising*, has started to take effect.

Flexibility

Together, the ten keys make up a set of actions which are essential for successful change. It is up to change managers to adapt these actions to the particular requirements of their business and of the changes they wish to make. Since every change is unique, it would be absurd and dangerous to try to apply identical procedures to every case. Our ten-key method is an essential resource to be used in its entirety by change managers to help them succeed. Each key will therefore be more or less important and will be applied in differing ways according to circumstances. How thoroughly each of them is applied will depend on the requirements of the situation.

Interdependence

The ten keys form a coherent whole. They are highly interdependent because each supports the others. Taken in isolation, each key has little effect; it is the combined action of all ten keys which makes it work. The keys are the means of setting the objectives and then implementing change. Change can only be achieved by combining the effect of the keys as opposed to simply juxtaposing them, since the whole (the method for succeeding in change) is greater than the sum of its parts (the individual keys).

In the remainder of this chapter we provide a brief overview of the ten keys to change as background for the more detailed exposition of the remaining chapters.

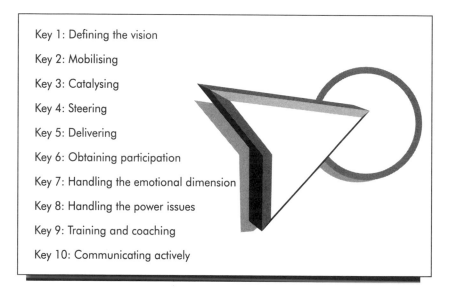

Key 1: Defining the vision

Key 2: Mobilising

Key 3: Catalysing

Key 4: Steering

Key 5: Delivering

Key 6: Obtaining participation

Key 7: Handling the emotional dimension

Key 8: Handling the power issues

Key 9: Training and coaching

Key 10: Communicating actively

Key 1: Defining the Vision

It is the initial vision that both prompts and justifies change. This vision will therefore continue to guide and act as a reference point throughout the change process. It is not concerned with the details of the process, which will be dealt with in due course, but touches on every aspect of change: its causes, the ultimate objective and the broad outline of the action needing to be taken. The definition of the vision must be based on a profound understanding of the business and its environment, as well as on a global appreciation of the issues at stake in change. The vision will in fact be used by change managers as a landmark by which to steer the process and ensure its successful outcome. So the vision defines the domain of change and takes the first step towards obeying the principle of globality by indicating how and to what extent the various components of the business need to be transformed. Moreover, the vision identifies the major issues of change and anticipates potential difficulties.

There are five stages to be followed when defining the vision:

1. formalise the need for change
2. identify the issues at stake in change
3. develop alternative visions
4. choose the appropriate vision
5 formalise the vision.

Key 2: Mobilising

This key initiates the actual process of change, once the vision has been defined, by making the business mobile; in other words by creating a dynamic for change. The need for dislocation (according to the principle of dislocation) is created by analysing the current situation and revealing the extent to which it differs from the vision. These differences effectively prove that the existing situation (in terms of organisation, thinking, behaviour, procedures and so on) is no longer appropriate. As the need for change becomes apparent, a sense of anxiety emerges, which is a necessary characteristic of the mobilisation phase.

The response to the new need is next defined by choosing the improvement initiatives to be launched in order to attain the vision. Three objectives can therefore be achieved by mobilising:

- sensitising employees to the need for immediate change;
- endorsing the issues at stake in change, identified in Key 1;
- choosing the improvement initiatives.

Although mobilising plays an essential part in instigating the process of change, it does not suddenly disappear once change is under way. The drive to mobilise continues throughout the change process, albeit less intensely. A mobile state is never achieved once and for all, and the dynamic for change can evaporate at any point unless awareness of the need for change is constantly sustained and reinforced. According to the laws of motion, initially substantial force is necessary to create movement; then a lesser force is needed to maintain that movement by overcoming ongoing resistance to motion.

Key 3: Catalysing

By catalysing we mean the process of setting up an organisation which will stimulate and manage change. Like any other project, change must be managed, but its peculiar nature means that considerable resources need to be made available and dedicated exclusively to it. To accomplish change requires constantly overcoming resistance, fighting against inertia and stagnation, creating support, and reaffirming the validity of the changes proposed. What is more, if employees' skills and expertise are to be exploited, a special kind of organisation is required to bring them out, channel them and structure them.

Part of the purpose of catalysing is to describe the type of organisation needed to direct change and the way in which it should operate. Under this heading we specify the groups who will be involved (e.g. senior management, the change executive committee, the change facilitation team, expert groups and support teams), the role of each, how they should function, and the relationships between them.

Key 4: Steering

Change is such a complex process that there is a danger of drifting away from the original objectives (in accordance with the principle of indeterminacy), whether by following the wrong path, taking too long or costing too much. Key 4 is focused on the guidance system which keeps the process on the right track, predicting dysfunctions and discrepancies, and using energy effectively.

The process of steering consists of the following activities:

- establishing the logical structure of the change process;
- planning the process;
- making sure it runs properly on a day-to-day basis;
- facilitating and accelerating change;
- providing impartial advice and suggestions;
- monitoring the attitude to change of key staff within the business;

- identifying the methods and tools needed and making them available to employees;
- initiating and following through on coaching;
- ensuring that the other nine keys are applied appropriately.

Key 5: Delivering

Delivering is the word we have chosen to characterise carrying out the process of change; in other words, effecting the transition between the current situation and the situation aspired to, i.e. the implementation of the vision. Delivery is a process which reinforces mobilisation by allowing individuals to understand how they can play a practical part in change, and help ensure that change, once achieved, is lasting.

Delivering consists of five main sub-stages:

1. making a detailed analysis of the existing situation in relation to the improvement initiatives and identifying all the opportunities it presents;
2. devising a detailed plan for each improvement initiative and specifying what must be achieved in each case for the vision to be delivered;
3. carrying out pilot testing;
4. using the results of testing to apply the process of change more generally;
5. setting up systems to ensure that change is lasting.

Key 6: Obtaining Participation

Delivering change requires the participation of the entire workforce (principle of universality). Key 6 is concerned with participation and how to obtain it. Participation is an important issue, because it enables the business to exploit the rich diversity of employees' skills and experience, helps to overcome resistance by involving employees directly, and ensures that change is lasting.

Under this heading we discuss how to obtain and maintain employee participation, and how to handle the variations in participation which are inevitable in any change process.

Key 7: Handling the Emotional Dimension

Individuals react to change in many different ways: they may either be intimidated or attracted by its novelty; they may be reluctant to alter their current ways of working or look forward to greater job satisfaction; they may feel challenged or be afraid of failure, and so on. Some of these reactions are positive, but unfortunately many of them are negative. Either way they must be carefully handled, because they can seriously interfere with the process of change and in extreme cases even obstruct it completely. These emotional factors run counter to the logic of normal business activity, which emphasises rationality and economic ways of thinking.

The objective is to find a solution to the apparent contradiction between, on the one hand, emotional resistance to change and the mental blocks people develop and, on the other, the need for employee participation in order to make change successful. This key therefore necessitates:

- identifying the emotional factors relevant to change;
- assessing the problems created by resistance and mental blockage during the implementation of change;
- handling the emotional dimension.

Key 8: Handling the Power Issues

Change often alters the balance of power within a business, which can cause certain individuals to oppose it or try to turn it to their advantage. Power and change are often at odds, and successful change requires that the balance of power within a business evolves in line with the ultimate objectives.

Using the key enables power issues to be dealt with in three stages:

- identifying the power issues
- handling power issues effectively
- altering the balance of power in line with the objectives of change.

Key 9: Training and Coaching

Change means acquiring and assimilating new skills, as well as new ways of thinking and behaving. Training and coaching (i.e. the individual support given to help everyone to change effectively and improve continuously) therefore play an important part in the process of change and eventually lead to a dynamic for self-development.

This key deals with the following training and coaching issues:

- determining and evaluating training and coaching requirements;
- training, in particular identifying the specific technical skills demanded by changes in jobs and responsibilities, as well as the interpersonal skills needed to support the process of change itself;
- coaching, describing how coaching techniques should be used;
- the dynamic of self-improvement which must be created to support change effectively and derive the maximum benefit from it.

Key 10: Communicating Actively

Throughout the process of change the entire business must engage in frequent and broad communication. This is one of the prime factors in making the process consistent and homogeneous as well as dynamic. Communication means not only informing people about the progress of change, thereby reassuring and motivating them, but also generating an explosion of ideas which enhance and accelerate the process. Communication about change must follow strict procedures if it is not to degenerate into a negative influence, but at the same time the need for information and self-expression must not be frustrated.

This key defines those involved in communication and their various roles, what is communicated at each stage as change progresses and the methods available for maintaining the level of communication.

***

As we have seen, the ten keys to change derive from the four principles underpinning our method, which means that there is obviously a strong connection between the keys and the principles, each of the former contributing to the application of the latter. For example, Key 1: *Defining the Vision*, embodies:

- *the principle of globality*: by defining which physical and psychological components are part of the domain of change;

- *the principle of dislocation*: by making evident the disparity between the current situation and the target objectives;
- *the principle of universality*: by allowing everyone to influence the process of change at their own level;
- *the principle of indeterminacy*: by describing an overall objective which will serve as a guide throughout the process which is otherwise unpredictable in its evolution.

Key 1 relates particularly strongly to the first, second and fourth principles.

Table 3.1 shows how each key relates to the four principles. Reading downwards will identify the keys that are crucial to the realisation of each principle, while reading across will make it easier to understand the function of each key and consequently how best to apply it in order to conform with the principles

Table 3.1   The Relationship Between the Ten Keys and the Four Principles

Keys	Principles			
	Globality	Dislocation	Universality	Indeterminacy
Defining the vision	✓	✓		✓
Mobilising	✓	✓	✓	
Catalysing		✓		✓
Steering	✓			
Delivering	✓		✓	
Obtaining participation			✓	
Handling the emotions			✓	
Handling the power issues			✓	
Training and coaching	✓		✓	✓
Communicating actively		✓	✓	

VARYING THE METHOD TO SUIT THE TYPES OF CHANGE

How our method is used will vary from one situation to another. In this section we shall show how it can be adapted to suit the two main types of environment in which change can take place: static and dynamic. A business which is not accustomed to change would be a static environment, whereas one in which change is an everyday activity (e.g., those many small changes the Japanese call 'kaisen') would be a dynamic environment. Static environments give rise to discontinuous change, dynamic environments to continuous change.

The method should be used in accordance with the specific requirements of each of the two situations. If a particular case falls between these two extremes, the keys should be applied accordingly.

In the case of discontinuous change, all ten keys need to be applied scrupulously if the business is to be transformed. It will require considerable effort to overcome inertia and generate the necessary momentum. Keys 1–3, *Defining the Vision, Mobilising and Catalysing*, will have a particularly important part to play, and considerable time and human resources will therefore need to be allocated to them.

Keys 7 and 8, *Handling the Emotional Dimension* and *Handling the Power Issues*, will also be critical in achieving successful change due to the extent of dislocation and destabilisation which will occur. Our method will accelerate and enhance the process of change so that performance can be improved far beyond existing levels, achieving for example a 50% increase in productivity or a 50% reduction in the development time required for new products.

If the business is already in a state of continuous change, the aim will be to accelerate the process either on a long-term basis, in order to strengthen its position, or on a short-term basis, in order to achieve a particular change more rapidly, such as introducing new technology or adapting to a sudden variation in business activity. In this case, Keys 2 and 3 will be less vital, as will Keys 7 and 8, since employees are already motivated and have overcome their fear of change. The original definition of the vision can remain unchanged if the objective of long-term acceleration is the same as before. On the other hand, the modifications required may be so great that they amount in effect to discontinuous change. This could happen in a business which normally increases productivity by 3% per annum but which decides that it must increase it by 8% per annum in future in order to remain competitive. In terms of managing change, this would equate to a case of discontinuous change where the vision would have to be redefined, even though the business is already in a state of continuous change. Figures 3.1 to 3.4 illustrate the impact of applying the keys.

Previous experience of change should enable a business to change more and more rapidly and effectively. Managers will be able to make quicker and better decisions, the organisation of the process will take less time to set up and will work more efficiently. Employees will become more involved more quickly, so that the vision will be consolidated sooner and at lower cost. The business will learn how to change and so get better and better at it; it will also be more

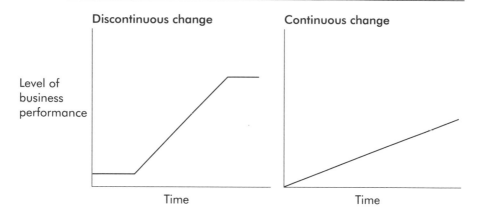

Figure 3.1   A Comparison of Discontinuous and Continuous Change

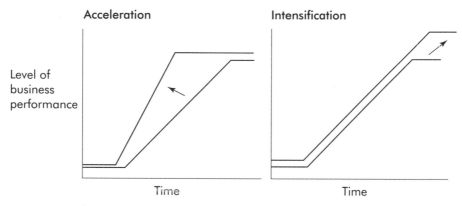

Figure 3.2   The Result of Acceleration and Intensification Combined

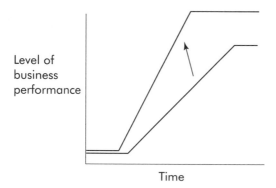

Figure 3.3   Potential Impact of Using the Method for Discontinuous Change

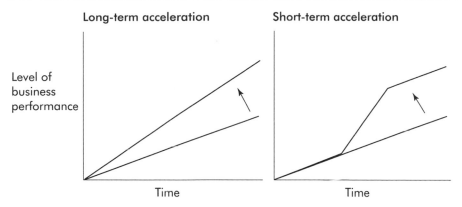

Figure 3.4 Potential Impact of Using the Method for Continuous Change

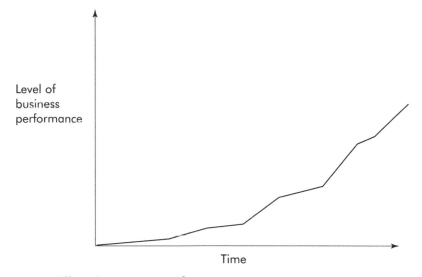

Figure 3.5 Effect of Experience of Change

productive during the process of change itself. In learning by experience, the business will be able to raise its level of performance more and more rapidly, as shown in Figure 3.5.

These few examples clearly show the importance, not to say necessity, of adapting the method to suit the situation in order to accelerate change, minimise its cost and maximise the chance of success. The way the method is structured allows it to be adapted easily to every situation, which is what makes it universally applicable.

Chapter 4

Key 1: Defining the Vision

THE ROLE OF THE VISION

Vision is what propels and directs change and provides its justification. The purpose of a vision is to ensure that everyone is pulling in the same direction, while still allowing individuals room for manoeuvre. It is not intended to inhibit initiative and must never be allowed to do so. The vision is what defines the ultimate objective of change, specifies which parts or elements of the business will be affected by it and establishes the main features of the process of change.

The vision shows the direction change will take and the goal it is to achieve. It is the one stable element in the process and acts as its guiding light from beginning to end amidst the chaos of change. It is the one determining factor in a process which is largely indeterminate (one of the four principles), for it determines the goal. Everyone who is affected by change, however slightly, acts with reference to the vision. Keys 2 and 5, *Mobilising* and *Delivering*, interpret the vision into practical routes for improvement and individual actions. It is its generality which makes it consistent with the principle of indeterminacy. The vision provides a framework within which everyone knows how to act and how to tackle unexpected situations by making decisions that are consistent with the purpose of change. As we see it, the vision is entirely compatible with the role of managers as leaders, directing and guiding the business.

The vision also justifies change by highlighting the discrepancy between the current situation and the target situation. It articulates the reasons behind the decision to change (e.g., changes in the business environment, inadequacies in the present situation, expected advantages of the target situation) so that it can be seen to be supported by identifiable motives and to result from a logical progression. The vision makes change meaningful and prevents it from degenerating into an arbitrary process. In this context, then, its role is to make it easier to create the necessary dislocation (another of the fundamental principles) for change to succeed, by demonstrating the weaknesses of the current situation and the advantages which change will bring, though it is not always able to create that dislocation by itself.

The vision also specifies the extent of change, i.e. how profound it will be, how long it will take and in which domains it will operate. It demonstrates the globality of change (the first fundamental principle) by stipulating the major issues at stake in the process, which will be developed in Key 2: *Mobilising*. The way the vision clarifies the change issues may cause apprehension among some employees, but it can also serve to mitigate this feeling and focus it in a positive way by lessening the sense of journeying into the unknown, which is always a source of anxiety and resistance. Similarly, it helps to prevent others from building their hopes too high and ending up disappointed and frustrated. In this way the vision initiates the development of employee ownership and accountability.

THE NATURE OF THE VISION

As we have already described, the extent of change varies greatly from minor adaptations or modifications to total business transformation. The nature of the vision varies accordingly.

In the case of total transformation, every component of the business will be in confusion for a long time. This puts managers in an uncertain and risky position. Except in exceptional circumstances, this kind of change can only be justified by absolute necessity. The business is to be 'recreated', which will probably be a violent, stressful, dramatic and shocking process. Those who have been through this kind of change often refer to it as being like surviving an earthquake or getting eaten alive. The vision is based on strategic intent (as defined by K.C. Prahalad and G. Hamel): to be 'the world's favourite airline' or 'to be No. 1 or No. 2 in the world in everything we do'. It directs all efforts towards the goal. As we shall see, this strategic intent is backed up by more specific objectives in each of the major areas of activity, but does not preclude the opening up of new avenues or the emergence of individual enterprise. Indeed, transformation depends on the ability to create, to invent and to experiment. Gradually the vision will be consolidated, the business will be transformed and less radical processes of change will arise. Then the vision will become more specific.

Such transformations, though spectacular and often the subject of widespread media attention, are rare. They are generally the result of businesses either refusing or failing to keep up with developments in their environment until their very existence has come under threat. In most cases change takes place under less dramatic conditions, in which managers can set their own deadlines and evaluate the risks involved. This sort of change is consistent with the strategic intent it is helping to implement. The merger of two companies or bodies, the reorganisation of a product-led business to become a market- or customer-led business, or the introduction of a total quality management (TQM) programme are three examples of this kind of change—a significant change which impacts the activities of the business as well as its development and its operation (i.e. its processes, structures, equipment, etc.), but which is to a certain extent controllable and programmable. The vision therefore clearly indicates not only the main objective, but also the general domains of activity and the projected timetable. In this context too, the vision should encourage mobilisation and participation among all concerned by offering them the opportunity to contribute in thought and deed to its implementation.

Finally, in cases of minor adaptation or modification (such as the introduction of new processes or behavioural changes), the vision is capable of specifying concrete objectives, whether in the field of results or procedures. There will be less uncertainty and risk than with major transformations because change will be short-lived (usually taking between a few months and a year) and will affect only a few clearly defined elements of the business.

THE CONTENT OF THE VISION

The vision, as is now clear, describes the proposal for change adopted to solve the problem that has been identified. The term 'problem' should not automatically be taken to mean something negative, but might refer to a desire to strengthen the position of the business, to continually improve its operations, to capitalise on a competitive advantage or to overcome a handicap. The vision comprises three principal elements:

- an explanation of the origin of change, i.e. the problem;
- a description of the ultimate objective of change, i.e. the solution;
- a broad definition of the course of action to be followed: the means.

ORIGIN	ACTION	OBJECTIVE
the problem	⟶	the solution
	the means	

The origin of the need for change, in other words the problem to be resolved, is an essential component of the vision and is no less important than the objective. It is worth taking the trouble to clarify the source of the need for change in order to:

- confirm the validity of the problem initially identified and therefore the relevance of the justification for change;
- equip oneself with the tools to explain and justify change;
- begin to formulate the process of change by identifying the strengths and weaknesses of the business in relation to the ultimate objective.

The need for change is often felt in a particular area before the vision has been formalised. It may even be that action has already been initiated. Whether or not this is the case, it is essential to identify the true problem, the real basis of change, at an early stage. It is not enough to rely just on observation or intuition. The apparent issue may not in fact be the underlying one, but merely the consequence of another issue which is what really needs to be tackled. A certain large group manufacturing mass-market goods provides a good example of this. One of its subsidiaries was losing market share and suffering a fall in profit, so the group's managers decided to merge it with another subsidiary, whose performance, although not as bad, was also considered inadequate. Following what had been achieved by other players in the sector, they hoped that the merger would improve the performance of both subsidiaries by giving them more muscle in the marketplace. However, when the situation was analysed in preparation for the merger, the results showed that the problem lay elsewhere and was actually a case of poor marketing and strategic positioning by both companies, neither of which had adequately scrutinised the way they were operating in a rapidly developing market. A merger would not have solved anything and might even have aggravated the situation, in spite of what had at first sight appeared to be the key to success, i.e. an increase in size.

During this problem validation phase it is essential not to over-simplify. A single problem usually has several causes and con-sequently many possible solutions. Any analysis should expose this complex web of causes and solutions rather than trying to find *the* cause and *the* solution. An example of this was a capital equipment company whose managers had reached the conclusion that their commercial setbacks were caused by excessive delivery times. Delivery often took several weeks, whereas their competitors were delivering within days. They therefore decided to re-engineer their whole order fulfilment and delivery system. However, their plans soon developed into a much broader change programme because they realised that shorter delivery times were not the solution to their difficulties. The real problem lay in their response to customers' needs. It was helpful to reduce delivery times, but they also needed to be able to offer a more appropriate product range and to provide better installation and user training. When they did so, they realised that they did not in fact need to reduce delivery times by as much as they had thought. In-depth analysis of the problem enables the benefits of change to be confirmed or denied and the initial approach to be properly targeted. At this stage many proposals for change are either abandoned or radically altered from what was initially envisaged.

Specifying the source of change is also an important stage in setting up the process of change itself. It is at this point that the disparity between the current state of the business and the way it would like to be should be investigated and its advantages and disadvantages, whether in relation to skills, market position, partnerships, operating methods or whatever should be identified. This will help to define the objective and the action that must be taken. Managers will need to reach an initial level of consensus over this description of the existing situation and the way in which it should be used to attain the objective. Usually there is only partial consensus and differences of opinion persist on certain points. This diversity is a positive factor, as long as it is properly controlled and does not develop into violent conflict over key issues.

Next, the vision must specify the ultimate objective of change. The exposition of the solution logically follows the explanation of the problem. As we have seen, however, these two processes are closely interwoven and interact with one another (as indeed does the description of the means, which will be examined next). The objective is both the core and the driving force of the vision.

The nature of the objective (or solution) depends very much on the type of change, but it is always defined in terms of three criteria. It must:

1. offer a credible and effective solution to the problem that has been identified;
2. provide all employees with the target and point of reference they need in order to focus their actions;
3. make the best use of both individual and collective skills and expertise in realising that solution.

The objective must therefore be inspiring as well as realistic, stable and fixed throughout the process of change (unless completely new factors arise), clear and easy to understand, accessible and stimulating. Some of these characteristics may seem contradictory or incompatible. This is not the case, but proving it is one of the main problems in defining the vision.

The way the objective is defined must immediately make clear how it diverges from the existing situation. The more pronounced the apparent dislocation, the more the need for change will be emphasised. The objective must be set alongside the expected benefits to all concerned (employees, managers, shareholders, unions and customers). These are the positive aspects of change which offset the drawbacks, real or imagined, that immediately spring to mind when changes are announced. Since the objective is to act as a point of reference, it must remain fairly general in comparison with the changes envisaged. This is the only way to guarantee its stability. At the same time, if it is to support and guide every individual's efforts, it must be quite clear and precise. So in the case of major changes involving medium- and long-term objectives it will be necessary to set up subsidiary or intermediate goals. If the business is to undergo a major transformation, its strategic intent will be the meta-objective, but it will be supported by shorter-term objectives which will initiate the process of delivery. We shall therefore make a distinction between the meta-objective and the shorter-term objectives, the latter being subject to change as the transformation progresses. These shorter-term objectives are vital to mobilise the workforce and deliver change—things which the meta-objective alone (which may take years to achieve) cannot do.

Defining the vision is only the first stage in the process of change. So the objective, as defined, must facilitate subsequent stages, particularly mobilisation. This will be achieved by the opportunity it affords all employees to make an effective contribution to change through their skills and expertise rather than through merely following a plan and carrying out instructions. Those responsible for formulating the objective should neither overstep the limits of their own competence and knowledge nor forego the potential contributions of other employees to enhance delivery of the vision.

Here are some examples of ways in which the objective of change might be formulated, from minor adjustments to major transformations:

- Maximise the potential value to users of our information system.
- Double our profitability within two years through better cost control.
- Improve our relations with customers by offering them a more appropriate product range and first-class service in order to increase our market share by 20% over five years.
- Strengthen our position as market leaders and technological pacesetters by establishing a closer partnership with our customers and suppliers.
- Achieve total customer satisfaction in the fields of cultural and leisure spending.

It is important that the objective adopted is in fact the real business objective and not simply a means of achieving it. In the earlier example of the merger of two companies, the merger was the global action adopted to achieve the objective of increased profitability. But, as we have seen, a global action is often mistaken for the objective of change, so that in this case the merger became the goal without anyone knowing exactly what they expected from it. The re-engineering of a process cannot be an objective of change; nor can overhauling an information system or creating a new distribution channel, for example, because these are not business objectives. Preliminary analysis usually circumvents this kind of trap by showing up any possible confusion between ends and means.

The third element in the vision is a description, in broad outline, of the course of action (or means) chosen to achieve the final objective. This will have a strong influence on the progress of change and the results obtained.

We shall not describe the means in detail here; this will be done under Keys 2 and 5, *Mobilising* and *Delivering*. Our purpose here is to specify the scope of change, to structure its course, and to establish how long it will take and how much it will cost. The scope of change means which parts of the business, and consequently which of its employees, will be affected directly or indirectly by the changes which are about to take place. Defining it within the vision makes it possible to take a global view right from the start and so minimise any false hopes or fears.

By structuring the course of change it will be possible to programme and coordinate the various actions required. It is a complex process, except in the case of minor adjustments and changes of limited extent. The structure adopted should ensure that all action taken is feasible, that change is consistent across all the different components of the business, that the existing situation and any action that has already been taken are integrated into the process, and of course that the objective will be achieved as efficiently as possible. In the case of significant changes and major transformations, the task is not unlike that of a town planner, who must take account of the existing situation with all its limitations and possibilities and exploit it, define the main principles and underlying framework of development and coordinate the inputs of a large number of people, each with their own role to play, their own interests and their own timetables.

Businesses are always on the move and action is constantly being taken, since no one can afford to wait for an official decision on making changes before doing something. The business of structuring change involves reinforcing and extending some of these actions, redirecting some, and perhaps halting others. Structuring change also involves controlling the development of the various components (physical and psychological), which evolve in different ways and according to different patterns. Finally, those in charge of structuring change must make allowance for the constraints of the business environment, i.e., time, money, social factors, and the ability to manage complexity. After all, the business must continue to operate even while it is being transformed. The structure adopted for progressing change must never lose sight of this fact. Should it tackle one problem at a time or all of them at the same time but in different parts of the business? Should it concentrate initially on improving the working of the business, by means of re-engineering, for example? Or should it also deal with development and growth in order to raise staff morale? These are just a few of the questions which must be answered by whoever is structuring the course of change.

The vision also states how long the process of change will take. We saw in Chapter 1 how important this is. The length of time allocated to change must be both realistic and appropriate. A lengthy process does not necessarily increase the chance of success. It is a question of timing: if the process is too quick, it will reduce the value of change; too slow and it will weaken motivation.

In addition, the vision must outline the type of organisation which will be set up to manage the changes. It will indicate what kind of organisation it should be, who should run it, its approach (stimulation, support, control, etc.) and the powers it has to act.

The cost implications of change must also be evaluated at this stage and should include not only direct financial costs, but also indirect costs, especially the amount of time to be spent by employees.

Defining the vision is a perilous exercise. We shall now look at four classic traps which must be avoided in the process.

Too Specific an Objective

The objective can be a handicap to change if it is too specific, because it may not prove durable and will fail to exploit the diversity of skills and expertise that enhance change and improve its chance of success. Managers may mean well in describing the objective in detail, feeling that they must be as precise as possible about the target situation in order to increase the probability of attaining it. Or it may be that they want to control the process of change and reduce the degree of uncertainty involved. Whatever the reason for it, too much detail betrays a lack of understanding of the indeterminacy of change.

A Vague Objective

The objective must act as a landmark to help everyone involved in change to target their actions, particularly when unexpected situations arise. If the objective is too vague, in other words if it does not act as a precise landmark, their actions may not be focused on the same target, which means that energy will be dissipated instead of being directed towards the objective envisaged by management. Increasing the synergy between two companies in the same group, optimising the use of production tools or improving customer services are all examples of vague objectives which make change less effective and lessen the chance of resolving the primary problem.

An Inadequate Objective

An inadequate objective is one that will only partially address the primary problem. The objective represents the resolution of the issue, but it may only partially solve it because of the choices that have been made. We are not referring to analytical errors, but to decisions taken by managers in full possession of the facts. Any change involves taking risks and upsetting what has previously been achieved. If managers are reluctant to do this, they may be induced to set an objective which only tackles part of the problem—a sort of intermediate objective. In fact in many cases a partial solution is unsatisfactory: either the issue must be tackled in its entirety or the attempt abandoned, because otherwise employees will misunderstand the objective and the implementation of change will not go smoothly.

An Unrealistic Course of Action

The vision establishes an outline of the course of action necessary in order to undertake change. It is essential, however, that the proposition should be realistic, or employees will be severely demotivated from the outset. When the projected costs and timescale are announced, they must not be underestimated, since they reflect management's commitment to change and their perception of how difficult it will be. Too great a discrepancy between the proposed course of action and employees' own perception of the difficulties may lead to rejection, which can be costly to overcome, both in time and money. If the means allocated are unrealistic, whether in an attempt to minimise cost requisitions or in attempting to move fast in response to urgent need, a lack of realism at the outset can be a major handicap to success.

DEVELOPING THE VISION

Defining the vision is a management responsibility, since it is managers who take the decision to embark on a process of change and who are ultimately responsible for seeing it through. They must of course ensure that the vision they have defined is relevant, but also that it is properly developed. If this development process entails taking a global view of what is at stake and involves most of the people who will be the principal players, it will greatly increase the chances of success.

Developing the vision is a task usually undertaken by a small team which carries out the analysis and researches managers' needs in order to make decisions and choices. It is recommended that some of the members of this team also belong to the teams subsequently responsible for implementation.

We suggest that a five-stage procedure is normally appropriate for developing the vision. To what extent this will be necessary in a particular case will depend on the nature of the vision required and the conditions under which change is to take place. Each stage represents a requirement that must be met in order to define the vision. The stages do not always follow one another in strict sequence, as they are sometimes closely interrelated. Whole books have been written on the subject of developing vision and it is not our purpose to repeat this material here; rather we provide a description of the stages we would expect to see included and a short description of each in turn.

Stages in developing the vision

1. Formalise the need for change
↓
2. Identify the issues at stake in change
↓
3. Develop alternative visions
↓
4. Choose the appropriate vision
↓
5. Formalise the vision

Stage 1: Formalise the Need for Change

The objective of this first stage is to understand why the business needs to change, or needs to change more quickly or in a different way, and then make managers aware of the reasons for wishing to do so.

By studying the commercial environment and the way the business is performing and functioning against these external needs, it is possible to describe the existing competitive situation and internal response and how these are likely to develop. This analysis is necessary because it enables the importance of the business issue to be confirmed and establish that it is indeed the primary problem and not the result of some underlying problem which has not yet been discovered. This analytical front-end, which often features the use of various kinds of internal and external benchmarking, provides the raw material from which managers can construct a shared view of the existing situation and of the need to change. This consensus is an ideal to be aimed at, which Japanese organisations especially put great effort into achieving. In reality there will often be differences of opinion between managers, who will not all interpret the facts in the same way, nor have the same idea of how circumstances will develop or what needs to be done. While often it is not worth trying to eliminate all these differences, since the sole purpose of analysing the present is to design the future, it is nevertheless essential to have compatible views of the *general* direction of change before proceeding further.

While the procedure can involve a considerable amount of analysis and research, most of the necessary information can usually be found within the business itself, although it is necessary to ensure that the external competitive perspective and environment receive fullest possible consideration. There is nothing like a perceived external threat to focus people's minds and create a crying need for change. Management thinking, supported by the work of the research team, must be a group activity as well as an individual one, since its aim is to create a shared view of the necessity for change. It may take several weeks to complete this stage, but it should not become an excuse for putting off decisions while more and more information is accumulated.

Stage 2: Identify the Issues at Stake in Change

Change is a complex and multifaceted phenomenon, so it is essential to have as complete an idea as possible of its potential consequences, both for the business itself (e.g., its strategy, culture and systems) and for the various parties affected (employees, customers, shareholders and suppliers). This presupposes an awareness of these people's needs and expectations as well as an understanding of their relationship to the issues in question. If, for example, the problem is a weakness in product innovation or market responsiveness, this means understanding the impact of making changes in these areas on customers, and suppliers: what positive aspects of change would increase their level of satisfaction, and what negative aspects might dissatisfy them and represent for them a loss of value?

A similar line of questioning must be followed for the various departments and functions within the business itself, with respect to structure, systems and management methods. It is very important at this stage for managers to work together, since many of the problems may exist or even result from departmental or functional barriers which have grown up slowly but inexorably over a period of time.

Stage 3: Develop Alternative Visions

After the previous two stages have been undertaken, it is still too early to define the vision, except in very simple cases. A number of alternative visions must first be developed to allow for the un-predictability of developments in the external environment (economic, technological and competitive) and the differing views managers may have held during the preceding stages.

There will be alternative end objectives and alternative courses of action, generally three or four of each, different enough to encompass the full range of possibilities envisaged at this stage, which will be sufficiently detailed to allow a choice to be made in the next stage. These alternatives are drawn up during group sessions on the basis of preparatory work carried out beforehand and attended to by all the managers involved.

Stage 4: Choose the Appropriate Vision

By the end of the preceding stage, alternative visions have been worked out in detail. Every outstanding question has been answered, the conditions under which each could be implemented have been examined and the costs and timescales have been evaluated.

Management will therefore now be in a position to choose the appropriate vision. The vision adopted is rarely identical to any of the alternatives put forward. In most cases it is the result of combining elements taken from several of them, because comparative analysis leads to the emergence of new ideas. Every manager involved in defining the vision must be committed to the chosen outcome, both to the solution and to the course of action it entails. In practice it is unusual for everyone concerned to be in total agreement with all elements of the chosen vision. This to be expected. Any change will generate resistance, even (perhaps especially) among managers, some of whom will soon change their minds and come to agree with the vision, others will continue to disagree. We shall deal with this problem in Key 8: *Handling the Power Issues.*

What is important is that the leader should make sure of having necessary and sufficient support (as the process of defining the vision should have ensured) and that, although there may be opposition to it, this is not such as to invalidate the vision. In some cases, the visionary leader alone among his team may see clearly what it is necessary to do. This occurs particularly in cases where new leadership is brought to a company from outside. The leader must in every case assess each manager's level of support as precisely as possible, and if lacking the necessary and sufficient level of support, seek to find new blood from outside before continuing further.

Stage 5: Formalise the Vision

Defining the vision is not an end in itself. It is only the beginning of the process of change. The purpose of this stage is to give proper emphasis to the extent to which the vision can stimulate, support and guide the process. Vision is the most powerful means available for driving change—without it the task would almost always be very much more risk-prone, difficult, time consuming and costly.

Formalising the vision consists of:

- formulating the vision in such a way as to make it clear and easily communicable;
- highlighting those elements of the vision which are essential to universal understanding of the issues addressed by it, the solution and the means of implementing it;
- drawing up a list of questions and answers relating to the vision in anticipation of likely queries from those it will affect;
- keeping the vision up-to-date as work on other areas proceeds apace.

CASE STUDY ON DEFINING THE VISION:
Rolls-Royce Aerospace Group

Rolls-Royce Aerospace Group, part of Rolls-Royce plc, one of the world's most renowned companies, is a leader in the development, manufacture and assembly and servicing of aero-engines, both for commercial and military use. Rolls-Royce as a whole had a turnover in 1996 of £4.5 billion with 42 000 employees. The engines made by Rolls-Royce and its US subsidiary Allison Engines Inc. are incorporated in many of the world's best-known aeroplanes such as those made by Boeing and Airbus as well as a wide variety of military aircraft.

The world of aerospace is complex in terms of the development of the products themselves, which are invariably at the frontiers of technology in order to gain commercial and other advantages and in terms of the sheer number and intricacy of the components which make up the final assembly. Product manufacturing lead times are long, while at the same time the product continues to evolve as improvements, refinements and even major changes are introduced. Finally, and particularly in the case of engines, the need for overhaul, spares and repair activities is considerable as various components within them are subjected to extremes of temperature, pressure and stress as a normal part of their working life. There are various means potentially available to cope with such needs, including sophisticated forecasting and planning systems, buffering against unavoidable uncertainty and maintaining close linkages with customers and suppliers in order to anticipate demands as early as possible.

The task of aero-engine development and manufacture is therefore demanding enough in its own right, even before the market environment is taken into consideration.

Market for Aero-engines and Spares

To all intents and purposes, the commercial market for aero-engines, particularly at the larger end, is dominated by three major suppliers: Rolls-Royce, General Electric and Pratt and Whitney, who by supplying each other, working together and subcontracting or partnering with a number of other well-known companies in the field with whom they are allied, dominate the industry. As a result, every time an airline places an order for an aircraft he has a choice of airframe and then for that platform a choice of two or three engines as the unit to power the aeroplane. In some instances the engine manufacturers share common suppliers for critical components such as shafts and discs, which at times of high demand makes the business more interesting still.

The choice of engine reflects the pressures placed on the airlines to provide the greatest possible comfort and service at the lowest cost per passenger mile flown. This inevitably touches on engine operating efficiency as a unit converting fuel into power as well as serviceability and maintainability, which impacts through direct costs and speed of learning on life-cycle costs.

Like many other industries underpinned by capital intensity, the industry suffers severe cyclicality of demand, not only in terms of aircraft and engine orders but also in terms of demand for spares, since to some extent the airlines themselves can manage their cashflows through the mechanism of pulling forward or retarding spares inventory replacement.

In the view of a number of observers of the industry, given the heavy development costs and the sales opportunities present in the market there may in the long run be only two survivors in the industry, with the third having to merge with one of the other two or disappear. It is the overriding concern of Rolls-Royce that it will be one of the two organisations left after that process is completed at some time in the future.

Process Benchmarking

In an environment where three strong competitors share the world market between them, in conditions that suggest that one of them might suffer its demise at the hands of the other two, there is little wonder that all of them pay close attention to the activities of their competitors in order to benchmark their own operations in as full detail as possible.

Work carried out by specialist consultants on behalf of Rolls-Royce Aerospace Group and its Allison subsidiary was used to draw up a detailed assessment of the Rolls-Royce market-facing and internal capability as compared with the perceived capabilities of the principal competitors. The initial drive to do this came from new top managers wanting to better understand where they were *vis-à-vis* the competitive environment so as to be able to set a vision of the new direction to head in. This demonstrates the power of the *external* competitive environment in creating a favourable *internal* environment for change.

From Benchmarking to Process Improvement Goals

To be aware of the need to act on a particular gap identified in a gap analysis is not necessarily synonymous with knowing how to close or reverse it. The next step is to break it down into its components to understand in what ways processes or functions contribute to the observed result. For Rolls-Royce this consisted in specifying five areas in which process-determined goals had to be improved and by what amount. Once this had been accomplished, as with manufacturing lead times and inventories for example, the contribution of sub-processes such as final assembly, component manufacturing and pro-curement can be taken into account by setting goals for the important sub-processes.

Equally, improvements in inventory availability translate into separate objectives for spares and for items delivered to final assembly.

Process Improvement Goals Generate New Processes

Once new process goals have been identified, it becomes apparent that existing methods may not be capable of producing the desired result, so a need to be radical and seek completely new ways of doing things becomes evident. Thus carrying working inventories of certain components in final assembly becomes unworkable as compared with the inventory performance figures that can be obtained from direct deliveries lineside. Equally, new rules of master scheduling are required if the conditions for highly effective manufacturing and assembly are to be met upstream. The new processes generated in this fashion demanded visioning and brainstorming from multi-disciplinary teams working to tight initial timescales. Inevitably they met resistance and doubt from those accustomed to the old ways of working.

New Processes Lead to New Systems Needs

In Rolls-Royce there was a perception that the implementation of new processes over a short time frame across a broad portfolio of business activity could lead to severe indigestion in the systems area. For Rolls-Royce this helped lead to the conclusion that a longer term IT partnership with a specialist IT provider would be needed. In the event EDS were selected for this role in an innovative outsourcing relationship, tied to process improvements and delivery of business benefits.

Systems Needs Lead to Business Partnership

Once the task for Rolls-Royce in the future was seen as rapid trans-formational business improvement against precisely defined performance metrics, coupled with a major IT outsourcing initiative, it became possible to structure an innovative ten-year arrangement, in which EDS took over the running of the existing computer facilities and the staff responsible for running them and A.T. Kearney provided management consulting support to achieve the improvements in business performance anticipated in a number of different business processes and business areas. Furthermore, the payment to EDS and A.T. Kearney for services delivered bears a direct relationship to the improvements achieved against a series of business metrics. In this way EDS and A.T. Kearney have entered into a business partnership with Rolls-Royce Aerospace, including Allison Engines (where a similar relationship was also established) with the rewards to EDS and A.T. Kearney made dependent upon the Rolls-Royce results.

Visionary Nature of the Arrangements at Rolls-Royce

There is little doubt that the bold nature of the Rolls-Royce move depended to a large extent on the visionary thinking of the business leaders of Rolls-Royce and Allison engines, who saw the need for radical change, and that a strategic partnership would be required in order to move forward with the resources, speed and drive necessary for business benefits to be achieved as planned.

The move has set a new agenda of change for the organisation which is a necessary condition for future growth and prosperity. With these arrangements in place the Rolls-Royce sales organisation is empowered to make aggressive deals in the confidence that a best-in-class competency is being built up behind them to deliver on the needs being expressed in the market.

Since this arrangement was concluded in 1995, the civil airliner market has come out from a trough in the cycle and is moving up strongly towards more buoyant conditions. Rolls-Royce and Allison are well-placed to obtain a strong market position in the years ahead in this complex, challenging and dynamic environment and the benefits from the new approach are already arriving.

In change management terms, several important essential conditions have been fulfilled. First, there are compelling external factors which drive the need for change and they are readily convertible into internal performance metrics. Second, the visionary leadership is in place to show the way and lead the change. Third, the vision developed is compelling and exciting and promises a decisive step forward. Fourth, by building the changes expected into planning, budgeting, etc., managers need to move forward with the new concepts quickly if they are to meet their own performance objectives.

Chapter 5

Key 2: Mobilising

As a result of the activity described in Chapter 4, the vision has been defined by management and is capable of being communicated to all concerned. However, if a major change is in prospect, in either operational performance or attitudes and values, communication alone is not enough to spur the business into action. The vital energies within the business must be released and directed in accordance with the vision. This is the aim of *Mobilising*, our second key to success in change management, which is the subject of the remainder of the chapter.

The New Collins Dictionary gives the following definitions for mobilising:

'preparing for war or another emergency by organising the armed services, etc.'

'organising for a purpose.'

THE OBJECTIVES OF MOBILISING

The five main objectives of mobilising are described in turn below.

1. Identify with the vision
The first objective is to ensure that the need for change, the urgency of that need and the purpose of change are understood and identified

with, not just by the people making the decisions, but by the majority of those who will be affected by change. They will then appreciate the implications of the process for their day-to-day activities and will be in a position to contribute proactively to its progress.

2. Change with and through people

People are a business's prime asset. They are the guardians of the knowledge about customers, markets, products and competitors, and of the expertise and skills which are the essence of the business; they are the source of its creativity and the trustees of its cumulative experience. The exercise and use of these attributes, i.e., the intelligence of the organisation, is not the sole prerogative of a few decision-makers but is in fact scattered piecemeal throughout the business. One of the major objectives of mobilising is to put this intelligence at the service of the change process in the broadest possible sense of the word.

3. Release of vital energies

Apart from explaining and articulating the vision, mobilising aims to create a shared confidence and enthusiasm with regard to the new business goal(s). Generally, when changes are announced, three groups of people emerge: enthusiastic supporters, opponents or dissenters, and waverers—the uncommitted. The vast majority of employees usually fall into this latter category, even in Japan. The aim of mobilising is to transform this group into proactive and enthusiastic advocates of change.

4. Confirmation of the issues at stake in change

A further reason for mobilising is to reinforce the desire for change, not only among the decision-makers but among all the players concerned, by justifying, clarifying and endorsing the objectives defined in the vision. Confirming the issues at stake in change makes it appear less and less desirable to maintain the *status quo*.

5. A structured process of change

By now the need for change and the urgency of that need are generally accepted and there is a shared vision to show the way forward. The final objective of mobilising is therefore to structure the process of change by outlining its course and the activities to be undertaken.

HOW TO TELL WHEN AN ORGANISATION IS CORRECTLY MOBILISED

Several factors will indicate to managers that their part of the business has been mobilised to good effect:

- the vision and the values associated with it have clearly been understood and are shared by the majority of staff;
- each individual understands how the vision is to be interpreted at his or her own level and how to contribute personally and proactively to it;
- *ad hoc* teams and work groups are continually being created and dissolved in response to independent initiatives to propose, try out and put in place new ideas for accelerating the development of the business in the direction specified by the vision.

Many of these initiatives are 'cross-structural' (i.e. they involve participants from different units or departments). Figure 5.1 below shows how in an organisation that has been mobilised effectively, the change activity multiplies rapidly, thereby contributing greatly to success, as follows:

- communication is simple, fluid, rapid and multi-directional;
- decision-making procedures have been simplified and decisions are implemented rapidly;

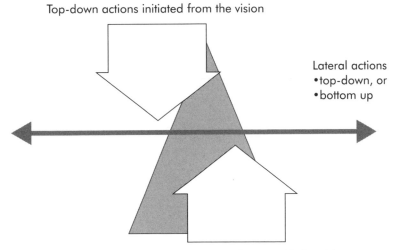

Figure 5.1 Multiplying of Change Activity in a Mobilised Organisation

– the goals of progress are ambitious, and there is perceptible enthusiasm and confidence in success.

Having described the benefits that mobilising generates, we next describe the three approaches that may be utilised.

THREE APPROACHES TO MOBILISATION

Much has been written about mobilisation as the first phase in the process of change. Table 5.1 below summarises the various theoretical models that have been developed. It is not our intention to set out the pros and cons of each of these, since they are in fact quite similar, but to describe methods of mobilising which we have experienced and which have proved their effectiveness widely, both in Europe and the United States. Only the Kurt Lewin model will be analysed in detail in this chapter. It will be noticed that, with the exception of the Tichy & Devanna model, all of them make mobilisation the first of three phases in the process of change.

The remainder of this chapter will describe three separate but complementary approaches to mobilising:

- a chain of seminars
- focused analysis and programming
- change workshops.

Table 5.1 Models of the Process of Change

Model	Process		
Kurt Lewin (1947)	Unfreezing	Changing	Refreezing
Beer (1980)	Discontent	Change	Target model
Kanter (1983)	Abandonment of tradition and crisis	Strategic decisions and initial action	Enactment of change and institutionalisation
Tichy & Devanna (1986)	Awakening	Mobilising	Reinforcing
Nadler & Tushman (1989)	Energy release	Target	Action

Source: Kanter, Stein, Jick: The challenge of organizational change

Approach 1: A Chain of Seminars

The idea of this approach is to set up a series of one- or two-day seminars for groups of between 20 and 40 people in order to mobilise what is known as a 'strategic community' which will implement change. This community consists of those individuals who potentially have the greatest ability and power to make change work (or on the other hand to obstruct it), and whose active support is therefore essential to success. The composition of the community will vary according to the form of change envisaged. For example, if it involves changes to working practices and attitudes throughout the business, the community might include all managers and senior staff; if the sphere of change is restricted to manufacturing, it might comprise only production unit supervisors and managers.

Structuring and Running a Mobilising Seminar

The seminar format is particularly appropriate for creating a sense of urgency, deepening understanding of and identifying with the vision, and plotting the course of the process of change to follow. It will reinforce staff support and commitment to change as well as their willingness to work together.

The graph in Figure 5.2, shows the typical development of attitudes during a mobilising seminar.

The seminar begins neutrally so that participants can get to know each other, exchange ideas and voice their expectations. In the second phase they will be rudely awakened to the realities of the situation and the urgent need for action. This is done by presenting the hard facts and every appropriate piece of evidence to account for the unexpected gravity of the situation. This is an extremely emotional part of the seminar and most participants will find it hard to cope with. One technique is to invite a dissatisfied customer to air his grievances and sing the praises of the competition. Another is to employ a consultant to play devil's advocate and pretend to be a competitor describing how he intends to set about outsmarting the business. Or perhaps a front page story from a leading business newspaper for some date in the future could be drafted and circulated, describing how the business went into liquidation.

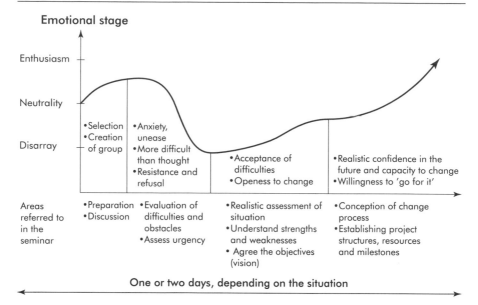

Figure 5.2   Development of Attitudes in a Mobilising Seminar

Participants might even be invited to engage in some role-playing to help them abandon their preconceptions and take a more objective view of the situation. For example:

'You are a competitor of your own business; how would you go about competing with it?'

'Your son decides to work for the business; what do you advise him?'

'Five years from now *The Economist* publishes an article on the success of your business; how would you write it?'

'You are about to retire from the business; what are you most proud of achieving?'

The aim is to make everyone painfully aware of the real problems, to create an awakening, a sense of dislocation, or even a crisis. Participants will then be more inclined to look for real solutions.

The next phase of the seminar involves analysing the present situation in greater detail, looking in particular at the weaknesses or limitations which need to be overcome as well as the true strengths which can be built upon. From an emotional point of view, par-

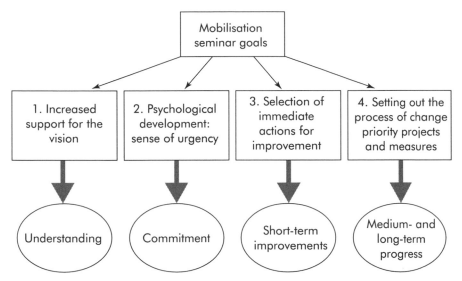

Figure 5.3   Goals of a Mobilisation Seminar

ticipants need to 'climb back up again'. They might perhaps discuss the vision in more detail, justifying it and enhancing it. This reinforces support for the vision. Difficulties are acknowledged and accepted, and willingness to change is strengthened, or in some cases created.

The seminar then ends by selecting and detailing the principal decisions or courses of action that will enable the business to evolve towards the vision. This is what we call designing the change process. Participants begin to show optimism, enthusiasm and commitment, and group bonding is strengthened.

Figure 5.3 shows the usual format of a mobilisation seminar.

Chain of Seminars

The idea of creating a chain of seminars is to mobilise the whole target community while ensuring that the message imparted and the decisions reached are consistent throughout. For example, in order to mobilise an entire line of management, representatives from two levels of the hierarchy must always participate in each seminar. Levels *n* and *n-1* will participate in the first seminar, and the second

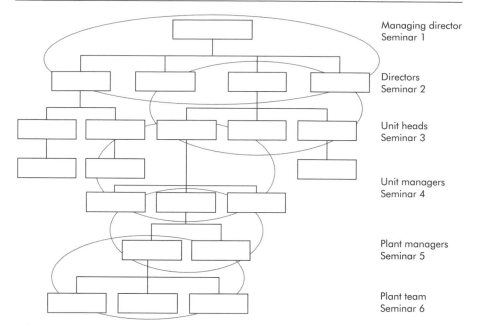

Managing director
Seminar 1

Directors
Seminar 2

Unit heads
Seminar 3

Unit managers
Seminar 4

Plant managers
Seminar 5

Plant team
Seminar 6

Figure 5.4   Using a Chain of Seminars in a Hierarchical Structure

will bring levels n-1 and n-2 together, plus a few representatives of level n as observers. The reason for including observers is to ensure that neither the message nor the decisions are diluted, curtailed or manipulated in any way. The third seminar will bring together levels n-2 and n-3, plus a few observers from level n-1, and so on down the chain, the principle being to achieve consistency by overlapping the various groups of participants. Figure 5.4 illustrates how it would work.

The worldwide change programme launched in the early 1990s by the president of Philips, Jan Timmer, was an attempt to relaunch the business and overcome the major difficulties it was experiencing. It was based on just such a chain of seminars.

Several international businesses have created special centres where these seminars for their executives are held—a structure symbolic of mobilisation. Crotonville, where a transformation of attitudes and values was famously forged by General Electric, is a case in point, as is the Motorola University, used widely by Motorola for major campaigns of change, which is also available to third parties.

Approach 2: Focused Analysis and Programming

This approach, which we have developed and applied during our work with many service and manufacturing businesses, is based on Kurt Lewin's theory of change (see Schein, Edgar H. (1992), *Process Consultation*, Volume 2, Addison-Wesley OD series). It relates to the first phase in Lewin's model, which he calls 'unfreezing'. First the underlying theory and then the procedure itself are summarised here.

The Underlying Theory

According to Lewin, change is a sequence of three phases:

- unfreezing
- changing or transformation
- refreezing or consolidation.

The unfreezing phase corresponds to mobilising and produces a group of individuals or a business which is convinced of the need for change and ready to commit to a process of change, despite the risks it entails. Unfreezing can in turn be broken down into three stages:

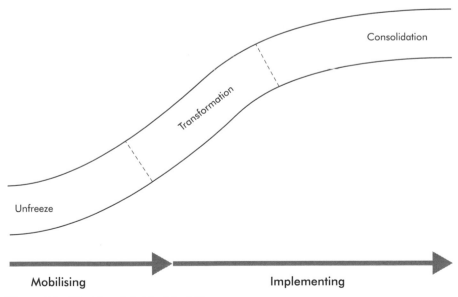

Figure 5.5   Kurt Lewin's Model of Change

- dislocation or rupture
- anxiety or guilt
- security.

Dislocation or rupture

Dislocation comes with the realisation that the situation the business has been in up to now has profoundly changed. For example:

- the competitive situation has been transformed by the appearance of new and better equipped competitors, or the launch of cheaper alternative products;
- profitability has fallen because of higher supply costs;
- new processes have been introduced;
- the ground-rules have been changed by deregulation.

Anxiety and Guilt

Feelings of anxiety or guilt arise when individuals realise that, given these new circumstances, what they are doing is no longer compatible with the best interests of the business or even runs counter to them. This realisation can be extremely unsettling, since it implies that they must suddenly abandon the traditional working methods, established practices, arguments, attitudes and opinions which they have previously relied on and adopt instead new, untried and unknown methods, a process which inevitably seems extremely risky.

An example taken from one of the leading electronic components distributors in the United States clearly illustrates the point. The company sells six product groups (active components, passive components, connectors, etc.) representing some 40 000 items which they distribute to several thousand customers across a wide range of market segments, including brown goods manufacturers, arms manufacturers and local retailers. As a result of an Activity Based Costing exercise, management realised that 80% of orders fell below the minimum volume required to reach profitability targets. Worse still, half of these orders did not even cover the direct costs attributable to them. This realisation came in a situation in which the salesforce's monthly targets were measured in volume terms, regardless of profitability. Moreover, their appreciation of how to maximise the profitability of the orders they generated was at best limited and at worst erroneous. Management therefore developed a software system to calculate the profitability of each order, which the salesforce was asked to use. From then on all negotiations were subject to an analysis of the order's contribution to profits. This course of action, backed up by an extensive programme of communication and explanation, created severe dislocation for the salesforce, whose credo had always been 'never refuse an order', followed by strong feelings of anxiety and even guilt that a large proportion of their sales were costing money instead of making money. This was one of the factors that led the business to initiate a process of change calling into question the whole basis of its sales methods and the way its sales operation was managed.

Security

By this stage of the process people have understood the need to modify their duties, their working methods or their behavioural patterns, an understanding which is associated with feelings of anxiety or guilt. However, the process of developing the understanding of what constitutes a new state can create just as much anxiety through the uncertainty prompted by the risks inherent in anything new or different from the present situation. Individuals are therefore faced with an unavoidable choice between two risks: to persist in their current ways, or to confront the unknown. They will only be willing to submit to change when they feel that the new course of action is the low-risk choice or when they are protected against the second risk, in other words when they are offered a safety net. In the case of the distribution company already mentioned above, the safety net provided by management consisted of significantly lower-volume targets for the following year than for previous years, on condition that the new profitability targets were met.

The three components of the unfreezing stage (dislocation, anxiety and security) apply not only to individuals but also to the organisation as a group of individuals. Essentially, unfreezing takes place when individuals (or organisations) are alerted to a dislocation in the current situation, made to understand that it is no longer possible to remain fixed in their present state, and finally given an assurance that precautions have been taken to assist and protect them in case of

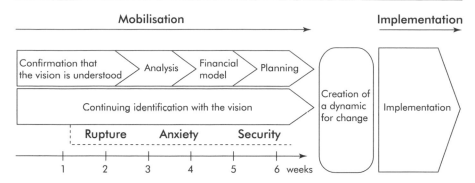

Figure 5.6   The Mobilisation Sequence

difficulty or failure so that they can go ahead and take the risk of changing to the new state. Unfreezing is therefore equivalent to mobilising, and we shall now look more closely at how it is undertaken. The procedure is modelled on Kurt Lewin's unfreezing phase and depends on a four-step sequence, as shown in Figure 5.6.

Confirming that the Vision Has Been Understood

The first objective is to confirm that all staff not only know what the vision is, but also understand it. Management should therefore already have started communicating extensively about the vision to explain and justify it. It is vital that this sort of communication is not seen as being empty of substance, with management continually putting forward visions and major change programmes without following them through.

Management can easily measure how well staff have understood the vision by means of structured interviews or questionnaires. Open questions such as 'What are the factors that will most affect our industry and our business during the next few years?' or 'What should our business do to adapt to these influences, and what strengths does it have in its favour?' or again 'What are the weaknesses that our business needs to overcome?'; questions like these will generally give a good indication of the level of understanding among staff. If this early study shows that the vision is not fully understood, it will have to be explained more fully before launching into the process of change. After all, the vision must be the constant guiding light of that process. On the other hand, if the vision has been properly understood by all staff, mobilisation can go ahead.

It is worth noting, incidentally, that these interviews/questionnaires have other benefits too:

- first of all they demonstrate to everyone in the business that something new is happening;
- second, they are an indication that the process of change will be highly collaborative at every level of the business. If staff are involved from the word go, it will be all the easier to encourage them to participate actively later on.

An unorthodox example of this is provided by a large French manufacturing group which wanted to find out whether staff identified with its new vision of 'increasing productivity by 20% and improving quality by reducing the number of defects to nil within two years'. They had the 50 most common questions about productivity and quality printed on a pack of cards and then held a series of group information sessions at which each participant drew a card and read out the question to the rest of the group. In this way they were able to assess the extent to which staff identified with the vision and at the same time to enhance people's understanding of it. Turning the process into a game also helped to ensure a high level of participation.

However, understanding and acceptance of the vision are not in themselves enough to create a dynamic for change among staff. Although they may be sufficient to create a sense of dislocation, they are often insufficient to create the feeling of anxiety which leads to a willingness to evolve from the existing state, which may be after all still a comfortable one, towards a new and apparently dangerous situation. The European automobile industry is a good example. Extensive communication on the subject of Japanese competition and how it threatened the very existence of the industry meant that the majority of employees in vehicle and component manufacturing understood the need to improve the performance of their businesses. One such business then launched a change programme with the aim of accelerating the rate at which its productivity increased, the stated vision being to reduce to three years the time it would take to wipe out the competitive advantage of its Japanese rivals, whose European factories then had 15% lower manufacturing costs. But although all were aware of the Japanese threat, most employees were not ready to embark on a programme of global change. The business therefore had to implement an intensive mobilisation phase involving extensive communication, analytical work and large-scale meetings in order to motivate employees and persuade them to participate.

Analysis

The objective of analysis is to reveal the improvements that will result from implementing the vision. It is neither a question of conducting exhaustive research, nor of solving problems, but simply of collecting enough evidence of the opportunities available to create a sense of dislocation and anxiety among employees, the potential for improvement being in proportion to the unacceptability of the existing situation.

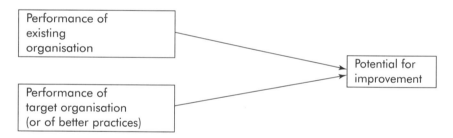

Figure 5.7   Conducting an opportunity Analysis

The analysis, set out in Figure 5.7, is carried out by systematically investigating each dysfunction of the business, each missed opportunity, and showing how they hinder the performance of the existing organisation and how implementing the vision or introducing 'better practice' would improve it. This approach is orthodox in its logic but unorthodox in its application, being both collaborative and rapid.

- *Collaborative analysis*: the approach uses analytical tools based on the collaboration of all levels of employees, including both executives and the workforce more generally.
  - Structured interviews are designed to collect ideas for improvement, taking maximum advantage of the experience of all em-

ployees and their knowledge of the business. The most valuable answers are generated by open questions like 'In which areas should we concentrate on making improvements, and why?' or 'What are the major obstacles to improvement, and why?' This kind of questioning is very much like installing a suggestions box, which many businesses do. It is often surprising how much information and how many good ideas are produced, helping to identify areas with the greatest potential for improvement which can then be analysed further.

– A group description and illustration of the processes:—administrative procedures, activities, interdepartmental relations, etc.— is made by the users themselves on large sheets of paper placed on the walls. A facilitator is appointed to help them set out methodically all the difficulties and problems they have encountered and any opportunities they may have identified. As a tool, this has several benefits. It allows a wealth of ideas to be collected in a few hours or days, because individuals can express themselves openly and without fear. It helps to motivate staff, since users are generally happy to talk about their activities, their role and their problems. It is also a highly visible activity and therefore a further indication of the will of management to implement the change. The first challenge is to ensure that employees make the list of problems and opportunities as long as possible, without attempting to offer solutions to any of them. The second challenge is to select the processes or areas in which the most clear-cut opportunities for improvement are likely to arise. We shall be looking more closely at this technique when considering Key 5: *Delivering*, in which it is extensively used.

The way in which the analysis is carried out is just as important as the results it produces. It is essential to devise tools which, as well as supplying the required data, serve as methods of involving the users in the analytical process and making them aware of the scope for improvement. From this point of view, an analysis is quite different from an audit: it is made by those directly involved in day-to-day operations, not by independent internal or external evaluators. The aim is to get enough employees to participate so that everyone in the business has at least one close colleague who has taken part in the process and who can vouch for the collaborative approach adopted. A participation rate of between 10% and 20% is usually enough to achieve this aim.

- *Rapid analysis:* analysis can and must be done quickly. It is not an end in itself, simply a means to an end to make blatantly obvious the wealth of opportunities that exist and the need for a change programme to be executed. It need not be exhaustive because the issue is simply to show up enough areas for improvement to bring about a reassessment of the way things are done. Besides, most of the effort put into the process of change should be focused on delivery, i.e. on realising opportunities. For this reason the analysis must be done as quickly as possible. An exhaustive and detailed analysis of the existing situation will be carried out later during the delivery stage. It is important to recognise, however, that analysis should be predominantly fact- and not theory-driven. Some organisations set great store by this and rightly so. It is all too easy to fail to act with the necessary rigour, which can create a serious credibility gap and therefore an obstacle to change from the very outset.

Analysis, when properly undertaken, severely destabilises the situation by bringing a wealth of problems and opportunities to the attention of a large number of staff within a short time. Many employees will regard these opportunities as a threat or a criticism and will be afraid of finding their role called into question, or simply resent the fact that the job they thought they were doing properly is now under review. To senior and middle management, the number of problems and opportunities and all the issues they raise will come as a shock, but this is in fact what is supposed to happen when the results of the analysis are collated and presented to management. The analysis is normally considered to have achieved its objectives when the reactions of managers are along the lines of:

'I didn't realise things were so bad.' (dislocation)
'Why didn't we tackle these problems before?' (sense of urgency and perhaps anxiety and guilt)

Although the results come as a shock, the fact that the analysis has been carried out by the staff themselves gives it the necessary credibility and reduces the chance of it being questioned. The problem has been identified, continuity has been broken and feelings of anxiety and guilt have been aroused, which will be strengthened by the next stage of mobilising, financial modelling.

An example of this effect is a European industrial equipment manufacturer whose vision was to improve his new product development cycle by reducing development time as well as manufacturing cost. The conclusions of the analysis were as follows:

- Our development cycle takes 30% longer than our competitors' and this disparity is on the increase.
- Our new product development process ignores development methods, causing constant to-ing and fro-ing between manufacturing and engineering, and regular delays to new product launches.
- Our investment in new production techniques is partly or even totally misdirected because production considerations do not feature in the new product development cycle.
- Conflicts between engineering, research and production methods are preventing an integrated approach to new product development.
- Conflicts with suppliers, caused by shopping around for the lowest prices, are also leading to regular delays, additional costs and quality problems.

Modelling Financial Savings

Analysis reveals the opportunities for improvement which would be realised by accomplishing the vision. The objective of financial modelling is to quantify the results of possible improvements and their impact on the profitability of the business. Here again it is imperative to involve the people normally concerned in such matters, in this case accounting staff, as well as the employees who drew attention to the opportunities. The calculations should not be made by managers alone, but also by executive, white-collar and blue-collar staff, who will later be responsible for implementing the change process. So it is appropriate to use a method which the people concerned can take part in and identify with. One way is to start by getting the users to translate the implications of the improvement opportunities into performance indicators such as increased market share, increased margins, reduced labour-intensity of manufacture, etc. The financial implications of movements in these indicators can then be evaluated by the accountants. The greater the collaboration between the operational and accounting staff, the quicker and more effective the whole exercise will be.

Clarifying the scale of the financial implications will add to the feelings of anxiety and guilt already aroused, especially since the calculations have been made on the basis of data developed by the users themselves. In the earlier example of the manufacturer who was trying to improve his new product development process, financial modelling showed that the development period could be reduced by 40%, development costs by 50% and the manufacturing costs of future products by 20%.

Planning

In this next stage the aim is to create a feeling of security by demonstrating through plans and actions that it is possible to achieve the improvements identified and evaluated in previous stages.

By this stage a significant number of staff will have understood the necessity of implementing the vision. Employees will have taken part in a rapid analysis which has revealed a surprising degree of dysfunction and significant opportunities for improvement. In addition, the improvements have been quantified in collaboration with the accountants and business analysts. The logical next step is to draw up a plan to enable the opportunities to be exploited—in other words, to undertake the necessary changes.

Planning will define:

- the articulation of the vision into improvements which must be defined in detail and activated in order to realise the objectives of the vision;
- the principal stages of implementation, timetabled as precisely as possible. The timetable will be broken down in detail for each improvement initiative at the start of the delivery stage, as we shall see in Chapter 8;
- the composition of the teams responsible for developing each improvement initiative;
- the results expected from the implementation of the improvements. The results expected from achieving the vision can therefore be confirmed at this stage. If there is any discrepancy, the vision can be redefined and the analysis and the financial modelling subjected to a further iteration.

Programming must be carried out by senior management, higher-level executives and the employees directly concerned with the activities under review.

Example: In the case of the example described at the end of the previous section, the improvement initiatives were defined as follows:

1. developing an integrated approach to new product development, combining research, engineering, manufacturing, purchasing and marketing;
2. developing partnerships with suppliers;
3. realigning the manufacturing function with research and development activities;
4. defining the role of senior management in the new product development cycle.

For each of these initiatives, the following additional activities were undertaken in the programming stage:

- detailed analysis of the existing situation, development of the desired organisation structure, implementation planning;
- selection of the relevant expert teams, including the names of the leaders and individual members;
- the likely benefits, both quantitative and qualitative, and examples of the indicators to be used to measure them.

Despite the ambitious nature of the vision, it took just four weeks to mobilise. Because the company did not at the time have resources dedicated to change, the exercise was carried out with the help of external consultants. One of the first stages in the implementation plan was to train just such internal resources.

Continuing Identification With the Vision

At each stage in the process of mobilisation we have insisted on the fundamental importance of staff involvement, and described how their participation can be obtained in practice. This is one way of getting employees to identify with the recommendations made.

Another way is to present the results of each stage to a steering committee for endorsement and guidance on the content of the next stage. If each committee member is first briefed individually, the process will be made simpler and surprises avoided. They are each responsible in turn for informing their own staff of the content of the presentation.

A third way is to pass on the results of analysis as they emerge to the personnel concerned, who will validate them and incorporate any new ideas. In the context of a process which is supposed to be carried out quickly, this continual validation might seem excessive and a waste of valuable time. In fact the team in charge of carrying out the process will spend 30–40% of their time on it. It is nevertheless vital to ensure identification with the vision because the value-added by involving the users in continuous reassessment lies in asking them to come up with new ideas and practical solutions. Validation is much more productive when carried out collaboratively.

Continuing identification with the vision ensures that it and the change process do not become the property of a few managers but belong to the majority of employees.

The process of focused analysis and programming is particularly well suited to launching extensive change in a specific area which has a clearly defined scope but which involves a wide range of participants from different parts of the business. Examples of this type of change are a reduction in the time taken to develop and launch new products, a reorganisation of the supply chain and logistics systems, and the introduction of a customer-focused strategy.

Approach 3: Change Workshops

The third approach to mobilising consists of setting up workshops whose aim is to kick-start a dynamic of change at a local level.

The advantages of this are:

- using local change management means that the programme, project or action is conceived, defined and executed from the outset by the people who will be most directly affected by it;
- the project is intrinsically in sympathy with concerns at the grass roots;
- the workforce and their middle managers are all the more committed and determined to succeed because it is *their* project;
- senior managers have less need to monitor and control the process: their main concerns are to verify at the start that the initiative is appropriate to the ultimate purpose of the vision and then to ensure that any positive results it has are communicated more widely;
- more lasting results are achieved.

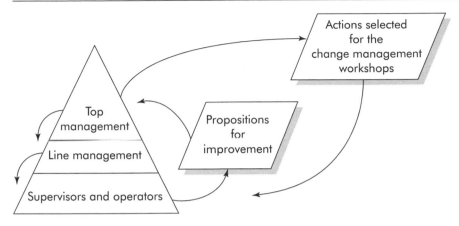

Figure 5.8 The Logic Behind Change Workshops

By this means a dynamic can be created as a chain reaction out of which suggestions for progressive action consistent with the pursuit of the vision will emerge and move up in importance and wider impact.

These suggestions will be analysed by the managers of the relevant part of the business and retained if they conform to the direction of the vision. They are then developed in change workshops by the people who had the original ideas. The workgroup is taught problem-solving, teamwork, analytical skills and how to carry out change, and a facilitator is officially appointed to help them (compare with the role of the facilitator in Key 3: *Catalysing*).

We have found the workshop approach particularly effective in generating high-impact operational improvements at grass-roots level (e.g. a 60% reduction in order fulfilment and delivery times, an increase in sales efficiency, cost reductions and so on) while also mobilising the grass roots and generating enthusiasm at this level. A critical success factor in this approach is to choose subjects for improvement where most of the decisions can be taken at a local level. Workshops are also a vehicle for spreading new values and ultimately a new culture such as teamworking or a results- or customer-led approach.

Table 5.2 'Making workshops work', explains how they operate.

Many major businesses now use change workshops to create a dynamic for change at local level. A similar approach is taken at General Electric, where it is called a 'work-out', and at Motorola, who

Table 5.2 Making Workshops Work

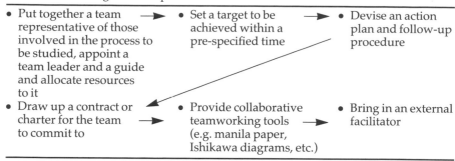

- Put together a team representative of those involved in the process to be studied, appoint a team leader and a guide and allocate resources to it
- Draw up a contract or charter for the team to commit to

- Set a target to be achieved within a pre-specified time

- Provide collaborative teamworking tools (e.g. manila paper, Ishikawa diagrams, etc.)

- Devise an action plan and follow-up procedure

- Bring in an external facilitator

have organised hundreds of workshops, the Motorola University calls these Total Client Satisfaction (TCS) teams.

The three approaches to mobilising we have described in this chapter allow businesses to respond to different types of change according to the particular problems they present as shown in Table 5.3. They can be used independently or concurrently as required.

Table 5.3 Choosing the Right Approach

	• Transformation of whole organisation • Global change in attitudes	• Transformation of one area of business (e.g. restructuring of logistics system)	• Proliferation of initiatives for change at operational level
Chain of seminars	XXX	XX	X
Focused analysis and programming	XX	XXX	X
Workshops	X	X	XXX

XXX = highly effective lever; XX = moderately effective lever; X = lever of limited effectiveness

Critical Success Factors

Several conditions must be met if mobilising is to be successful. Our experience indicates that if they are ignored, mobilisation will fail.

A Dedicated and Competent Team

Because a lot of work needs to be done in a short time, the team of people involved must be dedicated to conducting the approach in a dynamic way. The team must possess the appropriate expertise and skills. It may also prove expedient to call in outside experts on a temporary basis so that the necessary skills can be acquired more quickly.

The Change Facilitation Team is the unit responsible for steering and animating the process of change, while of course it is up to the appropriate line managers and staff to put the plans into action. The role and composition of the Change Facilitation Team will be defined more precisely in Keys 3 and 4, *Catalysing* and *Steering* respectively.

Management Commitment

During periods of change, managers are under even closer scrutiny than usual. Every one of their decisions and attitudes is being analysed and interpreted by employees. They need to set an example by demonstrating their own willingness and ability to mobilise and their commitment. They must therefore give up their own time to the process of mobilising and take the decision to make available the necessary human, material and financial resources.

A Positive Attitude Among Top and Middle Management

Both top and middle management must adopt a positive attitude towards subordinates when dealing with the problems and opportunities that have been identified. Under no circumstances should they try to find out who is responsible for past weaknesses or mistakes in order to 'punish' them. This sort of attitude would not only dry up the source of ideas but, worse still, instantly destroy the climate of universal participation and the whole dynamic of change which the mobilising process aims to create. The 'Let me sort out whoever is responsible' approach is suicidal for approaching a process of change.

A Short Timescale

Mobilising is not an end in itself, but a transitional phase leading to delivering, which has as its objective the changes to be made, on which the energies of the business must be concentrated as soon as possible. The timescales in mobilising must therefore be shorter rather than longer. The focused analysis approach, for example, can be completed in four to six weeks, even in very large organisations (i.e. more than 10 000 people).

***

Key 2: *Mobilising* enables a dynamic for change to be created within the business. This dynamic forms the basis for subsequent activity, i.e. the implementation of change. Nevertheless, it must always be borne in mind that an organisation can never be definitively and singularly mobilised; mobilising must therefore be continued throughout the implementation process and repeated as and when necessary, using the methods described in this chapter.

CASE STUDY ON MOBILISING: PHILIPS ELECTRONICS

Philips is one of the world leaders in electronics with $40 billion in sales in 1996 and 260 000 employees worldwide. Philips is organised in product divisions: lighting, sound and vision, components and semiconductors, professional products and systems, software and services and other. Philips is a strongly innovative company and this tradition is being continued with emerging products such as WebTV and the CD-ReWritable and telephone products.

At the end of the eighties, however, Philips went through a serious crisis which endangered its position. The company was not competitive against companies such as Sony and Matsushita and went into major financial loss. Turnover per employee was less than half that of its competitors and its operating income per employee was one-tenth that of Sony. Jan Timmer, the incoming president, launched a company-wide programme for change in the fall of 1990, called Centurion. Timmer's objective was to mobilise rapidly all Philips resources to ensure recovery while ensuring full compatibility with current actions. One hundred top managers met to assess the situation and begin the process of rebuilding. This meeting, called Centurion I, identified numerous issues in the company such as customers' needs and satisfaction, new product development, finance, and relationships with suppliers. As a result of the meeting, task forces were established to rapidly and deeply improve on the existing situation. Centurion I was the first of many meetings which would ultimately involve thousands of managers, as for example in Centurion II, III and IV.

Centurion meetings were organised by product divisions, National Organisations and staff departments. Each new Centurion made it possible to go deeper into the organisation and involve more and more managers. There were three hierarchical levels usually attending the two- to three-day meeting, which was very important in obtaining cohesion. At each meeting some had already participated in a previous Centurion. The goal of the meetings was to make sure that participants realised that change was needed and that there was a need to mobilise rapidly. The meetings followed the pattern described earlier in this chapter and were very intense. Each meeting was carefully prepared so as to guarantee its effectiveness. Financial and market data necessary for each meeting were gathered and analysed, interviews were carried out and estimates prepared. Thus, participants had all the necessary elements for a good and objective understanding of the situation before deciding on what actions needed to be undertaken. All seminars were targeted at contributing to the Philips rebuilding process. The conclusion was always an action plan implemented from the next day forward aiming at reaching very ambitious improvement objectives. After the seminar each individual knew exactly what he had to do to build a new future for Philips. In this way the atmosphere at Philips improved. In this serious situation, managers were confident in the future when they saw changes in working methods being proposed and the capacity being made available to make changes immediately.

In its first year Centurion focused on profitability improvement. Re-engineering actions concerned cost reduction, improvement in productivity, and optimisation of the activity portfolio. Re-engineering was painful for the company—45 000 people left the company in this period. Once these early actions had been taken other developments relating to customers, quality and competencies were introduced and implemented so as to revitalise the company and prepare for the future. The first Centurion (Centurion II and some Centurion III) meetings, were therefore focused on rebuilding while in the later meetings (Centurion III, IV and V) the emphasis was on revitalising initiatives.

Between the end of 1990 and the beginning of 1993, about 200 meetings took place worldwide, thus allowing the mobilisation of thousands of managers. Although the objectives remained unchanged (changing the mindset and creating actions to make change happen) the focus varied. Centurion III focused on particular topics such as zero defects, total customer satisfaction, or a targeted return on investment. Other Centurion III activities were focused on implementing the Centurion I task force recommendations. The consumer electronics division dedicated several Centurions to reaching excellence in supplier relations and in purchasing cost reduction. The method of approach brought added value to the existing change programmes of some entities while keeping their original name. In Taiwan, for example, Centurion is called Company Wide Quality Improvement, while Philips Lighting calls it The Winning Spirit and Philips Medical calls it PROMIS.

The flexibility and pragmatism of the Centurion implementation were essential to success. Global objectives were set and adapted to each level according to the specific nature of each entity and its internal priorities. The Centurion cascade process is an extremely powerful mobilisation tool for Philips. Beyond its contribution to improved profitability and operational effectiveness, the Centurion cascade impact has been very positive on team-working, communication, customer orientation, cooperation between entities and in sharing of information. These benefits have been revealed through special surveys of Centurion projects.

Chapter 6

Key 3: Catalysing

The business environment is constantly evolving. Customers' needs change, competitors introduce new products, new legislation changes the rules, and developments in fashions and habits alter customers' expectations.

Businesses cannot escape these influences and must therefore constantly adapt. The real challenge is to evolve quickly enough to maintain or increase market share, growth rate and profitability when competitors are themselves continuously evolving. In other words, each business must find a way of speeding up its development, and increasing its rate of transformation. Unfortunately this does not happen automatically. On the contrary, each unit, department or division of the business is preoccupied by its own day-to-day tasks and responsibilities. They have neither the time nor the resources, let alone the skills, to coordinate a process of change which will help the business to develop more quickly. It is up to the business leadership to devise and set up structures and mechanisms designed to do just that. This is what we call 'catalysing', after the scientific term meaning to accelerate a chemical reaction by the influence of an agent (the catalyst). To catalyse the change process therefore means to accelerate change by the influence of an organisational structure and mechanisms designed for the purpose.

STRUCTURE AND MECHANISM

A structure which enables catalysis to take place is one which ensures that:

- all the departments and parts of the business affected allocate the appropriate resources and the necessary time to the change process;
- the relevant skills and methodological support are brought to bear;
- the various measures involved in the process are co-ordinated;
- a sufficient level of participation is generated.

The model structure and mechanism we shall propose will enable the desired objectives to be achieved in the vast majority of cases (see Figure 6.1).

The new organisation is put in place once the improvement initiatives have been defined, in other words at the end of mobilising and before embarking on Key 4: *Delivering*. The change management steering committee and the change facilitation team were in place during mobilising to monitor its progress. This formal structure is applicable to a major change involving dislocation as opposed to slow, continuous change. In the latter case a change facilitation team would probably be enough. Its role will be explained later in this chapter.

ROLE OF SENIOR MANAGEMENT

The overall strategic direction and the master plan for the development of the business are defined by senior management. The principal function of defining the strategic aspects of the change is discharged at the time of establishing the vision (see Key 1: *Defining the vision*). After this, senior management bears the ultimate responsibility for ensuring that the change process is consistent with the vision, and that the necessary conditions for the success of the change process are met. Beyond defining the vision, the role of senior management therefore consists of:

- setting up the appropriate mechanisms to support the change process;
- allocating high-quality human resources to the process (i.e. change facilitation teams, expert teams, support teams, etc.);

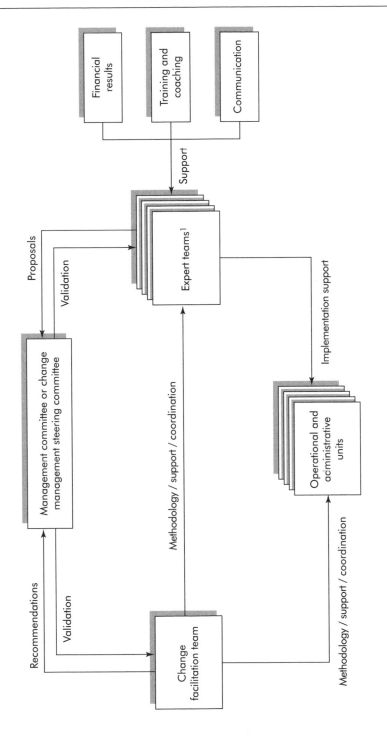

(1) One team per improvement initiative

Figure 6.1 Structure and Functions in a Change Programme

- validating the broad direction (principal stages, organisation, resources, timetable, etc.)
- regularly validating the development choices made by the business to ensure their consistency with the vision;
- breaking down the barriers to change in cases where high-level intervention is needed (e.g. where certain managers resolutely oppose all changes in the business despite every effort to bring them round. In this case they have to be found another position within the organisation or even let go);
- checking and analysing the financial results of the process;
- ensuring that the staff are appropriately informed of progress;
- ensuring that the necessary training is undertaken.

One of the objectives of creating a special structure for change management is to provide senior management with the means to fulfil the role. The management committee of the business or a subcommittee might equally well act on behalf of senior management, or a steering committee for activating change can be specially constituted for the purpose. This latter option is usually the most effective. Consisting of between eight and twelve people, the committee should include senior managers, the leader of the facilitation team and the managers of the departments or divisions most affected by the new vision and the changes needing to be introduced.

Meetings should be held every two weeks for the first few months, which is the most critical time for the success of the change process. Any waverers will be brought on board by the first signs of success, whereas any failure will make them break away and resist or oppose it. Moreover, if senior management are seen to be actively involved in the process via the steering committee, this will act as a clear sign of commitment in the eyes of the rest of the business. An even stronger signal can be given by informing the whole business of the agenda for each committee meeting and the decisions arrived at. It might be useful to invite one or more people involved in top management to take turns in attending the meetings, providing a direct and effective communication link with the rest of the business. In choosing to do this, it is obviously all the more important to ensure that there is a high degree of unanimity within the committee, who must be seen by the rest of the business to be firmly committed to and enthusiastic for change. Any dissent or opposition among them would damage the credibility of the vision and of the change process itself.

A simple but effective way of ensuring the smooth running of committee meetings is to appoint a 'facilitator', whose role is to brief every committee member before each meeting. This involves submitting all the presentations and subjects for discussion to them individually in order to get their backing for decisions needing to be taken before the meeting at which they are to be discussed. The leader of the change facilitation team or one of its members is generally best placed to act as facilitator.

THE CHANGE FACILITATION TEAM

The majority of staff will be preoccupied by their day-to-day activities. Employees will have little time to stand back and consider how the implementation of change is progressing. Besides, managing change requires specific social and managerial skills as well as technical expertise, which the average employee would not necessarily have. Finally, the implementation of change can generate resistance and often strong rejection, or simply questions prompted by fear of the unknown. A special unit needs to be set up to mitigate such negative attitudes and behaviour and to guide the development of the business through the power issues and emotional ups and downs. For these reasons we recommend setting up a team specifically responsible for facilitating change whose role is as follows:

- to assist senior management in defining the improvement initiatives on the basis of the vision already established and then setting the process in motion;
- to plan and develop the overall timetable;
- to provide the expert teams with tools for carrying out change and assist them in doing so;
- to participate in the working groups in order to help them identify and solve the problems they encounter;
- to assist in imposing overall consistency on the change process at both a strategic and an operational level;
- generally to 'steer' the change process (see Key 4: *Steering*).

Ideally the change facilitation team should report in to the top manager of the business. This will emphasise the message to the rest of the organisation that the change process is important as well as enabling decisions to be taken quickly. It also helps to reinforce the cross-functional role of the facilitation team. A less effective option (in our view) is to have facilitation reporting in to the board of directors.

The facilitation team should be quite small, comprising between four and at most ten people. It is the staff as a whole who will make change happen by adopting new working methods and assuming their new roles and responsibilities; the facilitation team will act as a catalyst in these developments.

Team Leader Profile

The team leader will be someone from within the business with at least ten years' experience in various roles and a broadly-based knowledge of the business. He or she will have to be:

- highly credible and respected by both top management and staff in general;
- a natural leader, capable of not only understanding but also sharing the vision, of identifying the improvement initiatives and communicating them to others in a convincing way;
- a born communicator, able to speak easily to anyone in the business;
- an arbitrator who can analyse and understand problems and situations from an analytical as well as from a political or emotional point of view;
- either a senior business leader or high-flying executive. Given that he or she will be in constant contact with management and that the team's involvement cuts across the whole business, the person must be in a fairly senior position in order to have the necessary credibility.

Team Member Profile

The other members of the facilitation team must know the business well, have a high degree of credibility, possess experience of project management (i.e. solving multifunctional queries and problems) and be capable of working in both formal and informal environments. They will be executives of stature. Their superiors will probably not be willing to see them transferred to another unit and senior management intervention may be required to make them available.

The team leader will be looking for executives with particular personal qualities and technical skills, including:

- willingness to work as a team and an interest in participating in cross-functional working groups;
- the ability to communicate at all levels, and make themselves understood at different levels and across the various functional departments and conversely to understand the problems and issues raised;
- the ability to mobilise and lead a team of people from different functions and different levels;
- a well-developed capacity for listening and 'reading between the lines' in order to grasp the true nature of situations and problems;
- a highly developed sense of responsibility, i.e. a willingness and ability to do the best possible job under any circumstances and within the allotted time;
- the qualities of a trainer and coach (see Key 9: *Training and Coaching*);
- a gift for 'seeing the wood for the trees', i.e. for identifying and emphasising priorities amidst a mass of data and information;
- an aptitude for summarising situations in the simplest possible terms;
- good knowledge of one or more business areas.

Ideally facilitation team members should be drawn from different functions of the business. This is another way of optimising their role as facilitators with all types of employees and, more specifically, when working within the expert teams.

The change facilitation team is the only body (apart from the change steering committee) which will have been in place since the launch of mobilisation. It is the kingpin, especially when it comes to analytical work, and reports directly to the steering committee. It is also the only team which will not necessarily be disbanded once the changes are complete. The steering committee, expert teams and support teams will all be disbanded once the vision has been realised, while the facilitation team will continue to act as a catalyst in the case of slow, progressive change or where a second change process necessitates the setting up of a more formal organisation such as the one described in this chapter. Some of the more important duties of the facilitation team are described in more detail under Key 4: *Steering*, while the remaining roles are described under other keys in later chapters.

THE EXPERT TEAMS

The role of the expert teams is to devise the solutions to be put into effect for each improvement initiative and to ensure that they are carried through (see Key 5: *Delivering*). We recommend that they should be 'cross-functional' teams (one for each improvement initiative) for several reasons:

- the solutions sought are often complex and require the active involvement of executives and employees at different levels and from different departments or functions of the business. Working as a 'cross-functional' group makes it easier to rise above potential difficulties such as rivalries between different departments or divisions and rigid hierarchical structures;
- solutions worked out by teams will be better for having benefited from a wide range of experiences and skills;
- team solutions will be more readily adopted, since employees will identify more fully with the vision and its objectives if they have been involved in formulating them;
- teamwork allows many barriers to change to be broken down by making employees who may not even have known each other before, work together. The more complex the vision is and the more it involves multifunctional changes, the more effectively these expert teams will be able to break down barriers to change. They are therefore particularly well-suited to changes involving the revision of major business processes (new product development, for example, which requires the integration of research, development, production, marketing and purchasing), since this necessarily calls for collaboration between the various parties concerned right across the business;
- run properly, they enable the improvement initiatives to be developed and put into effect more rapidly;
- setting up these teams gives yet another indication to staff in general that the business is committed to a process of change.

The expert teams report directly to the management committee or the change steering committee, and their specific purpose is to develop the improvement initiatives which were defined at the end of the mobilising stage (see Key 2). The members of these teams are drawn from both administrative and operational areas and we recommend that they continue to report to their respective managers in a matrix structure. Indeed, they will usually not be required to work full time with the team (between 30% and 50% of their time is often enough) and the matrix format helps to involve their normal line managers in the process, since they remain in contact with them. Furthermore, when the teams are disbanded, the members can return to their former positions where they will perform a particularly effective role in seeing to it that the changes they have helped to put into effect are lasting. This also avoids the need to reassign them, which can cause considerable problems in large organisations.

The life-cycle of the expert teams might follow the pattern described below:

1. management defines the improvement initiatives at the end of the mobilising stage and sets up an expert team for each one;
2. the expert teams define their tasks (aims and objectives, timetable, principal stages and means of implementation) based on the objectives and vision defined by management;
3. the expert teams work out a recommendation for each improvement initiative which is then validated by the steering committee;
4. the expert teams put the solutions into practice. Once the process has been launched and is well enough under way, their level of activity gradually diminishes.

They are eventually disbanded at the end of the delivering stage when the solutions adopted have been largely implemented. The operational and administrative management teams ensure that the changes are lasting. The teams therefore only exist for the duration of the change process.

The way these teams are structured is crucial to their success in carrying out their task, culminating in implementing the improvement initiative they are responsible for. The chances of success will be greatest if the various roles are clearly and appropriately assigned. There are three distinct roles to be allocated: those of leader, facilitator and team member, as shown in Figure 6.2 .

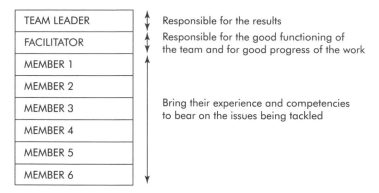

Figure 6.2   Structure of an Expert Team

Team Leader

The team leader is the person who has been given responsibility by the steering committee for providing a solution to a particular problem; for defining the target and structure of the improvement initiative his or her team is responsible for, putting it into practice and achieving results.

It is crucial that the leader should be an executive of some seniority with considerable credibility within the business, to indicate once again the importance of the change process and management's commitment to its success. Another reason for the leader to hold a senior position is that he or she will then be better able to resolve any inter-departmental problems the team may encounter by assisting them to gain access to important data or key personnel. It is also a good idea to choose a leader who seems to have a natural 'claim' on the particular initiative, i.e. the executive in charge, or at least partially in charge, of the function, process or area which is to be improved. For example, if one of the needs is to improve the quality of service the business offers its customers in order to gain an advantage over the competition, the expert team might be led by the sales manager or perhaps the marketing manager.

The question must be asked whether such people are available to act as team leaders. Should they neglect their jobs and devote themselves full time to the change process, or should they carry on their existing duties simultaneously? As we have already mentioned, we believe the second option is preferable. They will have to arrange for some of their normal responsibilities to be delegated, while taking advantage of help and advice in order to make the most effective contribution to their expert teams. As we shall see, the facilitator will provide the necessary assistance.

The Facilitator

Facilitators are experts in managing change. Their role is to make the team as efficient as possible by providing it with appropriate resources, techniques and tools, coordinating its activities (meetings, group problem-solving, etc.) and generally stimulating good group dynamics. They act as a sort of personal coach for each member of the team, helping them to make progress as a result of their experience with the team (see Key 9: *Training and Coaching*). They are also responsible for defining and providing the interface between the team and the rest of the business (or whichever parts of it are affected by the change) so that as many employees as possible feel involved in the work of the team and consequently in the change process. This is achieved by means of the tools and the working procedure introduced to the team by the facilitator (see Key 6: *Obtaining Participation*).

Usually facilitators are members of the change facilitation team who have been assigned to a particular expert team or teams. Each facilitator can work with up to three expert teams at once, but ideally only two. Their work as facilitation team members involves them 100% of the time in the change process.

The Team Members

The other members of the expert team are what we might call its life force. There should be between five and ten of them; any more would make the team less efficient because of the difficulty of getting them all together at the same time and of creating and maintaining good team spirit. Members are chosen for their skills or knowledge relating to the particular improvement initiative under consideration. They will come from several different levels and functions of the business, in order to bring together the maximum variety of experience and to ensure that the adopted solution is integrated as fully as possible into the relevant part of the business. So the teams are not only multifunctional and multilevel, especially if they are dealing with one of the business's fundamental processes which cuts across the current organisation of the business. This is one of the differences between them and 'quality circles', as well as the fact that the expert teams act at a more strategic and global level.

Team members will be chosen by the team leader, with the support of the change facilitation team, and endorsed by the steering committee. It is essential to select people who, as well as possessing technical skills, are able to contribute by having a positive attitude towards change and the ability and willingness to work as part of a team. If this is not possible, the facilitator's job becomes even more critical and a rather more flexible timetable will be required, since it will take longer to get the team all pulling in the same direction and working together effectively.

In terms of their commitment, we recommend that team members continue their original duties, as far as possible, but with a lighter workload. They too should devote between 30% and 50% of their time to the expert team, which will allow them to retain a significant proportion of their original responsibilities. This temporary matrix arrangement will obviously put considerable pressure on these employees, who will have to report to their team leader as well as to their usual superiors. On the other hand, it ensures that the people who are to design the change process are also the ones who will be actively involved in implementing it. Apart from allowing better communication of the adopted solutions to all staff, this matrix arrangement prevents the business being split between the chosen few who are to build the future and the rest, who are concerned only with day-to-day operational and administrative tasks.

An example of how it should be done is given by a leading US-based oil company, which recently launched a Europe-wide change programme. Management's vision was to integrate their entire European operation in order to benefit from potential economies of scale and to offer the best possible service to their customers all over the world. The challenge was to reorganise Europe from being territorially-based to being function-based, the whole organisation to be supported by a single IT system. It was a matter of replacing six independent ways of operating (one in each of the six main countries where they had plants) with an integrated and consistent approach which maximised efficiency of operation across all six countries. Management established that this development would involve designing and establishing nine management processes which would be common to all six countries and supported by the same IT system:

1. purchasing and relationships with suppliers in general;
2. order processing;
3. distribution and delivery;
4. stock control;
5. invoicing;
6. pricing policy;
7. sales reporting system;
8. budgeting;
9. sales and purchase accounting and general ledger.

Nine expert teams were charged with defining and proposing an outline target organisation for each of the nine management processes, which therefore constituted the nine improvement initiatives. The teams then spent six weeks developing the following elements:

- an articulation of the vision at process level;
- a description of the target organisation and systems;
- definitions of the new roles and responsibilities within the target organisation;
- a budget;
- an action plan for evolving from the existing organisation to the target organisation;
- specifications of an IT system capable of responding to the needs of the target organisation.

Each team was structured in the same way, comprising:

- a leader with responsibility for the relevant process at European level;
- a facilitator who was also a member of the change facilitation team;
- members who were executives managing the relevant process in each of the six countries.

The teams then saw the implementation procedure through in line with the target models.

THE ADMINISTRATIVE AND OPERATIONAL DIVISIONS

The administrative and operational divisions act as 'bodyshops' supplying the expert teams with competent staff. They play an active part in the work of the teams by inputting ideas, helping to solve problems and evaluating the financial implications of the teams' recommendations, and validating their decisions. Key 6: *Obtaining Participation*, provides the techniques designed to encourage involvement by these divisions. Managers play a crucial role here, especially if their division is to be in the front line of change. They must show the way by being enthusiastic supporters of the change process, while some of them will also be on the change steering committee. One of the functions of the change facilitation team is to ensure that these key players take an active part in the change process (see Keys 4 and 8: *Steering* and *Handling the Power Issues*, respectively).

Once under way, the centre of gravity of the change programme shifts progressively towards the administrative and operational divisions, which are responsible for putting it into effect. Continuity is assured by the expert teams, whose members and leaders have continued to report to their original divisional management throughout (see Key 5: *Delivering*).

THE SUPPORT TEAMS

The role of the support teams is to provide back-up to the expert teams. There are three of them:

- a financial results team
- a communication team
- a training team.

The roles and responsibilities of each of these teams are described below.

The Financial Results Team

The role of the financial results team is to evaluate the financial implications of the solutions developed by the expert teams and to devise and apply management metrics for monitoring the financial results as they emerge.

In terms of human resources, the financial group should comprise no more than two to four people, depending on the number of expert teams. In terms of expertise, at least one of them should be a highly qualified user, who can appreciate the operational implications of the changes recommended by the expert teams, and one a management accountant capable of translating operational developments into operational and financial data.

They will all continue to carry out their normal duties while devoting between 30% and 50% of their time to the financial results team.

The Communication Team

The role of the communication team is first, to provide the whole business with regular updates on the work of the expert teams and the change facilitation team, and second, to continually reassess communication needs so as to be able to meet them more effectively. Their job is to reassure people and overcome resistance so that the operational divisions will collaborate as fully as possible with the expert teams. The communication team is usually made up of communication or PR managers.

In Key 10: *Communicating Actively*, we shall be looking more closely at the role of communication in the change process.

The training team

The role of the training team is to carry out whatever training may be necessary for the vision to be realised, whether this means teaching the new technical skills required (such as how to use new IT systems, new procedures or new ways of canvassing customers) or skills relating to the management of change itself (such as group problem-solving techniques or handling resistance to change). It will of course be members of the expert teams and everyone involved in realising the vision, at every level of the business, who will be given training.

It is worth pointing out that any techniques which employees learn for managing change will subsequently be used, well outside the scope of the change process, in their day-to-day work. So it is beneficial for the whole workforce to undergo systematic training in these techniques. The training team is made up of members of the training department with the support, as required, of members of the change facilitation team, employees who have relevant skills, and external specialists.

In the case of a small business or where the change process involves a single division of a larger business (i.e. one with a turnover of less than £200m and only a few hundred employees), these activities can be supervised by and carried out either wholly or partly by the change facilitation team.

CASE STUDY ON CATALYSING: ELECTRONIC DATA SYSTEMS (EDS) CORPORATION

Electronic Data Systems, with a worldwide turnover in 1996 of almost $15 billion and over 90 000 employees on its payroll, is a leader in helping companies, government departments and individuals to make better use of information, communications and computing technologies. Headquartered in Dallas, Texas, it is the leader in its field, with a distinct management style and often used as a case study by authors such as Michael Porter and Gary Hamel.

The organisation has grown quickly, particularly so in Europe in recent times, where it has reached a turnover in excess of $2.5 billion, doubling its size in less than three years. One of the features of the organisation is that it grows by acquiring the resources of others, and is constantly assimilating whole new groups of people into its structure, culture and technologies in very short time frames. Significant changes such as these, which occur relatively frequently, whether in UK, France, Italy, Germany or Spain have created a very capable change culture. So much so that the opportunity to evaluate how EDS has adapted recently to major internal process changes becomes an interesting study for the purposes of this book.

Because of EDS' rapid growth throughout Europe and mindful of customer trends towards globalisation, it became evident to European and global leadership early in 1994 that there was a need to harmonise and integrate EDS' way of doing business in Europe. At the same time it was necessary to take into account the needs of the large customers making use of EDS on a global scale, such as General Motors and Xerox Corporation, as well as those of national government agencies such as the Inland Revenue in the UK.

Focus on Core Processes

Rapid growth through acquisition had led to a degree of diversity in EDS' core business processes in activities such as operations management, finance, human resources and procurement leading to unnecessary replication and inconsistencies which potentially could be expensive and difficult to deal with if not rectified. At the same time it was felt that EDS should be practising what it preached and doing to itself what it was so frequently being required to do for others. With these thoughts in mind European CEO John Bateman commissioned studies on the impact of migrating to common European business processes in the four areas referred to above, using state of the art information technology in support.

These first studies were top-down rather than bottom-up in nature but indicated that using a mixture of best practice benchmarks and the application of re-engineering principles over a five-year period, savings and benefits totalling many millions of dollars would be possible, thereby justifying a major pan-European re-engineering effort. Like all such schemes, the programme was soon to acquire a name: EARS, short for European Administrative Reengineering System. The word system here acquires a special significance, because in this case it was always anticipated that some kind of pan-European client-server delivery platform would underpin the new processes, operating throughout Europe.

There is little doubt that a lot of companies see their own process modifications in the same manner, despite the fact that a lot of re-engineering theoreticians would take exception to such an approach. For a company such as EDS with a very heavy concentration of systems expertise it is not surprising that new administrative processes should be seen in this way. In this sense one of the catalysts for action was a clear need seen by systems people that EDS needed a new, up-to-date systems infrastructure to support the four core processes in question.

Organising for Success

Once the benefits were seen to be attractive, the message was communicated by the chief executive that the programme would be put in hand and a steering committee appointed, consisting of representatives of European Business Leadership, as well as the European heads of the four process areas that were to be attacked. A consulting advisor was added to this group. The global leadership of EDS encouraged the Europeans to set out down the road on what was to be the first major effort of this kind to be initiated outside the United States. The Americans were very ready to help the Europeans in their bold efforts and Todd Carlsson, Chief Information Officer, acted as chairman of the steering committee. Project management skills and some consulting resources were also provided from the US. This was to prove most useful because by choosing to show its support in this way, the global leadership team gave important signals not just to Europe but also to the rest of the world, which led to other similar projects being initiated in Central and South America, and subsequently in Asia too.

Generating Enthusiasm in the Early Stages

The first job of the steering committee was to create four process teams to study in detail the four processes in question, to develop best-in-class (internal and external) benchmarks, and set about redesigning the business processes to achieve targeted improvements. It was impressive to see international teams, not just Europeans, but North and South Americans, come together and define radically new ways of working. This was accomplished in a period of around nine months. The next step which took place, partially in parallel, was to select application software best suited to meet the needs of Europe, which in this case proved to be SAP R/3.

The steering committee was itself subject to extensive training in change management concepts and principles and subsequently changed its name to the European Change Management Team (ECMT). At the same time European Process Owners were confirmed in their roles (as distinct from the ultimate sponsors at Board level) and made responsible for each of the four processes to be subjected to change and standardisation across Europe.

Early Piloting and Use of Reduced Versions

While the preceding activities were under way, it became necessary for the project teams by now working on creating the new processes to become familiar with the operations of SAP R/3 and in particular to examine the integration capability between the processes, since substantial benefits from good interfacing and integration were foreseen at an early stage. For these reasons, Belgium and Spain went live and then operational in December 1995 with sub-sets of the processes, deficient in functionality but sufficient to act as operational systems from which early experience could be gained. There is no doubt this was an essential preliminary step, of some catalytic value even though it was difficult for the countries to operate in an environment which was as yet only partially complete. This was, however, inevitable as the early SAP releases did not contain sufficient functionality for some major needs to be met. These improvements would only be finalised late in 1996.

So in early 1996, some of the features of the new processes were under test in Belgium and Spain, a re-engineering agenda and timetable had been set, benefits quantified and a full implementation of the new processes planned for the large and complex UK business, subsequently to be used as the template for roll-out afterwards in Europe as a whole. Plans had been made, budgets approved, and the green light given to the roll-out plan.

Issues and Challenges Which Led to a Change in Plan

As the project team grew to full scale early in 1996, a number of challenges arose to test the European Change Management Team and the EARS project manager and his international implementation team. First, the workload to meet the specifications grew more than planned; second, the functionality of R/3 could not in its earlier versions meet some very important process requirements; and third, it was hard to maintain the enthusiasm of countries who would not receive the roll-out until a long time in the future.

Additionally, until the team could be certain about the final functionality, which itself depended on the speed with which R/3 upgrades were made available by SAP, it was difficult to go into a heavy communicate mode with the first recipient of the new processes, the UK business. Finally, like any other group of people who are very busy with day-to-day activities, it was difficult to get the attention of the UK business until relatively close to the implementation deadline.

Maintaining Momentum While Replanning

A critical and useful part of the programme which had an important bearing on the outcome of the programme and people's commitment to it was a decision to revisit project benefits using 'bottom up' activity-based costing and other techniques in mid-1996. This demonstrated that planned processes were indeed going to generate the benefits anticipated, although not in quite the same way as had originally been supposed in the top-down assessment.

As a result of the new analysis and having made extensive use of risk assessment and risk management techniques, a delay of six months was introduced into the UK implementation, while seeking to speed up the European implementation as a whole. Once the template was proved in the UK there would be little reason to delay for very long the application elsewhere. At the same time it was decided to make another pilot site introduction in Italy in October 1996 because Italy needed support in a first phase well ahead of the original timetable.

In the event, the new European system went live in UK in January 1997 in accordance with the revised plan and at the time of writing the desire for a fast roll-out to take place throughout Europe during 1997 has been tempered by a revised assessment of the most acceptable pace of change. The processes introduced into the UK are a radical break with the past and it will take some months for them to be fully assimilated and for the forecast benefits to be obtained. Nevertheless the UK has transitioned to using the new business concepts which represent a radical departure.

Use of Country Change Management Teams

The method of introducing the new processes in the countries was to set up Country Change Management Teams (CCMTs), with one person from each of the CCMTs belonging *ex officio* to the ECMT. In each of the countries with an active implementation in prospect or under way, programme champions and project managers were appointed who then linked directly with their European counterparts at ECMT level, with the process owners, and with their peers responsible for implementation in the other countries.

Some Conclusions Arising from this Case Study

The most important lessons to be learned from the EDS Case Study with regard to catalysing the change are as follows:

- clear and visible commitment from the most senior levels in Europe and globally had an important positive impact;
- the commitment of the global leadership to provide resources and key personnel in some of the leadership positions was a powerful force for good;
- the European Change Management Team (ECMT) acted as a catalyst in pushing for change, aided by change management consultants;
- the Country Change Management Teams almost always picked up the baton and ran with it;
- in an implementation heavily dependent upon systems and technology, much effort needs to be devoted to the management of programme and project risk for which special techniques need to be applied;
- the EDS project was effectively catalysed and got off to a fast start. When the project encountered difficulties much later on, it was more in the area of the later keys where, with hindsight, more attention would have been beneficial. More will be said on this point in a subsequent chapter.

Chapter 7

Key 4: Steering

'Steering' is the act of guiding a business through the process of change. It means guiding the development of the business in accordance with the vision; in other words achieving or even surpassing the quantitative and qualitative objectives specified in the vision. It also means guiding the business from its present position to one in which the vision has been put into effect while keeping within the specified timescale and minimising the costs and risks involved. Given the possibly disruptive effect of change, any mistakes or shortcomings (such as the introduction of inappropriate structures or procedures with the result that the business cannot manage its essential functions, or a loss of morale which detracts from the efficiency of the organisation as a whole) can prove extremely costly and damaging. Steering is also about allowing the users sufficient flexibility to enhance the vision and to adapt its implementation to the specific contexts of different parts of the business.

Steering is essential to the success of the change process. As it evolves towards the vision, a business is engaged in a constant battle against invisible enemies: doubts as to its feasibility, widespread resistance among staff, obstruction by one or two key executives or managers, inadequacy or dilution of the solution effected by comparison with the original vision, delays caused by lack of planning, resources or coordination, and so on. Steering is all about overcoming these obstacles.

Steering is therefore a crucial but complex and demanding activity requiring the allocation of dedicated resources. This role is carried out by the change facilitation team.

The previous key, Key 3: *Catalysing,* defined the structure necessary for supporting and accelerating the change process. Key 4: *Steering* specifies one of the principal roles of the change facilitation team in this process.

Steering involves the following activities:

1. making a logical breakdown of the change process;
2. planning the change process;
3. day-to-day monitoring of the progress of change;
4. facilitating and accelerating change;
5. acting as an objective source of ideas and opinions;
6. monitoring changes in the power structure;
7. identifying and making available tools and techniques;
8. initiating and monitoring coaching;
9. harmonising application of the keys to change.

In the remainder of this chapter we shall describe each of these activities in more detail and suggest approaches and methods for successfully carrying them out.

MAKING A 'LOGICAL BREAKDOWN' OF THE CHANGE PROCESS

Breaking down the change process in a logical fashion is the means of ensuring that each task or activity carried out as part of the process makes a clear and positive contribution towards implementing the remainder and therefore ultimately the vision. All the resources of the business must be exploited to the full. The logical breakdown is the common thread running through the process, which all employees can use at any time to help them understand the significance of their role and the implications of their actions in relation to it. The logical breakdown also provides a feeling of security and acts as a tool for structuring the change process as a whole.

The logical breakdown is created by senior management with the support of the change facilitation team at the end of the mobilising stage. This breakdown is then filled out and applied to each improvement initiative by the relevant expert teams. There are different ways of drawing up a logical breakdown, but the method we recommend has the advantage of being simple and effective in creating a durable structure for the change process and ensuring that each activity brings clear added value. Because it is simple, it can be used by everyone: not only by members of the expert teams, but by all those who are involved to a greater or lesser extent in the design and implementation stages. It will give them a global view of the change process and allow them to visualise their particular role amidst the profusion of activity going on around them.

Our method of drawing up a logical breakdown is described below (refer also to Figure 7.1):

1. Senior management defines the business vision (see Key 1: *Defining the Vision*), which includes its quantitative and qualitative objectives.
2. Management then outlines the means or 'levers' to be employed to realise the vision and achieve the desired results, such as re-organisation, a new marketing approach, the introduction of a new IT system, the development of new skills, etc. In other words, a set of hypotheses is put forward.
3. These hypotheses are tested during the mobilising stage by rapid analysis and financial modelling. Mobilisation culminates in drawing up an action plan specifying in more detail the means by which the vision will be realised (i.e. the improvement initiatives) and how long it will take (see Key 2). Each initiative has its own expert team and its own objectives and outcomes, which will combine to achieve the global quantitative and qualitative objectives specified in the vision.
4. Each expert team develops a detailed solution for its particular improvement initiative (see Key 5: *Delivering*) which allows a new and much more detailed operational and financial model to be constructed, revalidating the objectives established in the vision. This process may have to be repeated several times before a solution is perfected which will, in theory, generate results of the quality required by the vision.
5. Each expert team selects a series of operational, economic and financial performance indicators with which they can monitor the results achieved and check that they match the target results.

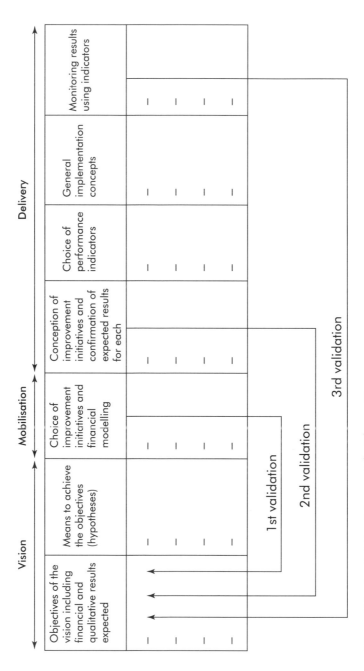

Figure 7.1 Logical Breakdown of the Change Process

6. The operational and administrative units implement the initiatives, using the selected indicators to monitor the progress of change and responding to any divergence from the objectives set out in the vision. Pilot tests can be conducted to check the validity of the proposed solutions before they are applied more generally.

This logical sequence ensures that the change always develops consistently with the vision. Any inconsistency is revealed by a series of validation exercises. Either the change facilitation team or one of the expert teams, or even one of the users who has been regularly involved, can then respond immediately to rectify the discrepancy. Unless the vision itself is unrealistic, the discrepancy can thus be rectified more easily because it is spotted as soon as it occurs. If the vision needs to be significantly modified (because it is either too ambitious or not ambitious enough, for example), the logic enables the deficiency to be revealed at the mobilising stage and the necessary modifications carried out (through analysis and financial modelling—see Key 2: *Mobilising*).

Figure 7.2 shows the logical breakdown developed by a leading French car parts manufacturer noted for its superior product design and development. In the face of increasing international competition, the company decided to launch a general productivity improvement programme with the aim of reducing manufacturing costs by an average of 20% over two years. By achieving this objective, the business would be able to beat most of its competitors on price as well as technical sophistication.

In order to ensure that the expert teams operate in an equally rigorous way and make the most effective contribution to the process of change, the change facilitation team also requires them to create and use a logical breakdown of their activities. The purpose is to define and demonstrate how each of the activities the team decides to undertake is linked to the vision. Figure 7.3 shows how the breakdown for each team fits into the overall breakdown at a higher level for the change process as a whole.

The logical breakdown acts as the perfect instrument for the change facilitation team and the steering committee to monitor and control the activities of the expert teams, which otherwise have considerable autonomy. In the case of the parts manufacturer we have reproduced as an example (see Table 8.5) the factory productivity team's activity breakdown (first improvement initiative). This shows how even a

Vision		Mobilisation		Delivery		
Objectives of the vision including financial and qualitative results expected	Means to achieve the objectives (hypotheses)	Choice of improvement initiatives and financial modelling	Expected results by initiative[1]	Choice of performance measures[1]	Implementation milestones[1]	Monitoring results using indicators[1]
–Accelerate rate of productivity improvement: reduce cost of goods sold by 20% in two years –Maintain product 'leadership' through an enhanced partnership with customers	–Rationalise the fabrication process –Research opportunities for economies in the product through working with suppliers –Research opportunities for partnerships both inside and outside the business	1. *Factory productivity* Reduction of cost of fabrication by 25% in 2 years, or 8% of standard cost of product 2. *Internal logistics* 3% reduction in standard cost of product in 2 years 3. *R & D* Development of joint approach with customers and suppliers, existing and future products. 5% reduction in product cost in 2 years 4. *Purchasing* Reduction of purchasing spend through supplier partnerships, 7% in 2 years. Technical improvement of product 5. *Management* Teamworking in groups	–Pinpointing and exploitation of productivity opportunities in utilisation of all available resources (plant, labour, materials, floorspace) –30% increase in output of key equipment –15% increase in labour efficiency –Reduction in rejects from 8% to 2% –Changes to operatives' remuneration scheme to encourage teamwork over individual performance	–Machine yield based on synthetic times –Added value (AV) per employee –Depreciation/ Added value –Rejection rates –Number of operatives affected by the performance of their team	–1 test in press shop (01/02/98) –1 test on assembly line no. 3 (01/02/98) –Finish general implementation by 31/12/98	*Evolution of machine yield* 31/12/96: 30/06/97: 31/12/97: 30/06/98: 31/12/98: *Change in AV/employee* 31/12/96: 30/06/97: 31/12/97: 30/06/98: 31/12/98: *Change in depn/added val.* 31/12/96: 30/06/97: 31/12/97: 30/06/98: 31/12/98: *Change in rejection rate* 31/12/96: 30/06/97: 31/12/97: 30/06/98: 31/12/98:

[1]For reasons of clarity, only the first improvement initiative is described in these columns

Figure 7.2   Logical Breakdown of a Change Management Process (example)

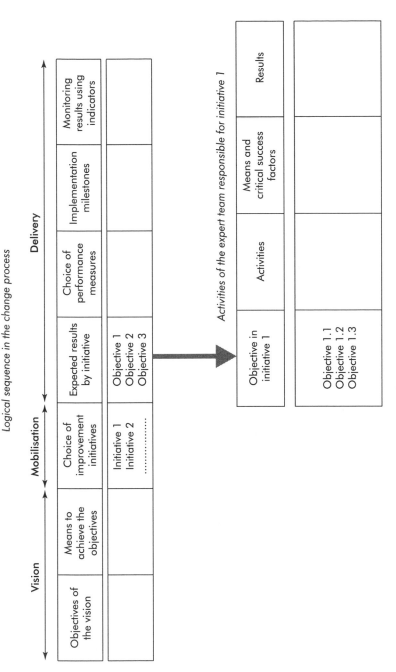

Figure 7.3   Integration of Expert Teams into the Change Management Process

purely operational and practical activity such as a machine's cycle time can be logically linked to the vision and can contribute to it, in some cases very dramatically. The business in question put up large posters (measuring 10 metres × 4 metres) inside the factories and office buildings, showing the overall logical breakdown of the change process and the activity breakdown for each expert team, so that all team members, and more particularly all employees invited to contribute to the design and then implementation of the improvement initiatives, could see and understand how their contribution related to the overall process of change.

PLANNING THE CHANGE PROCESS

Like any complex project, change management requires detailed planning. Being responsible for guiding the process, the change facilitation team must see to it that detailed but realistic planning is undertaken in order to minimise divergence from the vision. The aim of this section is not to describe planning tools, but to make a number of general points which are important regardless of the planning method chosen:

- overall planning of the change process is carried out by the change facilitation team at the 'planning' stage of mobilising. Each expert and support team then draws up a detailed timetable (for design and implementation). The initial planning has therefore been done before the delivery stage and it is regularly revised from then onwards;
- the change process should not be spread over more than two years, eight to twelve months normally being the ideal timescale (it is difficult to maintain energy levels over a longer period). A longer process should therefore be broken down by management into separate change programmes, each with limited but clear objectives and a timetable of its own;
- the overall planning process might follow the sort of progression outlined in Figure 7.4. This is in fact the timetable established by a company that designs and manufactures industrial copiers whose vision was to reduce its new product design cycle from 18 to 12 months. Each stage in the process will be looked at in more detail in the next chapter, Key 5: *Delivering*.

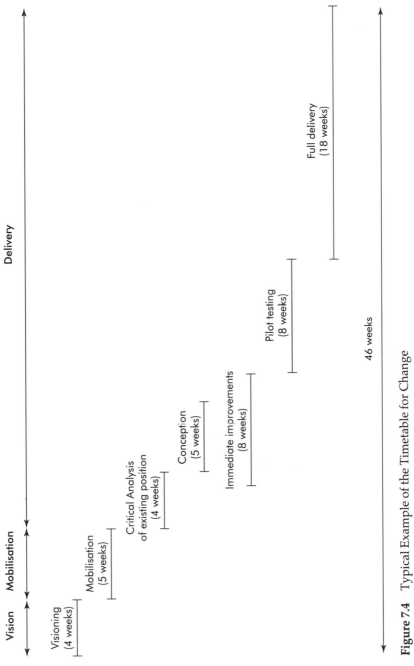

Figure 7.4 Typical Example of the Timetable for Change

DAY-TO-DAY MONITORING OF THE PROGRESS OF CHANGE

The change facilitation team identifies the critical path of the change process and checks regularly that each stage has been properly completed. It ensures that things are progressing in accordance with the plan established at the end of the mobilisation stage and reports all discrepancies to senior management for them to take decisions that might be necessary to rectify the situation. The critical path will of course vary according to the type of business and the way the process of change has been structured. However, the facilitation team should always pay particular attention to the following factors:

- Sufficient and appropriate resources must be allocated to the various expert and support teams at the latest immediately after mobilising, as soon as the improvement initiatives have been identified. Bearing in mind the major role played by these teams, it is essential for all members to be available as soon as delivery is launched. As was specified in Key 3: *Catalysing*, they must be both competent and well-known employees, which means that their superiors are usually extremely reluctant to let them go, even on a temporary and part-time basis, and so they delay their transfer. The facilitation team must be uncompromising and put constant pressure on senior management until the right people are made available. In short, they should target executives who are 'indispensable'.
- The time allowed for the analytical stages (i.e. a maximum of two weeks during mobilisation and four to six weeks during delivery) must not be exceeded. Analysis is a means, not an end in itself, the ultimate goal being implementation by the workforce. Nevertheless, many executives and managers will complain that they have not been given long enough to produce sufficiently detailed and accurate reports. There are a number of possible reasons for this attitude:
  - the complexity of the business environment and of the task in hand all too often represent a major stumbling block, causing them to confuse ends and means and to spend all their time manipulating data;
  - fear of the unknown makes them excessively cautious;
  - their resistance to change makes them keep asking for further information in order to defer decisions or deadlines.

Once again, the facilitation team must stand firm and make sure that each stage in the process happens on time, asserting the principle that the means must be just enough in relation to the objectives to be accomplished.

FACILITATING AND ACCELERATING CHANGE

The change facilitation team is critical to business transformation and must be everywhere at once, constantly stimulating and accelerating change. It must help to solve critical problems that obstruct the process of change, act as a 'model' for working methods and attitudes that are consistent with the vision and the routes for improvement (in the sense of overtly adopting and using them), and facilitate the work of the expert teams.

The 'agents of change' are in the first instance the team members themselves, but as the weeks pass, the role extends to a growing number of employees as they become involved in the process and take on the new working methods, responses and attitudes originally developed by the expert teams and the facilitation team.

As an agent of change, the facilitation team must:

1. see to the creation of small expert teams (ideally of between six and eight people, twelve at the most), which are autonomous and multifunctional (see Key 3: *Catalysing*). It must ensure that team members are of the highest quality in spite of the inevitable hindrances to their participation, such as lack of resources or time, and rival projects running concurrently with the change process;
2. ensure that all the employees assigned to expert teams or subsequently involved in the implementation process keep to the timetable laid down. This is specifically one of the duties of the facilitators seconded to the expert teams from the change facilitation team (see Key 3: *Catalysing*). A change process is in fact the product of a whole sequence of actions and contributions by individuals and groups of individuals. A delay to any one of them will have a knock-on effect on the whole timetable. The best way to avoid slippage is for the facilitator to use the 'action points' technique. This means, for example, that he or she will end each expert team meeting, which should be at least once a week, by listing the actions or tasks to be done next and putting someone in charge of each one. At the beginning of the following meeting the facilitator asks each of them to

give a progress report on their particular task. Although this system might at first seem rather coercive, it soon makes the team much more results-oriented, since it becomes almost imperative for each team member to fulfil those tasks within the allotted time. It is always difficult and embarrassing to try to explain in front of your colleagues why you have not done what you were supposed to do, especially when they have and you are the one holding the whole group back. The system has other benefits too. Members of the expert teams will become highly disciplined and will expect their colleagues to be the same in their day-to-day activities. This in turn will help to spread the new working methods (e.g. ending all meetings with a list of action points and clear responsibilities for them) and attitudes (e.g. always keeping to the agreed timetable) until they become part of the business culture above and beyond the process of change;

3. keep track of progress and regularly publish results, itemising all the benefits, both quantitative and qualitative, accruing from the change process, however small they may be. Continual communication of these results will help to maintain enthusiasm and consequently reinforce the dynamic of change. The change facilitation team should delegate these follow-up and communication duties to the 'financial results' and 'communication' support teams, which will have been set up following mobilisation (see Key 3: *Catalysing*);

4. encourage employees to think for themselves and find new solutions, however off-the-wall, by having the confidence to disregard the constraints of their environment which, though they seem real enough, are often in fact artificial, arbitrary, temporary and not insurmountable. It is a case of 'lateral thinking' or 'thinking outside the box', in other words seeing the big picture and trying to find the most radical and ambitious solutions. This kind of attitude can be fostered by regular brainstorming sessions in which members of the group adopt a respectful and positive attitude towards each other's ideas. Everyone, even the most timid or those who have the most unorthodox or avant-garde ideas, will thus be encouraged to contribute. Numerous experiments show that it is possible to develop these attitudes to a high degree by applying three simple principles which are nevertheless very effective if incorporated into the daily life of the business:

  – No idea is intrinsically bad. In other words all ideas, no matter how unrealistic they might at first appear, must be considered and analysed.

- Whatever idea or suggestion is put forward, its strong points are assessed first and its weak points are only considered afterwards. This means that a number of ideas which might otherwise have been thrown out on sight will in fact be looked at, but from a completely new angle in view of the strengths that have been identified. In our experience, this principle is particularly useful in a 'Latin' context, where the first instinct is usually to find the weaknesses or drawbacks of a suggestion and only after it has survived an inquisition to consider its strengths! Unfortunately, a lot of good ideas are rejected before they get that far.
- Assess the weaknesses or drawbacks of an idea or solution in a positive rather than a negative way, so that the question 'how can we...?' becomes the automatic way of framing a reservation. For example, 'how can we find a computer system which will give us data for each client segment and each product?' is a better response than 'computers never give us what we want anyway.' A positive approach opens new horizons by helping to solve problems rather than by simply making negative criticisms which are of no value to the business.

5. inculcate the idea that it is always possible to do better, so that no solution is definitive and there is always room for improvement;
6. consciously provide a model by exhibiting attitudes and behaviour that are consistent with the vision and the change process. All members of the change facilitation team must not only adopt and demonstrate such ways of behaving, but even exaggerate them, because at the stage of general implementation, when everyone is taking up the new working methods and altering their behavioural patterns as a result, employees will be looking for role models and will turn first to members of the facilitation team, who should act as the very embodiment of change.

ACTING AS AN OBJECTIVE SOURCE OF IDEAS AND OPINIONS

In Keys 7 and 8, *Handling the Emotional Dimension* and *Handling the Power Issues*, we shall see how the process of change inevitably generates agitation, anxiety and internal conflict. In such an environment it becomes essential to retain a bedrock of rationality and objectivity, independent of the inevitable internal conflicts all around, to act as a point of reference or as an arbitrator. The change facilitation team is just such a safe area. This means that its members are unreservedly committed to the success of the change process and of realising the vision as quickly and efficiently as possible. The role of every team member is in line with their current aims and expectations, and they have negotiated a future role for themselves, once their facilitating task is accomplished, which accords with their career objectives.

Members of the change facilitation team are aware of the constant danger of being thrown off course by the emotional and political resistance any development or transformation of the business will arouse. Their prime concern is to discover, understand and interpret any such divergence in order to ensure that the necessary analysis is undertaken and critical decisions made as calmly as possible, without being influenced by personal motives and in the interests of the business as a whole. Specific techniques for recognising and dealing with emotional and political resistance are described in Keys 7 and 8. The facilitation team can also serve to expose managers, executives and staff in general to new ideas or working methods by occasionally bringing in outside experts, organising talks or simply circulating relevant articles. Finally, the facilitation team is in a position to question the unquestionable and put forward novel ideas, to encourage the decision-makers, and employees in general, to re-evaluate their experience.

MONITORING CHANGES IN POWER RELATIONS

This aspect of guidance involves keeping track of how the attitude-to-change of key personnel develops. Which personnel this concerns will vary from business to business, but at the very least it will include all members of the steering committee, the executives in charge of units where changes are to be implemented, leaders of opinion and union representatives (see Key 8: *Handling the Power Issues*). The change facilitation team must see to it that all these people identify with the vision and overtly support the change process by their attitudes and ways of working and thinking.

These key people deserve particular attention because:

- their attitudes and behaviour are observed and often imitated by their colleagues, peers and subordinates. They therefore act as role models for their colleagues when the delivery process forces them to find new points of reference;
- it can sometimes be more difficult to change their behaviour and working methods than those of others. By definition they hold positions of authority and power within the business and may see the process of change and the vision as a threat. Some of them may therefore adopt a highly negative attitude towards the vision right from the start;
- throughout the change process it is important to know which side everyone is on.

We believe that it is imperative for the leader of the facilitation team to monitor changes in the attitudes of each of the key personnel throughout the change process. The leader must understand and respond to their concerns and, if necessary, help them to change their attitude as quickly as possible to one which is more in line with the needs of the vision. That is why the procedure needs to be systematic. Table 7.1 shows how this might be done.

Table 7.1 Chart for Monitoring the Attitudes of Key Personnel Towards Change

MONTH/ NAME	1	2	3	4	5	6	7	8	9	10	11	12
A	O	O	I	I	S	S	S	S	O	S	S	S
B	S	S	C	C	C	C	C	C	C	C	C	C
C	I	I	I	S	S	S	S	S	O	O	S	S
...												
X	O	I	I	S	S	S	S	S	S	S	S	S

O = opponent, I = indifferent, S = supporter, C = champion

The chart can be tailored to the particular characteristics of the business and to the stage the process has reached. For example, a fortnightly check might be necessary during the first few months.

At the beginning of the process a large number of key personnel might have adopted a position of opposition (O) or indifference (I), regarding the vision as the prerogative of the managing director and a few close colleagues. It is up to the facilitation team to work on them as early as possible to help them move towards becoming supporters (S) and eventually champions of change (C). After that, their individual development can be monitored regularly by means of interviews and brief conversations. Since the facilitation team always knows the current attitudes of key personnel, it can respond immediately to any negative developments. In most cases resistance or indifference is due to a misunderstanding of the vision or doubts as to the feasibility of implementing it, or perhaps to the (often misguided) idea that it will involve a loss of power (see Key 8: *Handling the Power Issues*). The facilitation team can generally encourage support by means of well-timed communication, by using the techniques for handling the emotional dimension and power issues (Keys 7 and 8), and through coaching (Key 9).

We would like to stress the positive function of the attitude-monitoring chart. It is not intended to be a way of conditioning or denouncing people. On the contrary, it is a means of drawing attention to changes in the attitudes of key personnel in order to enable the facilitation team to help them to remain in step with the change process. It is worth pointing out that the vast majority of problems of this kind can be resolved simply by talking constructively to the people concerned, and that the sooner the problem is tackled, the easier it is to resolve. Furthermore, when a supporter of change turns into a detractor, it must be recognised that this is most often due to a misunderstanding or misinterpretation of facts or decisions which is easily corrected if dealt with early enough.

IDENTIFYING AND MAKING AVAILABLE TECHNIQUES AND TOOLS

We are referring here to techniques for handling change rather than to scientific or financial management techniques. The aim is to provide, as early as possible in the change process, tools for group working, running meetings, dealing with resistance to change, and so on, which will maximise the effectiveness of the expert teams and the extent to which staff in general identify with the solutions adopted. These are the types of tools we refer to throughout the book:

- group problem-solving
- collaborative analysis of processes

- active forces analysis
- pre-positioning.

At the end of mobilising, the facilitation team identifies the techniques or tools which will be most useful and, with the help of the training department and the training support team (if there is one), makes sure everyone is familiar with them. Key 9: *Training and Coaching*, goes into this process in more detail.

INITIATING AND MONITORING COACHING

The change facilitation team is also responsible for initiating the process of coaching, in other words support for ongoing staff development. Priority is given to the key players in the change process, i.e. members of the expert teams. In Key 9 we suggest a method for coaching and show how it can be applied to all staff.

HARMONISING APPLICATION OF THE TEN KEYS TO CHANGE

As the guarantor of success of change and by virtue of the cross-structural role it plays, the change facilitation team is also responsible for ensuring that all the key factors for successful change are in place. In other words, it must see to it that each of the ten keys to change is appropriately applied, which means deciding how thoroughly each key should be implemented, what methods, techniques and tools should be used, and who should be in charge. We recommend that the team draws up a detailed chart for each key in order to record its day-to-day application and ensure that no crucial activity is overlooked. These charts should then be reviewed at each meeting of the steering committee.

***

It can be seen that steering change is one of the key functions of the change facilitation team. During the change process, the business needs to be steered away from its current position towards the target position, which is equivalent to delivery of the vision. Steering change, in fact, is all about 'making it happen'!

CASE STUDY ON STEERING: ELECTRONIC DATA SYSTEMS

The way that EDS approached the introduction of new administrative processes for Europe has been described in the previous chapter. Here the case is used to illustrate how the introduction of pan-European processes was monitored and steered so as to maximise the chances of success.

The EARS programme is one of the biggest in Europe of its kind and demanded that great efforts be made in order to create for EDS an advantageous set of common business processes, the benefits of which were clear at the outset from an initial benefits study. In the following sections, the measures taken to monitor and steer the development and introduction of the new business processes are described in more detail.

Maintaining an Up-to-Date View of Costs and Benefits

By repeating the cost-benefit analysis once the detailed process of design was complete, it was possible to confirm that the benefits could be expected to accrue as planned. Secure in this knowledge, it was possible to continue to proceed down a difficult and costly road with confidence. The detailed benefits study also identified the new process performance metrics which would need to be used to verify that progress was being achieved and to replace some of the older performance metrics that up to that time had been in use in the various countries. The study also revealed that to realise all of the benefits would probably require a degree of reorganisation after the new processes had been introduced, although in the first phase the main task to be accomplished would be installation of the new processes so as to be in a position subsequently to take advantage of some of the more subtle possibilities arising from change. This 'second round' effect through continuous improvement after a major change is quite common in situations where major discontinuities are likely to occur. It was the responsibility of the European Change Management Team to review the cost implications on the project of changes in scope and timetable, with the trade-off between value, time and cost being a particular preoccupation in programme management meetings and in periodic ECMT reviews. If either time or cost alone become the dominant consideration, as is often the case at various stages in the life of a major programme, there are risks that value will be the main sufferer. The ECMT spent quite some time in choosing the most suitable way forward, sometimes keeping timescale as the most important dimension and sometimes cost.

Tracking Process Functioning

The process owners played a particularly important part in monitoring progress as work proceeded. Without them it is possible that functionality within the processes could have been degraded too much in the interests of time or cost (always a danger) or that scope creep could have set in, causing cost increases and time delays. Yet there is one problem that process owners alone cannot tackle, the issue of inter-process integration. Although in EDS core processes are relatively easily defined, there are in fact many inter-connections between the four different processes of financial management, human resource management, procurement and business operations. It was the responsibility of the project manager to ensure that when the process owners met, in a group called the Process Leadership Team (PLT), that integration issues were never left out of consideration.

Managing Changing Process Scope

Reference has already been made to the need to avoid 'scope creep', the gradual adding to requirements as various interested parties seek ever-greater capability when they have had time to digest the changes being proposed. This natural tendency, while desirable as a means of entering into continuous improvement mode once the first implementation has been made, is destructive if carried to extremes, on the grounds that it is better to start faster, get 80% right and learn from actual usage, rather than delay to incorporate what are often marginal refinements better introduced later on the basis of some actual operational experience when other priorities might also become apparent.

Equally unnerving is the phenomenon of scope contraction as designers and implementors reduce functionality in an effort to meet time and cost. There comes a point where reductions in scope are so serious as to call into question the wisdom of an implementation at a particular point in time. It was for this reason that the ECMT called a six-month delay in implementation of the European template in the UK from early summer 1996 to January 1997, once it became clear that to meet the deadline would result in overly restrictive initial functionality. Conversely, some time later it was decided to accelerate the introduction of the European template into the rest of Europe on the grounds that the offering that was ready at the end of 1996 would generate over 90% of projected benefits (determined through a rapid update of the detailed cost-benefit study) and there was little reason to wait several more months for the last 10% of benefits which had been planned from the outset to be produced as a result of a second version of the template.

Risk Management

One of the most interesting features of the monitoring and steering process was a mandatory risk management review conducted regularly by the programme management team and presented to the ECMT. The objective was to identify all project risks, determine whether they were the subject of internally controllable or external factors, assess their likely impact on time and cost and understand their proximity in terms of time from the review point, so as to be able to deal effectively with near-term risks while keeping a wary eye on the clouds on the horizon. There is little doubt that this simple and elegant mechanism was a powerful technique in taking appropriate action in time to avoid time, cost or scope issues becoming troublesome.

Monitoring Plan, Including Time, Cost and Resources

It goes without saying that on a project such as EARS, which represented hundreds of man-years of effort, that considerable attention has to be paid to effective project planning. Costs were kept under regular review by Scott Krenz, the European controller, and projections of likely cost prepared by the programme team for review by the ECMT. In the countries, local budgets and plans were monitored by the country change management teams. Occasionally, if it looked as though costs were likely to exceed European-level budget targets, special investigations were made to identify revised planning assumptions to keep the budget within the agreed limits.

Reviews of time estimates were a regular feature of programme management, Process Leadership, and ECMT meetings, with new planning ideas receiving continual attention. Priorities for country implementation, timings of pilot introductions, needs of process documentation, training plans, software upgrade planning and a wealth of other matters featured regularly on ECMT agendas.

Resource management is a whole subject of discussion in itself. On major project work there are rarely sufficient resources available, either at the outset, or as work proceeds. When the necessary level of resource finally is available questions are then asked about whether they are being used effectively. On the EARS programme, all of these issues were encountered, with external resources from consultants and from SAP, the software provider, being needed from time to time to supplement EDS' own internal capability. At its peak the project required around 150 people dedicated to the task, covering user support as well as process and system design and development functions. Finding a team of this size is never easy, particularly in EDS which sets great store by responding first and foremost to the needs of its customers.

Evaluating Readiness to Implement

While the programme team was working away at developing the new business processes and the corresponding software customising and enhancement, there was a risk that the 'customers' might be left in the dark about what was about to befall them and what actions they would need to take to facilitate the change. Throughout the programme, change management consultants were present, working first with the ECMT and then with the country change management teams to help them gain understanding of the impact the changes were to have and how best to introduce them. A drawback in this process was the fact that the final statements of what was to be in the proposed processes could not be issued until relatively late in the day because much depended on late-arriving new software releases, without which the implementation in UK could not have proceeded. This meant that the UK received relatively short notice of the implemented functionality. This was compensated by a broadly favourable reaction to the new processes in the subsequent user training sessions.

Chapter 8

Key 5: Delivering

The vision has now been defined in broad terms. Mobilising has served to convince the participants that change is both necessary and urgent. The principal improvement initiatives along which the business will develop in the direction of the vision have been specified, detailed and quantified. The organisation has been primed and plans have been made and agreed. The next step is to deliver the desired changes; in other words, to ensure that they are realised effectively.

THE ISSUES AT STAKE

Achieving Both Physical and Psychological Goals

Delivering means developing the business from its current state to one in which the vision has been permanently and effectively established. This involves both attaining the quantifiable goals and putting into effect the desired changes in management practices and behaviour (the intangible goals), because only developments on both fronts can guarantee that the changes will last and will withstand the natural forces tending to pull the business back towards its original state. Examples of behavioural changes include:

- moving away from a management style based on command and control towards delegation, risk-taking and consultation;
- supporting or even actively pursuing change rather than obstructing it;
- acknowledging problems and asking for help rather than concealing them.

We believe that ignoring or underestimating the importance of these intangible goals is one of the prime causes of failure in change programmes. According to a study by Michael Hammer, of 're-engineering' renown, over 70% of re-engineering projects fail. We suggest that the prime cause is usually giving insufficient attention to human factors, for if such projects are to be successful, they require marked changes in behaviour. First, of course, the need for change has to be accepted, but in addition there must be development in culture and management style:

1. from a hierarchical style of management to one that cuts across the hierarchy;
2. from a purely technically-based culture to a more customer-oriented one;
3. from concentrating exclusively on the individual to highlighting the success of the team.

Figure 8.1 summarises the major issue of delivery, which is to create lasting change in an environment where major changes in behaviour and practices must be combined with a sharp increase in business performance.

The manner in which we seek to introduce change has a direct and significant impact on the way change is implemented. Since changes in practice and behaviour cannot be effected simply by decree or by issuing orders, the way we go about delivering change is itself the vehicle for creating the evolution to the new state of affairs.

If, for example, one of the objectives of change is to make the business more customer-oriented at all levels, the delivery process will give priority to customer contact by all members of staff and to appreciation of customers' needs and expectations. It was with this

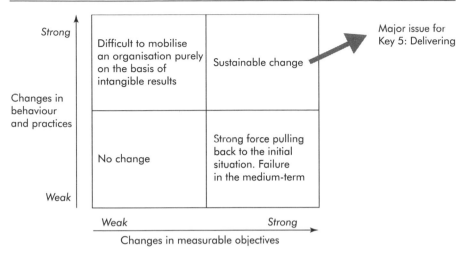

Figure 8.1   Area of Application of 'Delivering'

aim in mind that a major European telecommunications provider, as part of a change programme designed to reduce costs dramatically and increase sales, organised a customer contact day for all technical and administrative staff (over 10 000 people). After a short training session to brief them on some of the products and services on offer, the employees spent a day in public places such as stations, shopping streets and business centres, presenting the firm's products to passers-by. This is the same practice as used by Sony in Japan, who sometimes require their young engineers to work in retail outlets to understand how consumers react to their products.

Developing the Business's Capacity for Change

The Conference Board Europe has published the results of a study of change management involving 160 large European and American manufacturing and service businesses. One of its conclusions was that the number of change programmes is growing and that there is a need to increase the rate at which businesses change.

The businesses studied revealed six major developments which made it essential for them to adapt more quickly in the future:

1. greatly increased competition
2. severe worsening of financial results
3. introduction of new technologies

4. globalisation of markets
5. merger and acquisition
6. partnerships or strategic alliances.

Around 60% of the businesses analysed stated that, during the period 1985–87, they had taken steps to implement changes in response to one or two of the six issucs listed above, whereas fewer than 10% claimed to have taken action in relation to all of them. During the period 1988–93, on the other hand, 40% of these same businesses claimed to have reacted to all six developments by taking steps to implement changes, and fewer than 20% had reacted to only one or two of them.

This is why when delivering change we must not only enable a business to move towards the current vision but also develop the business's capacity to make more numerous changes in the future.

Combining Radical Change with Continuous Improvement

For some time the literature has been full of debate around two opposing theories of how to go about implementing change: transformation involving dislocation, or a sudden break with the *status quo* (organisational transformation or the revolutionary model) and transformation by a process of gradual reshaping (*kaisen* or the evolutionary model). Table 8.1 compares the two concepts.

The proponents of transformation maintain that when the ground-rules change radically (as a result of competition, technology, regulation, etc.), when the business goes through a crisis or when it takes action in anticipation of a potential crisis, only a change which brings about a quantum leap in terms of behavioural development and improved performance can enable the business to reposition itself. Business process re-engineering (BPR) is an example of how such transformations with dislocation can be brought about (see, for example, Johansson, McHugh, Pendlebury and Wheeler (1994), *Business Process Re-engineering, Breakpoint Strategies for Market Dominance*, John Wiley and Sons).

For their part, the proponents of transformation by gradual reshaping base their argument on the capacity of organisations to engage in a continuous and gradual learning process. Continuous evolution of this kind makes it possible to avoid dislocation and internal crises which, according to Peter Senje, 'can stimulate change but have a high social and human cost'.

Table 8.1 Dislocation and Gradual Reshaping

	Transformation with dislocation (revolution)	Transformation by gradual reshaping (evolution)
Underlying principle	– Change necessitates destabilisation of the existing state in order overcome inertia	– If the organisation moves forward gradually, dislocation is unnecessary – Dislocation has traumatic effects whose financial and human costs are too high
Objectives	– Major jump in performance in a short time (radical improvement)	– Continuous learning by the organisation, leading to gradual improvement in performance (continuous improvement)
Procedure	– Top down	– Bottom up – Training for action
Role of management	– Define the vision – Plan and follow up on execution	– Create conditions for continuous learning – Provide coaching
Risks	– Strong resistance – Possible traumas within the organisation – Underestimation of resources required	– Rate of change too slow to cope with possible dislocations in the business environment

These two approaches to implementing change are by no means mutually exclusive. On the contrary, they can coexist, and even re-inforce each other. Continuous improvement on the back of radical change is capable of taking the process beyond the initial objectives defined by management in the vision. The combined approach demon-strates that everyone in the organisation has genuinely identified with the change process, and helps to guarantee that the changes achieved will last in the longer term. It also demonstrates the enhanced ability of the workforce to take initiatives and act autonomously.

THE PRINCIPLES UNDERLYING DELIVERY

Effective, lasting and rapid delivery is based on four underlying principles:

1. changing roles and responsibilities before attempting to modify behaviour;

2. ensuring widespread participation as early as possible (the principle of globality);
3. allowing room for autonomy within the framework defined by the vision (the principle of indeterminacy);
4. adapting the delivery process to suit those taking part.

Changing Roles and Responsibilities Before Attempting to Modify Behaviour or Culture

There are currently two major theories on the mechanism which should be adopted for delivering change:

- programmed change and
- task alignment.

These theories are summarised below; for more detail see 'Why Change Programs Don't Produce Change', by Michael Beer, Russel A. Eisenstat and Bert Spector (1990), *Harvard Business Review*, November–December, and by the same authors, *The Critical Path to Corporate Renewal* (1990), Harvard Business School Press.

Programmed Change

According to the theory of programmed change, the transformation of the business begins with developments in employees' knowledge and attitudes. Once they have acquired new knowledge and changed their attitudes and the way they behave, their ways of working will begin to change. It will then be possible to define not only their new tasks, roles and responsibilities, but also the changes that will take place in the way the business, or a part of the business, is organised. According to the theory of programmed change, then, change can be brought about by means of seminars or training sessions designed to develop the necessary skills and instil the new patterns of behaviour.

Table 8.2 Steps in Programmed Change

1. Change skills and attitudes/ behaviour	2. Develop new ways of working	3. Redefine roles and responsibilities	4. Reorganise

We consider this approach on its own to be of limited effectiveness in most circumstances, because it creates too wide a gap both between theory and practice and between teaching and the practical application of what has been learned. Because the seminars and training sessions are divorced from everyday working life within the business, once employees are re-immersed in their day-to-day tasks and responsibilities they find that they have no reference point against which to measure changes in the way they work, and no power to make changes. They have no reference point because it is up to the individual to adjust to a new role and way of working, independently and without having a model to turn to, to make a self-assessment or look for support. They lack the power to change because their working methods continue to be influenced, or even dictated, by the systems and procedures in place and by their interactions with colleagues: those working closely with them and those in other parts of the business. Employees often find the training interesting at first, but soon come to see it as too theoretical and dismiss it as another good idea that is not applicable to the business in which they are concerned. There is even a danger that the vision will be discredited in the eyes of employees, seriously damaging management's credibility with their staff.

Nevertheless, this approach to change is widely adopted in business. Senior management defines a new vision, such as achieving the highest possible quality in the face of the competition, then launches general training programmes relevant to the new requirements identified (total quality management and so on) and sets up new appraisal schemes and sometimes new remuneration schemes linked to the new targets. Year after year, management finds that no real improvements have been made, and if they start introducing one programme after another, the results are even worse: total quality is followed a few months later by productivity improvement, and then by the introduction of a market-oriented approach to replace a product-oriented approach ... but without making sure that each programme is followed through successfully.

Task Alignment

According to the theory of task alignment, individuals' attitudes and behaviours are strongly moulded by the roles, responsibilities and

Table 8.3 Steps in Task Alignment

1. Change tasks, redefine roles and responsibilities, and reorganise	2. Change working methods	3. Development of attitudes/behaviour	4. Modification of culture

working methods assigned to them. This means that if individual and, as a consequence, corporate cultures are to change, they must first be assigned a new role and given new responsibilities. The business—its structure and its systems—is reorganised at the same time. As a consequence, employees' working methods will change, their behavioural patterns will alter and, finally, corporate culture will be modified. Any change programme therefore starts by redistributing and redefining tasks and responsibilities. This theory assumes, moreover, that if employees' performance is mediocre or their attitude is negative or at odds with the needs of the business, this is usually because the organisation is not providing them with the conditions for success.

Key 5: *Delivering*, is based on the theory of task alignment, in other words the need to modify roles and responsibilities systematically by means of a process of change in order to produce changes in employees' behavioural patterns. However, Key 9: *Training and Coaching*, picks up elements of programmed change theory by showing how training can facilitate and accelerate change. At the same time we also describe a coaching technique which can help employees to change their attitudes and behaviour.

Ensuring Widespread Participation as Early as Possible

The aim of this principle is twofold. First, to create an explosion of ideas which enables the business to take advantage of both the pool of skills at its disposal and the creative power represented by each individual employee. Such an explosion of ideas enables the best solution to be found and speeds up its design and implementation, by eliminating pitfalls and delays. Second, the people who will be putting the vision into practice and incorporating it into their everyday working lives are the ones who take part in the initial diagnosis and discussion. By obtaining their participation, potential resistance is reduced and the risk of failure is minimised, while the likelihood that the changes achieved will be lasting is increased.

Allowing Room for Autonomy Within the Framework Defined by the Vision

Some examples of vision are repeated here:

- to reduce the development cycle for a new automobile by 50% within two years;
- to move away from a product-based organisation structure towards a market-based one in order to increase market share by 30%;
- to reorganise in Europe from being territorially-based to being totally integrated and function-based, in order to benefit from economies of scale and offer the best customer service in the industry within three years;
- to reduce product costs by 20% within two years and to become the low-cost operator.

In all these cases, delivering the vision will require the active participation of all staff. Everyone must contribute: everyone must put their skills, experience and creativity at the service of the common goal and must work towards it. It is out of this profusion of ideas and actions that the solution will emerge and take shape in a form which is capable of achieving the objectives of the vision. It is therefore inconceivable to attempt to control every employee's every action during the change process. The big challenge for managers is to channel this vast number of activities into the initiatives defined by the vision. If delivery recognises this need for employee autonomy, the steering process described in the preceding chapter (Key 4) takes account of the need to direct the process of change.

Adapting the Delivery Process to Suit Those Taking Part

Many change programmes underestimate the difficulty of delivery because they fail to recognise the needs and characteristics of the various groups of people affected by the changes, and therefore give insufficient attention to them. The vision and the routes for improvement have been developed by a few brilliant minds, and delivering them is simply a matter of writing and circulating a few guidelines, and perhaps backing these up with some training and communication initiatives. Some groups of staff will oppose change; in certain cases with good reason because they stand to lose by it; in others for emotional reasons, because they fear the unknown or even because they see no need for change. Other groups of staff, usually the majority, will be undecided and will expect to be given some sort of explanation or perhaps to see some actions taken that symbolise management's commitment to the process of change. Yet other groups will come forward in support. These are generally employees who are used to taking a positive attitude to change or who can see specific personal advantages in the current changes. For change to be successfully delivered, it is essential to identify these various groups clearly and to put together a procedure which is appropriate to the needs of each one.

We have found it helpful to use two dimensions to analyse and differentiate the groups affected by change and construct an implementation procedure appropriate to the needs of each. The first dimension is an assessment of the impact of the current change on individuals. Employees measure the impact of change on their personal position in terms of potential changes in a number of tangible factors:

- place of work and hours of work;
- salary;
- job security: because of structural unemployment in many industrialised countries, this factor is particularly important today, especially in the context of privatisation of public utilities (telecommunications, electricity generators and distributors, etc.), where being a public sector employee was at one time a guarantee of employment;
- nature of work, tasks and responsibilities;
- status, position or status symbols associated with a particular grade;
- working relationships;
- working conditions.

Depending on the effect change is expected to have on these personal conditions, each employee will perceive the results of the change process as positive, negative or neutral.

The second dimension is the employee's intrinsic or *a priori* attitude to change in general. This may be positive, neutral or negative and depends on historical factors such as:

- the frequency with which changes have been made in the business in the past;
- the perceived effects of such changes, where experience of success tends to lead to an intrinsically positive attitude, and that of failure

(broken promises, inadequate support, etc.) to a negative one or at least to mistrust;
- confidence in management's ability to carry out the changes;
- corporate values: some businesses, such as Hewlett-Packard, rate change-related values highly.

By combining these two dimensions we can arrive at a clear-cut and practical differentiation of the groups involved in change (see Figure 8.2) and we can draw up an approach to implementation appropriate to the needs and characteristics of each of the major groups: supporters, waverers who are uneasy, waverers who are sceptical, and opponents. The choice of approach must be guided by a clear understanding of where each individual stands. By carrying out an analysis of the operational impact of change, backed up by a series of interviews, the position of each employee can be plotted on the 2 by 2 matrix shown in Figure 8.2. An internal survey could be undertaken to confirm or refine the analysis. Attitudes to change have to be measured by means of individual and group interviews, with a survey providing statistical validation.

It is usually helpful to draw up such matrices for each level of the business: top management, middle management, first level supervision and remaining staff.

POSITIONING OF DELIVERY

Delivering fits logically into the change process, capitalising above all on what has been achieved through Keys 1 and 2, *Defining the Vision* and *Mobilising* as can be seen in Table 8.4.

Table 8.4   Where Delivering Fits into the Change Process

Definition of the vision, including priority objectives	Choice of improvement initiatives and economic modelling	Detailed analysis of status quo	Design of improvements and implementation plan	Implementation and monitoring of results

Defining the vision

Mobilising

Delivering

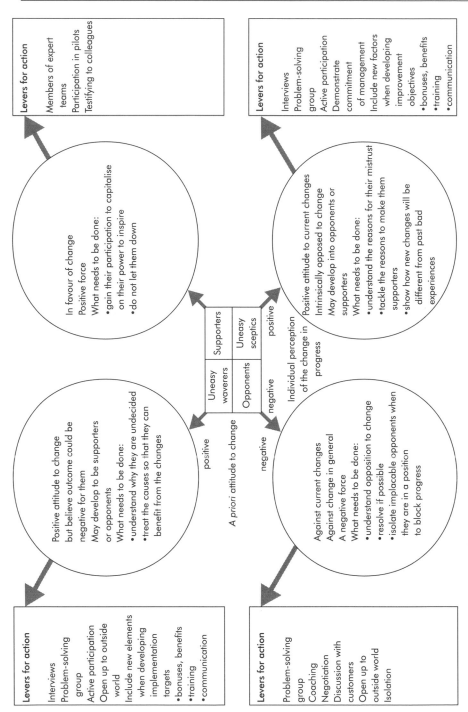

Figure 8.2 Participants in Change and Levers for Action

The targets defined in the vision and validated during mobilising will, as shown here, continue to provide guidance throughout the delivery stage. The success of delivery will be measured by how far the tangible and intangible objectives established in the vision and confirmed during mobilising have been achieved. Key 3: *Catalysing*, has already seen to it that the resources required for a smooth delivery process have been allocated.

The vision in its turn will be enhanced during delivery by new inputs from the expert teams. Equally, the drive to mobilise extends beyond the mobilising stage, as the energy and motivation needed to pursue change must be constantly maintained and strengthened.

Delivery can be divided into four main phases, which in turn break down into several stages (see Figure 8.3).

Phase 1: Modelling of the target state, which comprises the stages of launch, critical analysis of the *status quo*, design and identification of immediate improvements
Phase 2: Testing (experimentation or piloting)
Phase 3: General application and the subsequent monitoring of results
Phase 4: Setting up systems to ensure the permanence of the changes implemented.

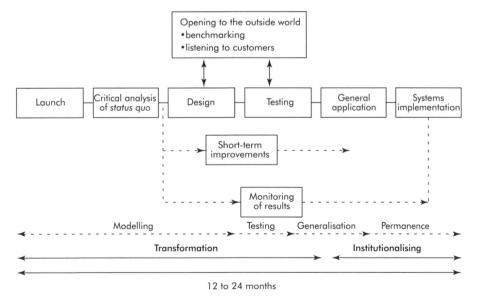

Figure 8.3 Structure of the Delivery Process

THE PROCEDURE IN DETAIL

The method described below tackles all stages of delivery. Both the suggested tools and the data or figures provided are intended to give practical examples of the sort of effort involved and the resources that will be required.

Launch

- *Aims:* On the basis of the conclusions of mobilising, each expert team draws up or fills in a detailed plan for its own improvement initiative, comprising:
  - the aims of delivery;
  - the expected financial and qualitative results;
  - the performance measures which will be used to monitor results throughout delivery and attainment of the objectives defined in the vision and, after that, to check that they are sustained;
  - the conditions for success and the obstacles to implementation;
  - the roles and responsibilities of each team member;
  - a detailed work schedule.

  Each item is endorsed by the steering committee and the relevant management team. This formalising process helps to ensure that the expert team's work is consistent with the objectives of the change process. During the launch phase, the expert teams receive training in two areas: the process of change itself (vision, improvement initiatives) and the techniques and methods which will be used to bring about change (see Key 9: *Training and Coaching*).
- *Activities:* The teams are engaged primarily in group discussions and analysing the data produced by the mobilising phase.
- *Tools:* Table 8.5 is an example of how the teams should analyse and document their tasks. Two weeks is usually long enough to put together an effective tool for systematically defining the scope of their activity. Team bonding techniques (welding a group of individuals into a team) and team working methods (guidelines for running productive meetings, group problem-solving, etc.) can also prove extremely useful at this stage.

Table 8.5 Logical Breakdown of the Activities of an Expert Team (example)

Expert team for factory productivity—global objective: 25% reduction in the standard cost of manufacture within 2 years

Objectives	Activities	Means and critical success factors	Results
Identification and evaluation of productivity improvements in all resource usage (machines, labour, materials, floor space)	Analyse shops focusing on critical resources and high usage of direct labour. Shopfloor observations, flow of materials, analysis of stocks and WIP. Analysis of indirects	Participation of all operators, admin staff, supervisors, technicians and line managers affected Utilisation of a group process mapping	List of problems and opportunities Objective data on production facilities Communication to all personnel on desire to launch a participative approach
Improvement by 30% in the yield of critical machines	Identify key plant and machines Measure machine cycle times Measure yields Elaborate improvement plan Define training needs Define performance indicators Launch the work and monitor	Obtain management buy-in to machine yield as a performance indicator Maintenance dept. to participate Promote team-working concepts	Actual yield of each machine List of failures and causes classified by origin Implementation plan for each machine studied Plan to monitor yield of each machine: 30% yield improvement in 18 months
15% improvement in labour productivity	Identify labour intensive operations Identify non-added value Assess improvement opportunities Draw up plan Launch the work and monitor	High participation by supervisors and operators	15% reduction in direct labour in 24 months
Reduction in rejects from 8% to 2%	Identify causes of rejects Pareto analysis Classify causes by origin: organisation or machine capability Define an action plan by cause Monitor implementation	Computer processing of existing data Development of computerised analysis tools for special analyses	Reduction of rejects by 6% in 12 months: • 2% in first 4 months • 4% in next 8 months
Changes in operators' remuneration to encourage teamwork rather than individual performance	Define organisation to favour teamwork Define team objectives Adapt the operators' remuneration scheme accordingly	Participation of all operators, admin. staff, supervisors, technicians and line managers in the shops	Implementation of new organisation for improved labour and machine performance Implementation within 24 months Improved collaboration at all levels

Critical analysis of the *status quo*

- *Aims:* It might be asked, 'What is the point of describing and analysing the *status quo?*'.

  The first aim is a full understanding of the existing situation, and its strengths and weaknesses; this is the point of departure in the drive for change. A second aim is to develop everyone's awareness of the inadequacies of the current situation, inspiring in everyone the wish to improve. Last, getting people right across the business to participate in group analysis of the *status quo* is a way of introducing them to the new management practices which are consistent with achieving the target.

- *Activities:* The task is to draw up a precise description of the *status quo* in relation to the objectives of change for each improvement initiative. This analysis may include the following:
  - a description of the operations carried out and their sequence (a description of the tasks involved in a process, for example);
  - a specification of the roles and responsibilities of those involved and the attitude to change of each group of employees, revealing potential obstacles;
  - a calculation of the costs and added value of each activity. This analysis can be particularly helpful in broadening the financial and management culture, or simply in getting participants used to measuring and studying performance with challenging new methods;
  - an evaluation of the IT systems currently in place and their development capacity;
  - a systematic listing of strengths and weaknesses.

This highly instructive analysis is applied to each improvement initiative. It can and does, however, take up an excessive amount of time if not properly handled, so it must be borne in mind that this critical analysis of the *status quo* is not an end in itself, but a means which contributes to developing the target and above all to implementing change. Involving participants as early as possible in the change process helps to ensure that everyone accepts and supports it, and users generally find it motivating, even flattering, to be asked to describe their present situation. They will be keen to take part in the exercise and will devote more personal effort to it than is strictly necessary, with the collaborative approach and mobilisation further boosting this natural predisposition. It is the facilitator's role to obtain agreement on bringing the exercise to a close once its aims have been achieved.

- *Tools:* Groupwork techniques are widely used. For example, drawing up a collaborative description and illustration of how a process, unit or department works, consists of describing all the activities involved in the familiar form of flow charts, but with some special characteristics:
  - instead of being prepared on sheets of paper, the presentation is made on strips of paper several metres long pinned to the wall. The symbols used in it are simple and standardised and can be understood by all. For the first time, those affected not only get an overall picture of their work environment, but they can also see where they fit in and how they contribute to the whole. Besides the interest it arouses, this global view is highly productive in generating ideas for improvement;
  - instead of being filed away in a cabinet and eventually forgotten by participants, the description is pinned to the walls of meeting rooms or corridors, offering a further invitation to everyone to contribute their ideas, which they can do informally or even anonymously, since all they have to do is annotate the chart, using sticky notes, for example;
  - rather than being carried out by internal or external auditors, this collaborative description and illustration is made by the people involved, with the help of facilitators. This further motivates them and encourages them to participate, thus acting as a catalyst for the generation of new ideas;
  - finally, this approach goes beyond simply describing procedures. It specifies who does what, where, when and how. It identifies the information required and evaluates the efficiency of the information systems. It reveals dysfunctions, bottlenecks, redundancies, shortcomings, activities with little or no added value—and it goes beyond the inefficiencies to act as a tool for gathering ideas and recommendations for improvement.

As an example, here is the view of a director of an American oil major who used this tool to analyse six major cross-structural processes crucial to his European organisation (product ordering-to-delivery, marketing, sales, billing, purchasing and logistics):

The first phase, which has just ended, consisted of analysing the *status quo*, what people are really doing and not what they are supposed to be doing. This painstaking step-by-step process helped to show up a large number of problems and opportunities for improvement. The collaborative descriptions and illustrations so popular nowadays are the physical underpinning of this huge investigation: they adorn the corridors of the offices on several floors and give every single person the opportunity to see how his or her role fits into the process being described, and so to enhance it. All the ideas, recommendations and opportunities we have identified using this method will now contribute to the stage of designing our new processes.

Another tool at this stage is active forces analysis (AFA), which consists of listing, for each improvement initiative, the positive forces (i.e. all the factors, such as activities and skills, which favour development towards the vision) and the negative ones (i.e. the forces opposing the development). Apart from its simplicity and effectiveness, this tool has the advantage of helping groups which are undecided (see preceding section) to talk about what they see as the obstacles to change or the risks involved in the process.

- *Contributors:* The critical analysis of the *status quo* is led by expert teams who see to it that as many people as possible participate, by encouraging them to add to or comment on the analyses. We recommend rounding off this study with an open day when all those involved in the area under analysis can come and familiarise themselves with the work and contribute to it. Quality analysis methods also offer useful support during this stage: for example, Hoshin, Ishikawa, and cause and effect diagrams.
- *Timescale:* Critical analysis of the *status quo* should not take longer than four to six weeks. The amount of work involved depends on how much has been carried out at the mobilising stage (see Key 2: *Mobilising*).
- *Results:* The *status quo* has been described in a communicable form. The major weaknesses and opportunities for progress have been identified, detailed and quantified by those involved. Their appreciation of the urgent need for change has been reinforced. An initial chart of attitudes to change has been drawn up (see Figure 8.2). The matrix of opportunities for progress in Figure 8.4 is one of the tangible, actionable outcomes of analysing the *status quo*.

Let us look again at the case of the expert team whose objective is to reduce the manufacturing cost price by 25% within two years (Table 8.5).

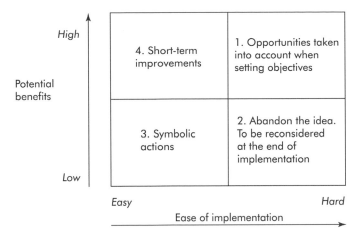

Figure 8.4 Matrix of Opportunities for Progress

The immediate improvements were better organisation of tool-change times and of the availability of parts to be machined, increasing the running time of key plant by 30%. This is a good example of how problems can be resolved quickly, often with the help of common sense and without the need for any investment, but only by mobilising employees, trusting them and benefiting from their expertise.

Selecting the target and objectives

- *Aims:* For each improvement initiative, a detailed definition must be drawn up of the target, the expected benefits, performance measures and the implementation plan. All of this must be consistent with the vision. The description of the target includes both the physical aspect (organisation, structure, processes, etc.) and the psychological (behaviour, values, management style). For implementation to be successful, it is also necessary to ensure that all future users identify with the target. One of the key issues is to set aside existing constraints so as to develop innovative solutions which break with the *status quo.*
- *Activities:* There are several ways of going about choosing the target, and many books have been dedicated to this particular topic. We do not intend to list or describe the possible methods here, but

rather to specify a number of activities which should feature in any approach:

1. Bridge the gulf between those making the decisions and those carrying them out (see Figure 8.5). Everyone is involved in both discussion and action. The decision makers are authoritative enough to guide and control the design of a target for each improvement route that is consistent with the vision. On the other hand, they allow participants enough freedom for each individual's experience and creativity to find expression. We have found that whenever this duality is respected, the target that is eventually specified and implemented goes further than the objectives originally set by management.

2. Search for an ideal target. Proceeding via an ideal target—that is, setting aside existing constraints at first—makes it easier to break with the status quo and develop more innovative solutions (see Figure 8.6). Using inductive ways of thinking is a helpful way of breaking with past tradition and evolution (by asking questions like 'How can we triple our revenues?', or 'If the business belonged to you how would it be run differently?' This can be contrasted with deductive thinking in which we are more concerned to improve by eliminating existing problems using a step-by-step approach.

3. Modify habitual ways of thinking. By listening to customers and analysing their expectations and undertaking external compar-

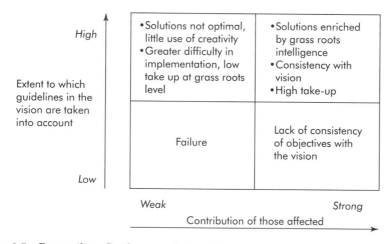

Figure 8.5   Reconciling Guidance and Creativity

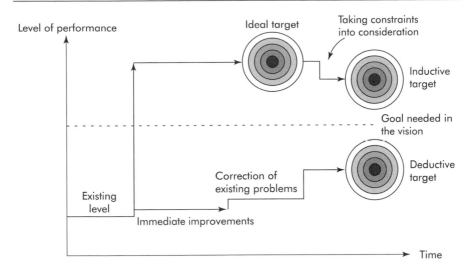

Figure 8.6 Creating a Target for an Improvement Initiative

isons (better known as benchmarking), new ideas can often be brought in and frameworks or habits which have become limiting can be discarded. This is an example of the dislocation which is often necessary if truly innovative solutions are to be found. Moreover, listening to the customer's point of view makes it easier to develop a target which accords with market needs, while external benchmarking (with competitors or with businesses in other sectors) helps to maintain or reinforce a sense of urgency and so to keep anxiety at the necessary level (see Key 2: *Mobilising*). Modifying habitual ways of thinking is therefore a particularly effective or even an indispensable lever for changing behaviour and practice, since it encourages reassessment by individual employees.

4. Make use of technology for innovation. The new technologies such as computing, telecommunications and multimedia are powerful levers for innovation. The Internet, for example, can change the ground rules for activities such as distribution and banking. Here again, one of the crucial issues is to find a way of exploiting these new technologies to attain objectives which at first sight seem unattainable, and not to be content with simply discovering ways in which they can improve on the *status quo*. What is more, the installation of a new IT system is in itself a very strong impetus for change, because it affects the daily work

of the people concerned. Managing change means being able to turn this to advantage.

On the other hand, IT systems can form an obstacle to change, if they enforce a vertical flow of information at the expense of a flow across the business—in other words, if they are constructed purely on the basis of a hierarchical analysis of the business. Merely automating the existing way things are done and structured also carries the risk of failure, or rather the certainty of failure to change. This scenario is unfortunately all too common.

By way of illustration, the following sequence shows how improvement targets can be generated.

1. Researching best practice relating to the initiative, either internally, among competitors or in other industry sectors.
2. Analysing customer expectations by means of a printed questionnaire, or through individual or group interviews.
3. Analysing and enhancing the ideas and recommendations produced by describing the *status quo*.
4. Brainstorming sessions to find an ideal solution. Besides using the results of activities 1 and 2, outside experts can be invited to contribute.
5. Developing the various options. Each option should specify the target of the improvement initiative, aiming five to ten years ahead. The target to be reached within a maximum of twelve months to two years is described in detail; this will be the objective of the implementation plan, after which a further change process can be initiated. Setting a five-year or longer-term target ensures that short-term choices are seen in the light of possible longer-term developments.
6. Analysing the strengths and weaknesses of each option in terms of their contribution to the vision, their expected results and the feasibility of implementing them.
7. Choosing a solution, enhancing and validating it with the help of interested parties throughout the business. This step, which is vital whatever design approach is adopted, may seem too demanding of time and energy. However, it must be carried out because it can lower resistance and increase the support of the majority of employees.

8. Finalising the adopted solution on the basis of the additional ideas and recommendations which have been contributed.

At this point, each improvement initiative has been chosen and specified in detail: its objectives, its contribution to the vision, its expected effects on the physical and psychological components of the business, the investment required and the return on investment, precise descriptions of the new working practices, the new skills (both technical and behavioural) to be developed, and the principal milestones in the implementation plan.

A formal process of integrating and harmonising the solutions for all initiatives can be carried out by means of:

- regular meetings involving all expert team leaders
- regular meetings involving all expert team facilitators
- using a central programme manager to integrate the initiatives
- validation meetings by the steering committee.

In addition, choosing high-flying expert team leaders who have a cross-structural perspective on the business gives a further guarantee that the adopted solutions will integrate well.

- *Tools:* Various methods and tools are employed in designing the target: benchmarking, listening to customers, dynamic modelling of the business, systems analysis, simulation, and so on. Group-work, brainstorming and problem-solving techniques are also extensively used.
- *Contributors:* The expert teams lead the discussions. They obtain the highest possible participation level among the people who will eventually be affected by implementation. As with the analysis of the *status quo*, it is useful on completion of designing the target to hold an open day when everyone is invited to familiarise themselves with the target and put forward their ideas. Key 6: *Obtaining Participation*, describes the levers for participation in more detail.
- *Timescale:* Since work has already been done in the course of defining the vision, mobilising, and analysing the *status quo*, by this stage the expert teams can concentrate on establishing the targeted objectives. In most situations, the design process can be completed in four to eight weeks.
- *Results:* The vision has been articulated in detail for each improvement initiative. The support of all interested parties has been obtained or strengthened.

Short-term Improvements

- *Aims:* Putting immediate improvements into effect as soon as the analysis of the *status quo* has been completed reinforces the dynamic for change, as it demonstrates management's commitment. It also helps to strengthen the support of the employees concerned, who can see the measures they suggested being put in place with immediate effect. On their own these changes often recoup a major portion of the investment involved in change.

  As well as dealing with the cost issues, we recommend putting into immediate effect improvements which may be less significant in financial terms, but which allow a large number of employees to become involved. The high visibility of the change process is thus maintained pending more general application.

- *Activities:* The first task is to choose the improvements which are easiest to put into effect and generate significant benefits. The matrix of opportunities for progress, described above, is a particularly useful tool for making this choice.

  We recommend passing the responsibility for implementing immediate improvements to line managers and putting one individual in charge of each measure, both to avoid increasing the expert teams' workload and to raise the level of participation in the change process. In addition, identifying a patron or sponsor, preferably a member of the steering committee or of the senior management team, ensures that the measures are carried out with the necessary thoroughness.

- *Tools:* These comprise all the levers for action: specifications, procedures, training, coaching, and monitoring documents.

- *Contributors:* It is the users who put the measures into action, helped by the expert teams or facilitators where necessary. The person to be responsible for implementing the improvement measure can be picked from among the supporters of change, and those who are undecided can be encouraged to participate in implementation, in order to convince them of the benefits of change and to give a further demonstration of management's commitment to the change process.

- *Timescale:* The implementation of immediate improvements can begin on completion of the analysis of the *status quo*. It can run in parallel with designing the objectives and can continue throughout the testing stage that follows. It should not last more than six months.

- *Results:* Immediate improvements help to justify the change process on economic grounds. They very often account for 10–20% of the overall financial return and by themselves recoup a major portion of the costs directly involved in the change process: for example, the costs of the change facilitation team, the time spent by those involved, and their out-of-pocket expenses. For managers, they constitute the first tangible financial justification for the current undertaking, and for all those involved in the business, they provide a source of enthusiasm which helps to reinforce mobilisation and universal commitment.

Pilot Tests

- *Aims:* It is useful to carry out testing if the targets are to be deployed in several parts of the business: regions, operational units, departments, subsidiaries and so on. It is highly recommended, and even essential, wherever the changes to be implemented are complex or risky.

  Testing has many aims. The first is to confirm and demonstrate the feasibility of the targets proposed by the expert teams for each improvement route, and if necessary to amend them. The second is to test an approach to implementation which can be applied generally, along with the target itself. The third is to strengthen commitment and mobilising by means of early successes.
- *Activities:* The significance of testing and its chance of success can be increased by taking the following measures:
  - define the aims of testing carefully. A formal specification should be drawn up, setting out in concrete terms the results to be achieved, the performance indicators to be used as the metrics, the modes of operation to be tested, the tools and other resources to be used, and the roles and responsibilities of those involved;
  - define a fixed minimum requirement at the beginning of testing or, at the latest, before the end of it. This is the set of requirements which must be fulfilled. Over and above these necessary minima (the basic solution), participants have the autonomy to identify and implement measures which are specific to their environment. This approach can strengthen their motivation, above all because of the confidence shown in them, and very often leads to the original objectives being exceeded;

- involve representatives of the areas of the business where the target will be deployed, to encourage their support;
- communicate frequently with staff, explaining not only the results but also the obstacles encountered and the problem-solving methods employed.

In addition, during this stage we recommend recording critical moments of the testing on video, especially the development of participants' reactions and standpoints. The video recordings will be shown during the general application stage. They will demonstrate, particularly to the waverers, that the people involved in testing shared their doubts and concerns, but that in the end they found satisfactory or positive answers during implementation.

Testing will normally proceed as follows:

1. define users' new roles, responsibilities and tasks with precision, making sure to understand and respond to their questions or concerns, identify and tackle the obstacles and anticipate and deal with resistance;

2. train users for their new roles, responsibilities and tasks. It is essential to lower resistance before providing training; otherwise, training will be more difficult and take longer because of the continual need to defend and convince. At worst it could actually stiffen resistance;

3. modify the physical components of the solution to be implemented, by installing new equipment, putting new procedures in place, deploying new software, creating a new organisational structure, putting new modes of operation into effect, and so on;

4. allow users to exercise their new roles, responsibilities and tasks;

5. work with users to assess their performance to determine how well their actions conform to the target model. In doing so it is necessary to understand both good and inadequate performance by analysing the causes. Exercising new roles and responsibilities, coupled with continuous prompt assessment of performance, will give rise to changes in working methods and lead to development of employees' attitudes and behaviour. It may be necessary to modify the system of rewards and sanctions as an aid to spreading new patterns of behaviour and practice. The most appropriate management style to be adopted may vary according to the attitudes of those involved;

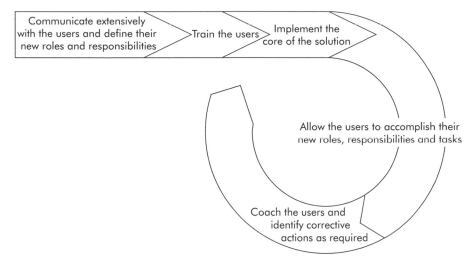

Figure 8.7 Iterative Process for Implementation

6. allow users to apply the results of assessment to changing their own ways of working and behaving in line with the objectives of the improvement initiative being tested;

7. repeat the assessment process and let users reapply the recommendations, until the desired changes are obtained following the iterative process of implementation shown in Figure 8.7.

- *Tools:* The description of the target objective and the detailed implementation plan drawn up during the design stage are utilised. The techniques of coaching and training and methods for handling resistance to change and controlling the power issues are also useful as described in later chapters;

- *Contributors:* All staff involved in the area under test contribute to the testing process. The managers directly affected by the experiment provide the leadership, supported as required by the facilitators or members of the expert team for the relevant improvement initiative;

- *Timescale:* The testing that follows on from development of the concept should not last longer than three to four months, so that general application can begin without further delay;

- *Results:* The feasibility of the improvement targets has been demonstrated. The minimum requirements and areas for autonomous improvement have been vindicated and validated. An approach to implementation has been tested.

General Application

Proceeding to general application is probably the trickiest stage of delivering. Many change programmes fail at this stage, even when fully successful during pilot testing. We have identified two principal causes of failure. The first lies in thinking that the success of general application is a foregone conclusion because the solution has been found and its feasibility has been tested. General application is reduced to simply sending out an instruction, which is very often not sufficient to overcome mental blockages and resistance and to convince the undecided. The second cause of failure lies in considering general application as simply a repeat of the preceding stages: analysing the *status quo*, designing the target and implementing it. Apart from the very high costs involved where general application covers a large number of sites, there is the risk of the organisation running out of steam during an over-burdensome or over-lengthy change process.

- *Aims:* General application pursues three aims simultaneously:
  - acceptance of the minimum requirements for each improvement initiative;
  - enhancement of the minimum, by including features particular to each application site;
  - dissemination of change management methods whose effectiveness has been demonstrated in earlier stages.

Figure 8.8 clarifies the objectives of general application and summarises this three-fold aim.

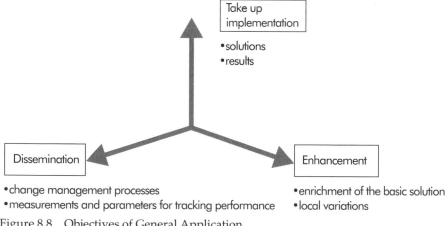

Figure 8.8 Objectives of General Application

- *Activities:* Depending on the complexity of the anticipated changes, their depth and their level of acceptance—to be determined for each individual location—acceptance and implementation require a greater or lesser degree of effort. For example, the straightforward communication of information, backed up by the testimony of those involved in pilot testing, may be enough. In other cases, workshops will be needed to analyse the *status quo* and define the target starting from the necessary minimum. In parts of the business where resistance to change is particularly high, a detailed analysis of the *status quo* should be carried out in order to convince staff of the need for change and to persuade them to identify with the minimum objective. In this case, implementation may go through the same stages as testing.

Figure 8.9 lists possible activities for general application, as well as the activities involved in setting the target. Activities are selected by the management of each general application site, with the support of the change facilitation team.

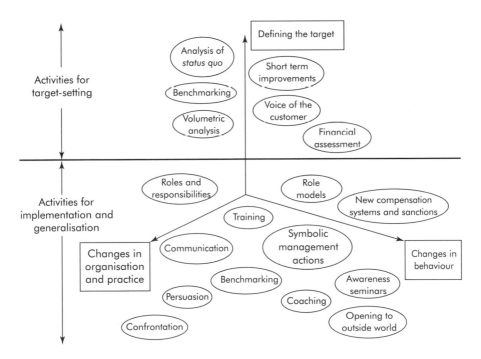

Figure 8.9   Activities Associated with Implementation and General Application

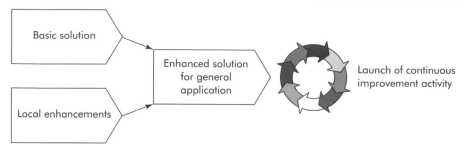

Figure 8.10   Utilisation of the Basic Solution in the General Application Phase

- *Tools:* Communication, training and coaching are extensively used. By using the minimum requirements as a starting point, the general application sites can give free rein to their creativity, the target being enhanced locally and a process of continuous improvement also being instigated (see Figure 8.10).

The local enhancement activities, leading eventually also to continuous improvement can be initiated by means of change workshops (see Key 2: *Mobilising*).

- *Contributors:* The management and staff of the general application sites are the prime contributors. They are supported by the change facilitation team and the expert teams.
- *Timescale:* The timescale for deployment should not exceed eighteen months, and the total duration of the change process should be no more than two years at the outside. It is difficult to maintain the required level of energy and motivation over a longer period. For changes which require a longer timescale, it is advisable to set up a sequence of several change processes, each with clearly defined objectives. With increasing experience, each process in the sequence will be completed more quickly than the last.
- *Results:* The target for each improvement initiative has been put into effect and committed to throughout the organisation. The business has developed its ability to manage change.

Monitoring Results

- *Aims:* For each improvement route, it is necessary to:
  - define the quantitative and qualitative results expected;

– define the economic impact of these results: additional earnings, cost reductions, investment required, annual profits, and return on investment;
– check that these expected results are consistent with the objectives stated in the vision;
– monitor the results obtained by means of operational and financial metrics.

How well the objectives of the vision are achieved as a whole is monitored with the help of the metrics or alternatively by combining some of the metrics specified for each improvement initiative, e.g., increase in market share up to the stated objective, cost reduction achieved, completion of a merger between two companies or divisions.

- *Activities:* The activities are carried out for each improvement initiative. For example, they could follow the following sequence:

  1. list the expected results for each improvement initiative, including also qualitative results and those whose economic impact is indirect or even slight;
  2. where possible, back up these results by means of historical data, and simulations incorporating best current practice or simply estimates based on experience or particular studies;
  3. choose metrics for monitoring the expected results and make them available to the users for follow up;
  4. monitor the changes in these performance indicators during the course of the implementation process;
  5. ensure that both the changes in the indicators and their positive impact on the business are widely publicised;
  6. continuously assess the results with managers and staff concerned.

- *Tools:* Operational and financial analysis and management control tools are used. It is helpful to set up a special file for each improvement initiative for following up indicators and results. The format is the same for each initiative, and graphs and other visuals are used regularly as an aid to communication. Figure 8.11 shows schematically how such results can be tracked.

- *Contributors:* Both the estimating of expected results and the choosing of metrics are carried out by the relevant expert teams during the design stage. However, arrangements must be made for the results obtained to be monitored by line managers and their staff. Where implementation is complex or the results are difficult to measure, an 'operational and financial results' support team studies the results closely and gives technical and methodological assistance to both expert teams and users. The change facilitation team can fulfil this role if it has the necessary time and skills at its disposal.

- *Timescale:* The estimating of expected results and the choosing of indicators takes place during the design stage. The indicators are put in place before general application, then monitored throughout the change process and subsequently. This is to check and confirm that the gains made are maintained.

- *Results:* This stage enables the results to be monitored and compared with the objectives defined in the vision. Progress can be checked and corrective action taken in case of drift away from the objectives.

Systems Implementation

- *Aims:* The results are starting to look favourable. The change process is now successfully under way in all or part of the business.

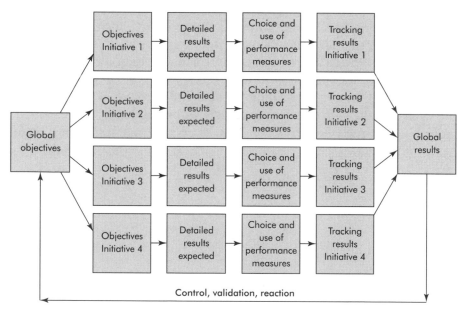

Figure 8.11   Method for Tracking Results

The new business structure is in place, and the new equipment or systems are working, as are the new management procedures. Employees are adapting to their new roles and responsibilities in accordance with the objectives of the vision and the improvement initiatives, and their behaviour has developed in line with the vision. This success was promoted by the training and coaching dedicated to achieving it. The time has come to embark on a new phase of the process: institutionalising. The aim of institutionalising is to put in place management systems designed to ensure that employees do not revert to their original ways of working, behaving or thinking, so as to guarantee lasting results. Such systems include, first and foremost, schemes for employee remuneration and performance, human resource management and career tracking, as well as systems designed to handle allocation of funds. The management systems which need to be put in place vary from one business to the next, depending on the type of change being carried out and the particular features of the business in question.

- *Activities:* In the majority of cases the essential activities are as follows:
  - identifying the management systems which have a major impact on the people in the business, their working methods and the way they behave;
  - structuring these management systems appropriately to support the vision and the new working methods. Employees whose attitudes or working methods are not consistent with the vision will, from now on, increasingly be seen to be at variance with the remodelled systems;
  - making immediate use of these systems to support, promote or reward employees whose behaviour continues to sustain the vision and, on the other hand, to transmit warning signals to the others. A coaching programme may be developed specifically to help the latter.

- *Tools:* The tools employed are first and foremost those of human resource management, management control and strategic management.
- *Contributors:* The management teams in charge of the major administrative divisions (human resources, finance, IT, etc.) are responsible for this undertaking, with the support of the expert team

leaders and the leader of the change facilitation team. Senior management and those in charge of the units most affected by change also play a decisive role in ensuring that the changes are lasting. They must be seen to be committed and set an example in maintaining and even enhancing the solutions put in place. They must also make sure that the managers who played a leadership role in implementing the vision remain in post long enough—at least a year—for the change to be truly institutionalised. This means that change must not be seen as dependent on the presence of a particular executive in a key position, with the result that their departure could lead to backsliding. This implies that in the short term such managers should be rewarded not through promotion, but by other means—which would in itself constitute a change for many businesses.

- *Timescale:* This process must be carried out during general application, to ensure that the new systems are in place by the time this is complete.
- *Results:* Change is now institutionalised in the business. The vision has been permanently achieved. Future change processes linked to new objectives can be launched with even greater effectiveness in the light of the experience gained.

In the remaining chapters we shall be providing more information on how delivering is supported by a variety of important means, including: obtaining participation, managing the emotional aspects, adjusting for changes in power structures, training and coaching and communicating extensively.

CASE STUDY ON DELIVERING: FRANCE TELECOM

France Telecom is the fourth largest telecommunications operator worldwide with revenues of $27 billion in 1997 and a workforce of around 150 000 employees. With its $2.3 billion net profit, France Telecom is also one of the most profitable operators, showing the best results of all French companies in 1997.

The France Telecom digital network is one of the best worldwide and its productivity is high compared to other large national operators. Its R&D department has broken new ground in the field of technologies with the implementation of Minitel, forerunner of the commercial development of the Internet.

Change in the Environment

In June 1993, the European Union created a revolution for all European telephone operators. From 1 January, 1998, all telephone monopolies in Europe will
disappear and competition, which was limited to a few sectors, will be open for
all services and installations. Although France Telecom has many assets, the re-
engineering of its organisation is necessary to face the complete deregulation of
telecommunications announced in Brussels. Company management has
defined three main directions along which changes must take place.

- increase market focus
- reduce response times and increase the capacity to adapt
- focus on productivity and performance.

'SCLSN' Change Action

Vision

As a consequence of the above requirements, the 'SCLSN' change plan
(*Satisfaction Client pour la Livraison des Services Numériques*: Customer
Satisfaction for Digital Service Delivery) was launched. The objective is to
reduce by a factor of two to four the delivery times of products and digital
services as well as a 100% improvement in fulfilling delivery promises. This
objective is crucial since digital services are delivered mainly to companies
and professional customers who in 1998 will become the primary target of
France Telecom's new competitors. Although the order-to-delivery process
is one of the most visible and critical in terms of service quality for
customers, external benchmarking has shown that France Telecom
performance is not yet best-in-class, especially with regard to Bell Atlantic or
South-western Bell in the United States.

Delivering

Jean-Claude Stambouli, change manager, has elaborated a four-step process
to improve performance as shown in Figure 8.12.

Forty eight regional districts are involved, in each of them 200 to 300
people participate in the programme. Representatives from each function are
playing a part from areas such as sales, sales administration, etc.

Delivering change was a great challenge when this project was launched,
according to Jean-Claude Stambouli :

- the objectives of the project were in total disagreement with the existing
   situation. Executives considered them to be unreachable and impossible

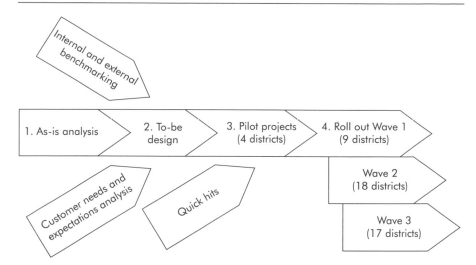

Figure 8.12 Process for Performance Improvement

in an organisation where nothing encouraged risk taking. They were consequently quite reluctant to commit themselves to the project objectives.

– because of the number of people involved (about 10 000), a participative process was necessary. This process contradicted the usual hierarchical culture where implementation was usually carried out by directives handed down from above.

– true performance of the process could not be evaluated through the management systems in place, therefore improvements against target could not be effectively evaluated. Because of the nature of the performance indicators in use, an actual improvement of the process registered as a decline in the performance of regional districts. It was then difficult to mobilise operatives and middle management!

According to Jean-Claude Stambouli, four elements were essential to the success of the delivery phase:

1. Trust in the expert teams   During the analysis of the existing situation and the target, the expert teams have had great autonomy in the four pilot districts to define target objectives. When only marginal improvements had been planned by the leaders of the regional management, the teams have proposed objectives that were true *performance* leaps (reduction of delivery delays by a factor of four for some products).

2. Opening up to the outside at all levels   Benchmarking was an important step in targeting. Several operators, including South-western Bell and Bell

Atlantic have agreed to benchmarking with France Telecom and have thus received France Telecom teams. These visits have allowed challenging targets to be set compared to the actual practices. One of the features of this process lies in the very constitution of these teams. Not only were managers from regional districts and general management members of the teams, but also key operatives who never had hoped to have such an experience. This symbolic decision had a great impact: it showed that general management would rely on creativity and operating experience to succeed. Moreover, the operatives, back in their departments, were extremely motivated, and became enthusiastic and convincing supporters in front of their colleagues.

3. *The voice of the customer* Customer groups were created to analyse customers' needs and expectations in terms of product and service delivery. Individual interviews and focus groups were made and led respectively by members of the expert teams in charge of the analysis of the existing situation and of defining the objectives to be targeted. This process increased participants' state of readiness and encouraged them to define ambitious objectives.

4. *Indicators* Since the existing information system could not measure process performance and improvements, the project management team developed and implemented a system to measure and monitor results at the district level. The development and implementation of this system required significant work and an important investment in time, but it was essential to the success of the project. This was the main answer to the detractors as well as the basis for tracking improvements realised by operatives. Such recognition was necessary for the success of the operation.

5. *Delivery* The delivery phase lasted close to two years and allowed delivery times to be cut between two- and four-fold while increasing on-time delivery rates by over 100%.

Chapter 9

Key 6: Obtaining Participation

Implementing change requires the staff of a business to think, behave and act in a new way, not as they have been doing before. This change can only take place if employees identify with the vision and the redefinition of every individual's roles and responsibilities that this vision implies. This in turn can only be achieved by involving employees on a large scale throughout the change process. Obtaining their participation on this scale in the process of change is the objective of Key 6: *Obtaining participation.*

THE ESSENTIAL ROLE OF PARTICIPATION

Participation is the starting point for creating a dynamic of employee involvement, support and success in the process of change. This is the virtuous circle of participation which all change programmes must seek to create (see Figure 9.1).

To create the initial conditions for entry into such a circle entails encouraging employees to participate by offering them the opportunity to contribute their ideas, express their concerns, and contribute to the ultimate choice of the solution or merely to influence the choices made. Employees must understand that they have the opportunity and the power—in fact, the duty—to influence decisions. Communication

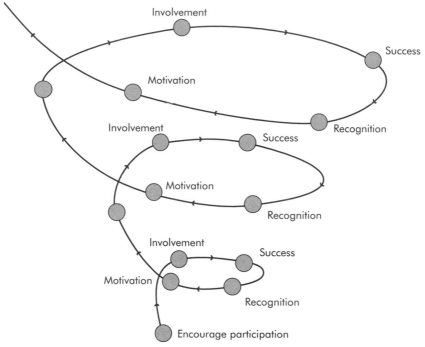

Figure 9.1   The Virtuous Spiral of Participation

therefore plays an important part in prompting all employees to participate in the change process. Emphasis needs giving to the collaborative nature of the process and the fact that everyone in the business should feel involved. We must show how everyone can contribute by putting forward ideas. We shall see later in this chapter how expert teams can activate and maintain the participation of the majority of employees with the help of tools and procedures designed for the purpose.

Employees start to take part in the change process, to contribute their ideas and to defend them. This initial level of participation creates or reinforces support for the vision, for the implementation procedure and for the improvement initiatives. From this point onwards, employees will of course identify more and more with the process, but their degree of commitment will above all be reflected in the level of their contribution and depend upon the extent to which they can see their own work having an impact on the adopted solution. Employees put forward their own ideas, defend them and enhance them with the help of their colleagues' ideas. Thanks to this commitment, they achieve early successes, which may for example be important strategic choices which are adopted for the improvement initiatives (as a result of their ideas and suggestions), or achievements on a much smaller scale, such as choosing and carrying out immediate improvements (see Key 5: *Delivering*).

This impression of success is reinforced when employees are shown appreciation of their performance, both by their peers and superiors, and by the change facilitation team. It is one of the responsibilities of the team, as well as of line managers, to recognise the achievements and contributions of individuals—or preferably of groups—and to see that they are publicised. They must identify those people doing well and make it known. Recognition can take the form of congratulating them verbally or in writing, mentioning them in the in-house journal or giving a bonus for ideas which generate significant financial benefits.

Employees' motivation is invariably boosted by personal success, coupled with recognition of themselves and their actions. This early experience of success pushes them to get further and further involved and therefore to participate more fully. They take on board the initial solutions and the new results, identify more and more strongly with them, and as a result make increased commitments which lead to renewed successes, and so on. Recognition, a key stage in this spiral, is all too often neglected, either because its importance is not appreciated or simply through oversight.

During a change process which was recently instigated in a German mechanical engineering business, we found that the personnel—blue-collar and white-collar staff alike—remained on the whole peculiarly detached from the change process. Very few (too few) ideas or recommendations were put forward. After a few days we asked a few of them why there was such a lack of ideas and creativity. The answer was quite simply that they did not have any ideas. We persevered, pointing out that this was the first time in our professional experience that we had met personnel who 'did not have any ideas'. This time the response was quite different: we discovered that they were refusing to contribute their ideas because their supervisors had already appropriated and implemented several of them without either informing or thanking the staff, who could only watch while their suggestions were put into practice. In short, their ideas had been 'stolen'. In the context of the change process, line managers must be especially attentive to showing recognition to those who deserve it, otherwise the impetus for participation that has been created will be destroyed.

The virtuous circle or spiral of participation has the following results, as far as its contribution to the change process is concerned:

- the higher the level of employee participation, the more the change process can capitalise on the fund of experience and ideas which each individual represents, and the better the ultimate solution will be, since it will benefit from the ability of every employee to make useful suggestions;
- participation ensures support. The solution ultimately adopted belongs to the participants and must not provoke the resistance which might be aroused by an imposed solution. This support in its turn makes it easier to implement the solution, as employees are more highly motivated and keener to implement ideas which they share, the more so since they contributed to developing them.

SOME TECHNIQUES

However highly motivated a manager or a group of employees may be, they cannot change the business without involving the majority of those colleagues who will be most affected by the desired changes. Individual participation is the key that unlocks and the motor that drives the virtuous circle we have described. It is the responsibility of the change facilitation team to create the enabling conditions for the initial involvement of employees. They have several methods and tools at their disposal.

Establishing Teams

One way of taking the first step in increasing participation is to create working teams involving people with different functions and at different levels. These are the expert teams or support teams described in Key 3: *Catalysing*. In the case of a global change process affecting a large business, there may be as many as eight to ten expert teams and three support teams, involving the participation of 100–150 people.

This first step, once achieved, should be built on—first, because this number represents only a small proportion of the staff who will eventually find themselves involved in or affected by the vision, and second, because it is important to avoid at all costs creating two categories of employees in the business: the select few who will participate in the change process using novel methods and tools, and the rest, who will watch from the sidelines and wonder what is going on. This rift would inevitably deepen with time and, however good the expert teams' recommendations may be, most employees would be unlikely to identify with them or be motivated to put them into effect. At this point an approach must be devised which allows the whole staff to participate, not just the expert teams.

The Interface Between the Expert Teams and the Rest of the Staff

The challenge is to move from limited activity involving only a few small teams, to a state of seething activity affecting all employees, where each individual feels involved in contributing to the detailed development of the vision and to its implementation.

One method is to create teams made up of employees who are not only open to the idea of participation but who also seek it proactively. The change facilitation team recruits employees of this type into the expert teams (see Key 3: *Catalysing*). A second method consists of equipping these teams with working methods and tools which promote widespread participation in the change process right from the start of the delivery phase.

The change facilitation team is the provider of methods and tools of this type. For example:

– *charting on large paper charts:* this is at once one of the simplest and one of the most effective tools for participation that we know. The expert teams chart the progress of their work on rolls of paper pinned to the wall, and all the users are convened regularly to familiarise themselves with the charts and to annotate them with their comments, ideas, concerns or suggestions. This method ensures that they are continuously involved in the progress of the work and that information about it is permanently available. In the case of a company in the chemical sector, where the vision required the complete transformation of all its management processes, the expert teams wrote their entire set of recommendations on large-sized paper, including a full description of the new procedures. This meant using several hundred metres of paper. Management then announced 'the paper event', with several days' suspension of normal work. The corridor walls on three floors of the headquarters building had been covered with paper, and all the company's employees were invited to come and comment, express their ideas and jot down suggestions. Besides bringing in many ideas for improvement, this event helped to make everyone aware of the state of progress, and to inspire widespread involvement, identification with the solutions and a high level of enthusiasm;

– *the matrix of quantifiable benefits, group problem-solving and active forces analysis:* these techniques are dealt with in Keys 5 and 7: *Delivering* and *Handling the Emotional Dimension.* They enable working groups to call on other employees, either as experts or simply as a resource to contribute to finding the optimum solution;

– *continuous use of communication* to keep the whole staff informed of progress and thus to make it easier for them to get involved and render their involvement more effective. At least one detailed briefing should be issued at each key major milestone in the change process:

- an announcement informing staff about the vision;
- a subsequent announcement outlining the general directions de-fined at the end of mobilising: how the change process will be organised, which improvement initiatives have been adopted, how the expert and support teams will be structured and the working principles that will be used for the change process (management commitment, universal participation, speeding up implementation, measurement of results, etc.);
- an announcement during the delivery phase, after detailed design, and before implementation is launched;
- several announcements during implementation, to inform people of the state of progress, the successes achieved to date and the difficulties encountered.

To summarise, these techniques are vehicles for spreading the involvement of staff beyond the activities of the expert teams and into the organisation at large.

By way of example, a big manufacturing company instigated a change process with the aim of speeding up its new product development cycle. A key factor in its success was institutionalising team working and the sharing of skills and expertise in a company where traditionally employees had worked in a very isolated way.

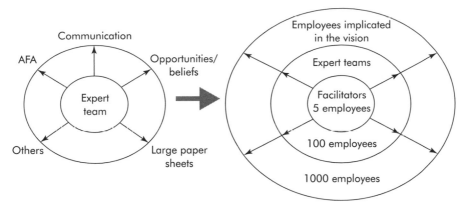

Figure 9.2   The Process of Extending Participation

As soon as the change process had been launched, management communicated widely with the whole workforce, exhorting them to work in groups. The aim was of course to obtain widespread participation in the change process, but also to create a corporate culture which was based much more on partnership and group working. Two plastic-covered cards were designed by the change facilitation team and distributed to all employees. The first card defined team working as follows:

Working in a team is ...

- willingly sharing your knowledge, your experiences and your expertise, justifying your ideas, listening to others' ideas and trying to understand them, analysing all the ideas, opinions and concerns put forward so that together you choose the best solution for the business;
- being able to work towards consensus, by taking care to choose the best solution for the business without continually accepting poor compromises to keep everyone happy;
- always bearing in mind that the solution does not really belong to the group, but to the rest of the business as well, so you need to be able to call on others to improve and endorse the solutions you have adopted;
- being able to bring in experts to solve specific technical problems which are beyond the competence of the team;
- defining clear roles within the team: leader, facilitator and resources;
- ignoring hierarchical barriers within the group;
- defining an objective, results, a timetable and responsibilities within the team.

The second card set out an approach to group problem-solving in six steps, which there is no need to reproduce here.

In conclusion, there are many tools for maximising participation. With a little creativity, the change facilitation team and the expert teams can develop further tools specially adapted to the particular features of their business. The only thing to bear in mind is that, to be effective, such tools must satisfy at least three criteria. They must be:

1. simple
2. targeted towards producing results
3. designed so that the maximum number of employees can make use of them to follow the progress of the work and generate added value.

RATES AND LEVELS OF PARTICIPATION

The rate of participation is considered in relation to the total number of employees in the part of the business undergoing transformation. Depending on circumstances, this may mean the whole of the business, or one of its divisions, or one or several smaller units. In the rest of this chapter, for simplicity, we shall treat the business itself as the domain of change.

As we see it, participation must be maintained throughout the course of the change process. During the period of defining the vision, only senior management and a few executives are involved. Next, the mobilising phase increases the participation rate and the proportion of employees contributing to the results of this phase can be regarded as being around 10–20%. To endorse the vision and its objectives and to make sure that the staff of the business as a whole are convinced that they are right, the change facilitation team carries out a rapid analysis during mobilising, with the participation of employees in the units affected and based on their experiences. All of them are invited to have their say on what they see as the dysfunctions and the opportunities for improvement. The number of employees involved in this way is large enough for every employee of the business to have a close colleague who can testify to: (i) the value of the change process; (ii) the desire of management to establish a collaborative approach benefiting from each individual's expertise; (iii) recognition of what the current situation really is; and (iv) the commitment of management to make change.

In addition, by issuing a general briefing (see Key 10: *Communicating Actively*) at the start of the mobilisation phase, announcing the vision and the launch of a change process—and also at the end of the phase, outlining the principal directions the process will take—helps to increase the majority of employees' awareness of what is going on and sensitise them to the process. The next phase, delivering, involves the participation of even more employees. With the establishment of the expert teams, dozens of people find themselves committing an average of 30–50% of their time to the process of change. The use by these teams of group-working methods and tools, as described at the beginning of this chapter, encourages a second level of participation: that of the many employees who will contribute to the work of the expert teams. It may be estimated that each team member involves at least five to ten outsiders, making a total of several hundred people taking part either in drawing up a detailed description of the *status quo* or in designing the improvement initiatives (see Key 5: *Delivering*).

The publication of a permanent display of the expert teams' work at every stage helps to keep every employee informed of how the programme is going and thereby helps to keep them involved. The final phase of delivering, testing and general application entails the involvement of all the employees of the business who are affected by the change process.

As an example, the chart at Figure 9.3 shows how the participation rate changed during the merger of two US regional banks with work-forces of 1500 and 1000 employees respectively.

We have been looking at participation from a purely quantitative point of view. However, involvement does not mean the same thing for all employees; it depends on their time, needs or personal interests. At one end of the scale are the champions of the change process who have identified with the vision, and consequently with the change process. They are always brimming with enthusiasm and act as engines or leaders of change at the implementation level. They are generally to be found within the change facilitation team and the expert teams, or are in charge of the units where pilot testing is carried out. This is a further reason for selecting high-flyers with lots of potential for the expert teams (as we stressed in Keys 2 and 3, *Mobilising* and *Catalysing*), so that they can exert the maximum leverage on those around them. At the other end of the scale is a quite different group of people, who are no doubt aware of the existence of a vision and a change process, but no more than that. In principle, if

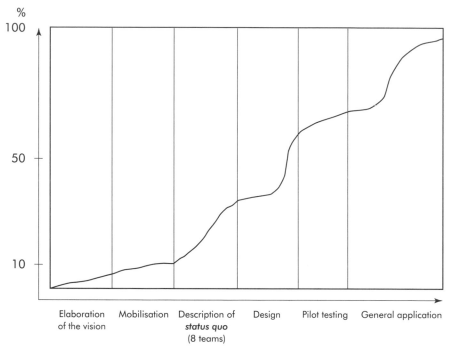

Figure 9.3 Development of Participation during a Change Process

Note: The participation rate is defined as the percentage of employees with respect to the original number employed by the two banks, i.e. 2500 persons. It is not a snapshot of the number participating at any particular moment but the total number of people who have participated in the change programme up to that time.

communication is carried out appropriately (see Key 10: *Communicating Actively*), every employee should at least be aware of the vision and the process of change once the vision has been established.

We have identified five levels of participation.

Level 1: Employees who are already *sensitised*. They are familiar with and understand the vision and the broad outlines of the change process.

Level 2: Employees who are *convinced* of the urgency and prepared to participate. They support the vision in broad terms and are persuaded of the urgency of launching the related change process. They feel themselves to be affected by the development of the business and its potential implications at their level. They are *prepared to participate* in the process if called upon.

Level 3: Employees who *have participated* at least once or are currently *participating* in the change process. They took part or were trained, but do not actively seek fresh opportunities to become involved.

Level 4: Employees who are *motivated* by the vision and the change process. They have participated on several occasions and regularly seek out new opportunities to participate and contribute.

Level 5: Employees who have become *champions of change*, initiators of the change process. They are constantly rising, moving round or up the virtuous circle or spiral described at the beginning of this chapter. They act as locomotives in the process of change.

Everyone at a particular level has also reached all levels below it. For example, a champion understands the vision and the change process, is convinced of the urgent need to act, participates in the process and is highly motivated.

Of course, at each stage of the change process, the chart of participation levels will change (Figure 9.4). During the development of the vision, for example, only a few executives and senior managers take part in the change process. They are all highly motivated and some fall into the champions category. Once the vision has been defined, it is conveyed to the whole staff, who are thereby sensitised to the vision and the change process. They are all aware of its existence and most of them understand its purpose. Next, at the mobilising phase, an initial level of participation among employees—of the order of 10–20%—can be established and, above all, there is the opportunity to convince the majority on the issues at stake in the vision and of the urgency of the change process. They all feel themselves to be affected and involved. They are prepared to participate and to assist in the change process, which they support if invited to do so. This rise in the graph of participation levels between the stages of defining the vision and mobilising is at its most marked where change with dislocation is involved. It is mobilising (see Key 2: *Mobilising*) which raises general support above the level of mere awareness or understanding.

In another case, a major change is proposed by management in circumstances where the position of the business is not under threat. Although it makes better profits than its competitors and enjoys leadership status in the eyes of its customers, its managers decide to launch an ambitious improvement and productivity programme, because they believe that they must prepare to face what they forecast as an inevitable economic decline. The vast majority of employees understand this vision and the need always to do better, although most of them are not by any means convinced of the urgency of launching a change process, a step which is especially difficult when the circumstances are still perceived as generally favourable.

The directors of this business therefore decide to instigate a mobilising phase to convince reluctant employees of the need to embark as quickly as possible on the change process and to participate actively in it; in other words, to raise them towards level 2 participation. The various stages of delivery will subsequently lead to the emergence of new champions but, most importantly, will ensure the participation of a growing number of employees (often between 30 and 60%) during the detailed description of the *status quo* and then the design of the targets and improvement initiatives. During the general application phase, the entire workforce of the affected part of the business participates in the change process.

The concept of critical participation rate by participation level is an important one. At each stage of the process, a minimum number of champions, motivated employees, participants, employees prepared to participate and employees sensitised to the vision is essential for satisfactory progress. The critical rate, which differs from one business to the next, varies as a function of several parameters: how ambitious the vision is in relation to the *status quo*, the current values of the business, the relationship between the forces sustaining change and those which are hindering it, past experience of change, and so on. It is up to each business and each change facilitation team to evaluate this critical rate. The graph in Figure 9.4 was developed from a manufacturing business faced with implementing a major change within its sales division which involved dislocation: a complete break with the ways of working which people had been used to until then. The graph shows the changes in the critical participation rate within the division as change progressed.

CRITICAL CONDITIONS FOR SUCCESS

In the remainder of the chapter we set out some other requirements which are important in achieving high participation.

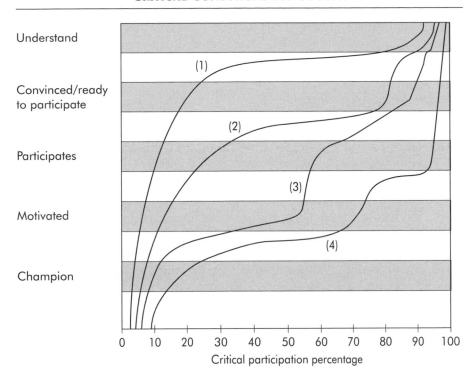

Understand

Convinced/ready
to participate

Participates

Motivated

Champion

(1)
(2)
(3)
(4)

0   10   20   30   40   50   60   70   80   90   100

Critical participation percentage

1. Critical participation rate by participation level on completion of establishment of the vision.

2. Critical participation rate by participation level on completion of mobilising.

3. Critical participation rate by participation level during the design stage of delivering.

4. Critical participation rate by participation level during general application stage of delivering.

Figure 9.4 Critical Participation Rate by Participation Level as Change Progresses (example)

Guiding Without Attempting to Control

The change process generates an explosion of ideas, initiatives and activities through the work of the teams and from the measures for obtaining mobilisation and participation. It is obviously unrealistic to attempt to control the activity of every single employee. It is better to rely on the creativity of individuals and their ability to make the most of their skills and expertise, and to direct this intelligence towards the vision which is to be realised. This is one of the aims of the change facilitation team and the organisation which has been set up (see Keys 3 and 4, *Catalysing* and *Steering*). But it must also be the concern of every manager in the business to allow his or her staff sufficient freedom and flexibility. There are two expressions to describe this approach: 'top down' and 'bottom up'. 'Top down' means that management, with the help of the change facilitation team, defines the framework within which employees can develop their ideas. For example, at the end of mobilising, management establishes the improvement initiatives, their targets and the teams allocated to them. 'Bottom up' expresses the reverse impetus: within the context defined by management, the expert teams and employees in general are allowed complete freedom to design the best solution. Each of them can make suggestions that influence management, by making use of their own experience, expertise and skills.

Handling Expectations at the Lower Levels of Management

It is often at the lowest level of management—supervisors, foremen and first line management—that there is the greatest reluctance to give their staff the necessary autonomy. They see any freedom granted to their rank and file and the resulting reduction in their control as a loss of authority and power which could threaten them personally. The change facilitation team can help to redefine their role in the new context. They need to learn to move from a straightforward supervisory role to one of team leader and coach. (See Keys 7 and 8, *Handling the Emotional Dimension* and *Handling the Power Issues*.)

Following up Ideas and Initiatives

Once employees have been invited to participate, it is important to make sure that their ideas are taken into consideration. The dynamic of change would soon be destroyed if employees saw their ideas being filed away and not followed up. One of the roles of the change facilitation team is to ensure that every suggestion gets a response. In one US manufacturing business, for example, management achieved this by making it one of the obligations of all those in positions of responsibility to respond to every suggestion or idea put forward by their staff, on condition that these were properly worked out and supported (by simple economic analysis and an assessment of feasibility). The response had to be made within five days, and observance of this rule was made one of the assessment criteria for management at year end.

In addition, we recommend setting up a bonus system to reward the best suggestions. The challenge is to work out a system which promotes group working rather than individualism.

Granting the Right to Make Mistakes

Participation rates will be higher if employees realise that they have the right to make mistakes. They will feel encouraged to express ideas and try out new ways of working as long as they believe themselves to be reasonably well protected in the event of failure. This right to make mistakes is therefore crucial to participation. We have also seen how it contributes to a sense of security during mobilising. Later we shall see that it contributes to training and coaching, since if employees are to engage in continuous learning, they must apply their newly acquired ideas or expertise, and therefore take risks.

CASE STUDY ON CREATING PARTICIPATION: ROLLS-ROYCE AEROSPACE GROUP

It has already been described previously how, in 1995, the Rolls-Royce Aerospace Group created a broad and challenging vision concerning how the business was going to be run in the future and what new metrics they would have to measure themselves by and perform against, to become a leader in the aerospace industry in the future. Once agreement had been reached between Rolls-Royce and EDS/A.T. Kearney to partner for ten years, it became necessary to define how the companies would participate in the business improvement initiatives as well as in the transfer of IT resources to EDS. While all this was going on, similar arrangements were being concluded at the Allison Engines Company with a similar kind of value-added partnership idea. It is important to realise that the vision of Rolls-Royce is global in nature, with the potential to embrace any existing or future theatre of operations of the Rolls-Royce Group.

Securing Top-level Support

Once agreement had been reached, the participation of staff from Rolls-Royce Aerospace Group in the change programme was first secured in a top-down fashion by using various board members to take responsibility for championing individual components of the business initiative programme. Thus Paul Heiden, then Group Finance Director, was placed in overall charge of the business initiative programme, while Wal Budzynski, then Director of IT, was responsible for the IT transitioning. At individual initiative levels, the various board level representatives were assigned responsibility for specific areas and charged with ensuring that the expected results would be obtained.

Because the financial management processes in a quoted company such as Rolls-Royce are necessarily very strong, the active leadership of the finance function in securing the overall outcome ensures that there is no creeping misalignment of performance objectives as work on the initiatives proceeds. This is a very critical matter because on many other change programmes in other organisations work has ground to a halt because people will not change if the means by which they are measured conflict with the new measures required in the change programme but which are not yet formally institutionalised (the same point was made in the France Telecom case study at the end of the preceding chapter).

From Top-level Support to Initiative Teams

The nature of the reward-sharing partnership between Rolls-Royce and EDS/A.T. Kearney meant that from the beginning there was a strong interest by both partners in contributing their best resources in appropriate quantities to the success of such a critical relationship. Bill Thomas, a senior executive of EDS, was made Global Account Director for Rolls-Royce, and specialist A.T. Kearney vice-presidents, principals, managers and staff were drafted in from around the world to help create the business initiative teams of which there were initially five, subsequently increased to seven. The A.T. Kearney presence was managed by Dan Shine, who has long-standing experience in the aerospace industry both as executive and consultant. Similarly, the same kind of approach was also adopted in Allison in Indianapolis.

The quick mobilisation of the EDS/A.T. Kearney team was to require a similarly fast mobilisation from within Roll-Royce, because it was essential that the initiative teams were staffed equally by Rolls-Royce and EDS/A.T. Kearney. This ensured the participation of a strong Rolls-Royce team from the beginning, many of whom were taken from important daily jobs to work on what has become a redefinition of the ways Rolls-Royce will be working in the future. It should be added that in other companies failure to find the right resources is an all-too-frequent initial source of difficulty which dogs the chances of success of the programme from the very beginning.

This visible support of the initial vision, by demonstrating great resolution in action, and a willingness to make a degree of short-term sacrifice, characterises the way in which leading companies approach business transformation. By demonstrating this unflinching resolve, the rest of the organisation not directly involved in the process see from the start that it is important to participate in what is going on, provided ways can be found quickly for them to do so.

From Initiative Teams to Spreading the Gospel

If one were to participate in an initiative team at Rolls-Royce, one would soon become aware of the extent to which the teams are working on a daily basis with their counterparts responsible for the day-to-day operations of the company. Teams should never be working in ivory towers or in isolation— rather, as at Rolls-Royce, they should be undertaking analysis jointly with counterparts in the operational areas or testing pilot applications of concepts they would like to see further applied.

Also noticeable at Rolls-Royce is the extent to which operational man- agement welcome the new ideas, frequently as the embodiment of ideas they themselves have been trying to introduce in the past. There are also of course cases of the opposite, where managers may doubt the wisdom of what is proposed and may wish to challenge it. In such cases, the initiative teams, because of the business nature of their own goals, go to great lengths to circumvent such blockages, with their own ideas often evolving to the point that they see eye to eye with line managers who by then may also have modified their own positions. If this fails to work they have easy access up the line to Paul Heiden and Colin Green, then Aerospace Group Managing Director, where final decisions can quickly be made.

These processes encourage and generate the full participation of the company. Virtually no-one is left untouched by the business initiatives and no-one can say their views cannot be taken into account. All levels of the company have opportunities to work on business improvement since in many of the shopfloor areas, for example, foremen and experienced operators possess a great store of knowledge, and participate in the redesign of activities in their areas.

Other Ways of Generating Participation

One interesting aspect of the work and progress of the initiative teams which is a powerful force for good is the use of 'blue teams', which are set up at periodic intervals to challenge the work of the business initiative teams and propose alternative ways forward. The blue teams are drawn from sources outside the company, from other non-involved specialists, as well as line managers in Rolls-Royce and Allison, on initiatives in which they are not directly involved. By allowing the participation at such meetings continually to evolve over time a considerable cross-fertilisation of ideas is gradually generated.

If the blue team reviews generate additional requirements for work then new initiative teams are spawned so as to react to the need to meet the additional requirements. Similarly, once their mission is accomplished the teams are dissolved or put on hold. A second force for good has been the creation of an Aerospace Centre of Excellence at the EDS facilities at the Rolls-Royce site in Derby. Here a lot of the systems and support tools are available for demonstration to Rolls-Royce personnel and to potential customers, suppliers and third parties.

Chapter 10

Key 7: Handling Emotions

THE EMOTIONAL DIMENSION OF CHANGE

The greatest difficulties encountered during a process of change are those that arise inside people's heads. Any change unsettles them and challenges them to some extent, because it affects individuals directly by impacting their view of the world, their role in their environment, and the way their identity is constructed. Change provokes emotional reactions such as fear of failure, self-doubt, hopes of greater personal development, and so on. Change creates new conditions, which can be either intimidating or attractive but which the individual finds unfamiliar, especially if the current environment is stable.

The initial break with the *status quo* (in accordance with the principle of dislocation) is particularly unsettling for employees, whether they have already accepted change or not. The novel and destabilising nature of change therefore gives rise to symptoms of resistance and the development of mental blocks on the part of the people affected by it.

The emotional dimension must be handled in such a way as to overcome this resistance and break down the mental blocks, thereby ensuring that employees participate, enabling the best possible solutions to be devised for delivery of the vision. The emotional dimension remains present throughout the change process, so it must be permanently managed. Resistance is of course particularly strong at the outset, then diminishes without ever being completely eliminated, although it causes change. As for the mental blocks, these also tend to grow weaker, but without ever disappearing entirely.

Resistance is the normal and most common reaction when confronted with a projected change, whereas strong and immediate support is the least common scenario. In general, 'resistance to change is the reasonable and legitimate expression of the risks which change entails for all participants' (Crozier, M. and Friedberg, E. (1980), *Actors and Systems: The Politics of Collective Action*, University of Chicago Press, Chicago). Since the way in which the vision has been defined has a strong influence on the level of resistance encountered, if vision is the result of information and suggestions coming from employees affected by change, their resistance may be extremely weak or even non-existent.

This was the case for the agricultural produce business quoted as an example in Key 1: *Defining the Vision*, where the whole staff had been encouraged to supply information about the competition and to make suggestions for improvement. The decision to change the delivery system so that it responded better to moves by the competition aroused very little resistance when it was announced, because it had been suggested by the employees themselves, but resistance of another kind emerged later, provoked by the sort of difficulties encountered in implementing any change process. This will be dealt with later in the chapter.

Initially, change is almost always perceived by employees as a threat, even if the existing situation is considered unsatisfactory. The transformation from seeing change as a threatening phenomenon to seeing it as one offering opportunities is an essential element in making a success of change, because without this transformation employees will resist change, through fear of suffering its negative consequences, and will disguise its positive aspects. A perception of the need for change as well as of its justification must be developed right from the beginning of the change process, but at the same time it must be recognised that these perceptions can never be established once and for all and need constant reinforcement.

The possible causes of resistance to change may be linked to the problem, to the solution or to the means, or even to a combination of all three elements of the vision. In the case of each element, resistance

Table 10.1 Causes of Initial resistance

	Problem	Solution	Means
Amount of information	–	–	–
	–	–	–
Level of rejection	–	–	–
	–	–	–

can be due to insufficient information or to rejection: the problem is denied, the solution is disapproved of, the means are rejected. The causes can be classified using Table 10.1.

The most common causes of resistance are described in more detail below, not in order of importance but in terms of ease of presentation.

Common Causes of Resistance

Awareness

The first cause of resistance is lack of awareness of the problem. When the existing situation is perceived as satisfactory, people do not understand why change is necessary. The amount of information here is zero and the decision to change is considered unjustified.

Relegation

Relegating a problem which has been identified to one of secondary importance constitutes another means of resistance. The problem is acknowledged, certainly, but is considered secondary in relation to one or more other problems which monopolise attention. The amount of information is average, whereas the level of rejection is high. People consequently refuse to dedicate themselves to a process which does not tackle what they consider to be the real problems, perhaps resulting from a poor understanding of the priorities of the business.

Familiarity With the Solution

Lack of familiarity with and understanding of the solution is also a cause of resistance. The problem is accepted, but change is resisted because the solution is not understood. Where the objectives are un-known or vague, people will reject the project, since they understand its origin but not its purpose. An unclear definition of the vision or poor communication of it is generally the reason for such resistance.

Rejection of the solution

Rejection of the solution is another example of resistance. In this case, the problem is recognised and the solution known, but the latter is rejected because it is not considered appropriate. People do not think the solution to be adopted is satisfactory, and they refuse to give support to implementation. If this is due to their lack of knowledge of the process, it will be easy enough to overcome such resistance by explaining more thoroughly the choice of solution. On the other hand, if rejection is the result of a solution being imposed from above on staff who refuse to accept it because their experience on the ground tells them that the proposed solution will be inappropriate, then it is generally a good idea to reconsider. It may in fact not be the best solution, and the users will not help to implement it in any case.

Fear of the Consequences

Resistance to change can also be caused by fear of the anticipated con-sequences of the solution. The problem and the solution are implicitly or explicitly acknowledged to be well defined, but the outcome of the solution is intimidating. In this case, people resist essentially because they are afraid of not being able to adapt to the new conditions or of losing advantages or power. The level of information on the three aspects of the vision is high and the level of rejection of the problem is low. On the other hand, support for the solution is more complex, be-cause the solution is considered good, but is nevertheless not upheld. This is one of the commonest problems that confronts change man-agers attempting to handle the emotional factors and the power issues.

The Means

The means are also a common cause of resistance, but often a false cause because they conceal resistance of the type just described.

Where this is not the case, all levels of information and support are high except support for the means (high rejection level). The features of the current change are not considered appropriate in terms of its timetable or cost, for example. This inappropriateness leads to change being resisted because people think that the means made available are not conducive to its success, or because they do not feel that management really considers it a priority.

Level of Interest

Finally, resistance can be simply the result of a lack of interest, whether real or affected. People are interested in neither the problem, the solution, nor the means. They do not want a change in the situation, because any change implies reappraisal and requires energy. This attitude generally arises from lack of interest or involvement in their work, or from widespread scepticism, or from a sense of frustration with the decision to commit to or implement change.

All these forms of resistance therefore impact on support for the changes managers want to achieve. To remove them will require measures expressly suited to each case. We discuss such measures later in the chapter, as well as elsewhere, in the chapters dedicated to mobilising and to communicating actively. Resistance is particularly strong at the beginning of the change process, since it is at that point that dislocation occurs, but it never disappears completely. It will never be possible to convince all employees of the validity of change and the need for them to participate in its implementation. The proportion of opponents decreases as implementation progresses, unless serious difficulties are encountered. However, constant efforts of persuasion must be made, above all to retain the support of those who are in favour of change but who, when suddenly confronted by unexpected situations, could suddenly come to reject it.

Transforming a situation is always difficult and requires a great deal of effort on the part of all staff concerned. The seriousness of the effort required and the difficulty of the tasks to be accomplished are often underestimated, and this will reflect on the levels of support and resistance encountered throughout the process. One of the objectives of this key and of Key 6: *Obtaining Participation*, is to maintain a high level of support and participation. Individuals' reactions depend very much on:

– the level of difficulty which they anticipate when they have fully grasped the vision and when the routes for improvement have been chosen and communicated to all;
– the gap between the difficulties actually encountered and what they had anticipated.

The anticipated level of difficulty will vary as change progresses. The successes obtained will raise the level of confidence and, in consequence, reduce the supposed difficulty of future tasks. Conversely, difficulties which are unexpected—or greater than expected—will probably increase the perceived difficulty of subsequent tasks. Employees' anticipation is therefore not linear, but can vary greatly as the process is undertaken.

The difficulty of the task to be accomplished may be greater than, equal to or less than what the individual had anticipated, consciously or otherwise. In general, greater-than-expected difficulty will tend to reduce the level of active support for change, while a lesser degree of difficulty will increase it, because it will boost individuals' confidence levels. Certain individuals, who are stimulated by challenge or who lose concentration when things are too easy, may contradict these general trends. We shall see later in this chapter that a view limited to the personal level is inadequate for an understanding of individual reactions, because group phenomena are always significant too. The business is not simply the sum of the individuals which comprise it, but a *group* of individuals, which is a very different matter, for action at group level is essential for handling the variations in active support which arise out of relationships and interactions between individuals.

This variation in levels of support was apparent during the process of transforming the large oil company which decided to reorganise in Europe from a country-based structure to a continent-wide one based on major functions. The sales and marketing people anticipated medium-level difficulties and strongly supported the project, which they could see had many advantages, while the administrative and IT staff foresaw great difficulties, which made them doubt that the change would succeed, despite the benefits which they acknowledged it would bring. The sales and marketing staff in many cases encountered greater difficulties than foreseen because of the diversity of types of organisation among their customers at a European level, which brought them to doubt very strongly the wisdom of this change, and therefore to question and resist it, before satisfactory answers were found. The administrative staff encountered situations quite similar to those they had imagined and therefore did not develop serious symptoms of rejection. The IT staff, on the other hand, were confronted with even greater difficulties than they had anticipated and had only very few pleasant surprises. They needed constant support and coaching from senior management and the change facilitation team, both of whom devoted a lot of effort to this task, to keep the IT staff's support and active participation.

The change facilitation team must pay a lot of attention to monitoring the level of support, thus avoiding big dips in support, which could cast doubt on the success of the project. Any transformation process, after all, goes through highly critical periods which can even cast doubt on the envisaged change itself. These periods correspond to points in the process where the difficulties are particularly great and it seems that they cannot be resolved, at least not in the way that was forecast. At these points the opponents of change will be listened to and doubts will develop, sometimes even reaching the level of senior management and the change facilitation team. The latter needs to equip itself in advance with the tools which will alert it immediately to the onset of such risk periods, so that it can react effectively at the first signs.

Loss of support and resistance to change need to be monitored in detail, because they give rise to symptoms of withdrawal, which can be concealed as well as asserted. Asserted withdrawal consists of expressing openly one's scepticism and one's withdrawal of commitment from the process of change. People may continue to participate in the tasks allocated to them, but cease to be active supporters and oppose change, which they depict as useless, unrealistic or too costly. This type of withdrawal is easily identifiable and can therefore be countered with the appropriate techniques and tools. Concealed withdrawal, on the other hand, is by its nature much more insidious. Individuals who withdraw in this way do not show it, or barely do so. They no longer believe in successful change, or at least in their personal ability to participate effectively in its success. Their participation becomes superficial; they do not openly oppose, but do what they have to do badly or not at all; they adopt a defeatist attitude, putting forward obstacles and contesting the proposed solutions. This concealed withdrawal, which is harder and takes longer to discover, must be dealt with as soon as possible to avoid the individual withdrawing from the process, which would without any doubt have a negative effect on colleagues.

Mental blocks are the other major emotional factor which must be managed during the change process. Unlike resistance, mental blocks do not represent an explicit refusal to sustain and support change, but an inability to sustain the process effectively by transforming oneself or by working out the best solutions to the problems encountered. This incapacity does not apply to the whole process, but arises selectively and affects only some elements of the process, in particular the search for solutions. Mental blocks will therefore generally be found in employees who favour and support change. The change facilitation team is responsible for eliminating these mental blocks once they have been identified, because they will slow down and impoverish change.

Mental blocks represent dead ends, inextricable situations which the individual has created and then perpetuated by magnifying the difficulties. Interactions between individuals are generally a very important factor in these situations, so it would be wrong to associate mental blocks with exclusively individual problems. To understand and resolve mental blocks, the relationships of the individual with his environment, especially with fellow employees, must be considered. This tendency to magnify the difficulties has three main causes:

1. Denial that a problem exists, leading to an essential measure being rejected because the complexity of relationships and interactions within the business (or any other social system) has been oversimplified. Individuals who put themselves in this situation generally say that they want to stick to the facts, to rely on their own eyes, and not get involved in a lot of analysis.

2. The will to modify a difficulty which does not exist or which is by its nature unmodifiable; the individual sees a solution where there is no problem and intervenes when he should not. The individual wants to impose his solution, which nobody before him had managed to find.

3. A logical error which permits no resolution. This arises from intervening at the wrong level; looking inside the system itself when the solution must be looked for outside the system, or vice-versa. Two types of change can be identified, with different emotional implications and requiring different methods of management: changes which take place within a given system, but leave the system unchanged

(called type 1 changes), and changes which modify the system itself (called type 2 changes). Type 2 changes must be introduced into the system from the outside and cannot be understood or recognised from within the system. If we take the case of a business which wants to develop its market share, a type 1 change would correspond to expanding the product range, lowering prices, improving logistics, etc., all these being actions which take place within the existing system, while a type 2 change would be invoked, for example, by acquisition of the business's most dangerous competitor. In this example, a type 2 change requires moving out of the business and into the level above it: the sector. In the case of a sales person trying to increase his sales performance, any alterations he could make in his way of approaching customers, his sales talk, his follow-up of customers, etc., would come under type 1 changes, while turning to a new category of customers would correspond to type 2; he would have moved from the level of his usual customers and prospects to the higher level of the market as a whole.

Source: Analysis taken from the work carried out at the Mental Research Institute of Palo Alto see Watzlawick, P., *The Language of Change and How Real is Real?* as cited in the bibliography.

The quality of the change process depends in part on how well these mental blockages can be resolved. They frequently prevent problems being solved optimally because either they lead to very elaborate solutions being devised or they get in the way of finding the right solution. We have already seen that the effectiveness of the change process relies on utilising the skills and expertise of the whole work-force to deliver the vision by the best and quickest method.

Problem-solving often consists of taking corrective action in a direction opposite to the tendency that one wants to halt: if, for example, quality deteriorates, quality controls and assurance will be increased; if costs increase, cost-cutting measures will be taken; if stock outages increase, procedures for monitoring stock levels will be stepped up, and so on. All these solutions seem obvious, and yet often they contribute to aggravating the problem instead of solving it, which prompts a redoubling of the effort, and so on. In the example of quality deterioration, putting new controls in place might slow down the output of finished products, since a much larger number will be rejected. This will disrupt production, because the causes of poor quality must be found within the production process. It will force certain products to be produced under more difficult conditions in order to respond to demand despite the new quality requirements. The solution could therefore lead not to an improvement in quality, but to a redoubling of control.

This example shows that the solution must sometimes be sought elsewhere and not where one might first expect to find it: perhaps in a greater sense of responsibility among technicians and operatives, or in an improvement of the interfaces between production and marketing. All this presupposes overcoming mental blockages, which otherwise will restrict reasoning and creativity to the sphere of what is known and familiar.

It is the role of the change facilitation team to disseminate the techniques and tools which enable the net to be cast wider in the search for solutions. Their involvement will be heavy at first, while they help people to use the tools and ensure that the solutions they come up with are optimal; later they will merely exercise a supervisory role, once employees have understood how to use the tools properly and are applying them effectively.

Problem-solving often necessitates looking at the area in which problems arise from a different viewpoint. As we saw above, it is often necessary to move to a higher level to find the right solution, since creativity and reasoning often require such a change of level. The classic example of the nine dots which must be joined by four straight lines drawn without lifting the pen from the paper is a good illustration of the mental blocks which arise in the search for a solution and of the need to think outside the confines of the system (Figure 10.1).

The ability to take into account the different levels of a system in

N.B. the solution is given at the end of this chapter (Figure 10.5) for those who do not already know it.

Figure 10.1   The Nine-dot Problem

the search for solutions is essential if the problems encountered are to be solved effectively. (It is worth pointing out here that in some improvement methodologies, great care is taken *a priori* to specify the system boundaries of a system under review.) Here, too, the role of the change facilitation team is decisive. Employees must in fact be able to identify the various levels with precision (which is not always easy because of the possible overlaps between them), to understand the effect that moving to another level has on analysis of the problem encountered and to place the solution on the right level—which means, among other things, that the higher level must not be perceived as automatically permitting a better solution. In the example of strengthening a business's market share, cited above, the type 2 change, which demands the acquisition of the most dangerous competitor, could be catastrophic if the acquisition led the most important customers to take business away from them in favour of a third party, so as to avoid being overdependent on a single supplier (that is often the situation where customers are big players who do not want to be too dependent on their suppliers). A type 1 change, on the other hand, which is based on internal growth, would still be perfectly appropriate and could provide the best solution.

HANDLING THE EMOTIONAL DIMENSION

The emotional dimension may be handled by means of a three-stage approach:

- diagnosing the current situation
- identifying and monitoring resistance and mental blockages
- dealing with resistance and blockages.

All three steps are necessary to win initial support, to maintain it and to work out the solutions which will optimise the results of the change process. They enable changes to be better structured. It must not be forgotten that change has a structure, which follows directly from the structured way businesses organise and behave.

Stage 1: Diagnosing the Current Situation

This diagnosis serves to evaluate how the business and its employees are likely to accept change and react to it. Businesses have very different starting points in relation to change, so it is necessary first to assess their level of adaptability to change. This analysis of the situation is based on simple criteria, but their interpretation is sometimes complex, for it requires multi-criteria analysis to classify employees according to their intrinsic adaptability. The main criteria to be considered are:

- the socio-demographic profile of employees: age, service, standard of education, category (middle management, white-collar and blue-collar staff, etc.);
- the hierarchical structure of the business and how it operates: the number of levels, how people relate between levels, the respective roles of formal and informal structures, etc.;
- the management style: authoritarian, delegating, participative, consensual, etc.;
- the business culture: bureaucratic, technocratic, individualistic, introvert, extrovert, flexible, rigid, etc.);
- the familiarity of change and how it is valued: types and frequency of change in the past, successes and failures, perception and positioning, etc.;
- competitors: competitive position, changes they have carried out, etc.;
- the economic and social context (economic development, employment situation, local projects, etc.).

Not all these criteria will have equal importance, depending on the changes envisaged. Purely internal criteria take precedence when reorganising a business, while a merger of two businesses associated with extensive restructuring involves paying more attention to external criteria.

Such an assessment provides the basis for handling the emotional dimension. It enables the business or parts of the business to be placed on a scale of adaptability to change. At one extreme are businesses which emphasise immobility, rigid relationships and attachment to tradition, businesses which have not yet embarked on major change programmes and whose employees are unaccustomed and/or hostile to dislocational change. At the other extreme are businesses constantly on the move, whose capacity for change is an essential value experienced in practical terms by employees almost every day. By means of an assessment of this kind, it is possible to evaluate

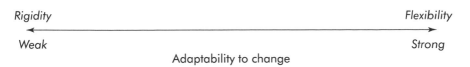

Figure 10.2   Level of adaptability to change

accurately the nature and degree of the effort required if change is to be accepted by the employees concerned. In businesses on the move or undergoing frequent transformation, this assessment must already have been made; it may need updating, but it should not be necessary to rework it completely.

Stage 2: Identifying and Monitoring Resistance and Mental Blockages

The aim in this second step is to define in advance the types of resistance and mental blockage which will possibly or probably emerge during the change process, in order to minimise and help to remove them. This is essential, wherever the business stands in terms of practical experience of change, because every change is unique. The resistance and mental blockages which can arise during the change process cannot simply be deduced from previous experience. They must be identified right at the start of the change process, and then updated regularly in the light of observations as progress is made.

We saw in the first chapter that the issues at stake in change very much depend on its depth, its speed and how it is implemented. These three variables must also be taken into account when identifying possible resistance and mental blockages, but they must be complemented by another: the *nature* of the change concerned. This makes demands on employees in terms of augmenting their technical and social skills, and their ways of thinking and acting and their attitudes.

Transforming the skills of employees generally creates only minor resistance and blockages, easy enough to resolve as long as they are identified early enough and tackled properly. On the other hand, transforming attitudes and ways of thinking and acting creates much greater difficulties, because it implies a much more profound reassessment by individuals of their world view, which has been defined as 'the greatest and most complex synthesis an individual is capable of creating out of the multiplicity of his experiences, convictions, influences and interpretations, and from their consequences on the value and significance he attributes to objects he perceives' (Watzlawick, P. (1978), *The Language of Change*, Basic Books, University of Chicago Press, Chicago). The transformation demanded of individuals means that they can no longer integrate their new perceptions or experiences into the world view which they have held until now; they must therefore change this view, a change which is never complete and which entails a risk of refusal on their part. Since an analysis of the impact of change on individuals must naturally take account of the diversity of the situations in which they find themselves, it must be a segmented analysis.

Changes which alter the system itself (type 2 changes) generally cause greater resistance and mental blockage than changes which take place within the system. It must, however, be borne in mind that changes of either type can become changes of the other type as soon as one moves from the global level of the process to the level of individuals or established groups.

This evaluation of the expected level of resistance and mental blockage can be combined with an evaluation of adaptability to change, to create a combined assessment of the emotional issues, using the matrix in Figure 10.3. This matrix must be drawn up for the various types of employees defined in the analytical step where the intrinsic level of resistance and mental blockage was identified.

Once the change process has begun, the risks of resistance and mental blockage can be monitored with the help of a second grid (Figure 10.4), which enables variations in the level of support to be anticipated. The grid gives general indications which, in the

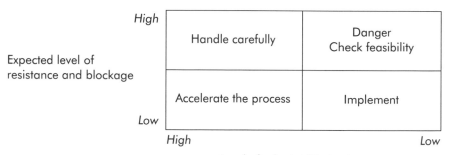

Figure 10.3 Matrix of Emotional Issues

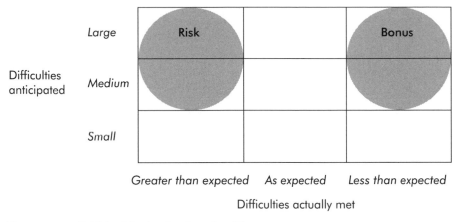

Figure 10.4 Grid for Monitoring Levels of Support

situations causing most concern, can be fleshed out by individual interviews. This grid is used by the change facilitation team.

Below we discuss the emotional issues which are associated with three types of business change commonly encountered at the present time. They are not mutually exclusive and may naturally occur in combination. They are as follows:

- changes which challenge the concepts of Taylorism
- changes which introduce an outside dimension
- changes which prompt headcount reductions.

Abandoning Taylorism

Reappraising the organisation of work may require the individual to accept a broader role and much greater responsibility. The individual moves from having tasks to be completed to having a mission to fulfil. He was formerly asked to confine himself to executing tasks which others had defined. Now he is expected to organise himself (on his own or in collaboration with colleagues), to take decisions and to allocate resources within the area of responsibility allocated to him. His world of work is turned upside down. All his values must be reversed. What his superiors say to him today is in complete contradiction to what they said yesterday. The qualities of obedience, absence of initiative and limited participation formerly expected of him are now replaced by autonomy, initiative and responsibility. There is, then, a lot at stake in the emotional issues.

There is a risk that the individual will reject the attitude and the way of thinking and acting expected of him, because they deny his whole past and are completely at odds with his world picture. All that was his pride and joy, everything he believed in or tried hard to believe in, is suddenly demolished and, even worse, regarded as negative and wrong. The individual may therefore either fail to understand this new demand or be unwilling to accept it, out of refusal to renounce his past learning or out of fear of being unable to develop towards the new situation. This movement towards carrying out more complete and varied tasks, which those in charge see as a source of enrichment and greater work satisfaction, can easily seem to the people affected to be nothing but a threat.

Hierarchical relationships risk being damaged as well, because an individual may lose all confidence in his superiors when what they say changes completely. The employee no longer knows who to trust, and his managers lose their credibility or even their authority. This situation can be very traumatic for middle managers, if they themselves find it difficult to accept the new objectives and feel that the changes are robbing them of their credibility and authority with their subordinates. The change facilitation team must rapidly identify such situations and respond to them, so that middle managers, who play an essential role, do not sabotage the change process. These symptoms are especially dangerous when the difficulty of implementing the changes is great, which makes them vulnerable to attack. Similar symptoms can appear when the aim is to establish an organisational structure based on small units of a few dozen autonomous employees who are responsible for their own performance.

Introducing an External Dimension

Introducing an outside dimension is another sort of change which can be very unsettling. The outsider is the customer or the user. The decision to make the customer the business's top priority and his satisfaction its main objective, the one towards whom every effort must be addressed, can also create severe emotional problems. In organisations where technical competence and the respect for standards and procedures dominate, putting the outsider first generally provokes considerable resistance among employees. Their resistance is more or less marked according to their role in the business; some employees may even experience feelings of relief and gratitude, such as the sales and marketing people, when, in a business where technical factors have previously come first, it is decided to act primarily on market factors. However, for most employees such changes create considerable disruption, because they are suddenly going to be appraised and judged according to criteria unknown to them. The task well done, the well-conceived product, might suddenly and inexplicably be judged otherwise.

Their whole value system is called into question. Competence, precision, rigour ... these are now evaluated according to how well they respond to the needs of the customer. Since the standard and the point of reference have begun to fluctuate and shift, the individual has the impression that the goal he is aiming at no longer exists in itself, because it depends on customers, with all their diversity and 'irrationality'. The employee is judged externally, by people who are less competent than he, by people 'who do not know'. If the specialists feel that they are undervalued and their true worth is not recognised, the result is often a decline in their skills. This can be seen especially clearly when, as is often the case, the business is organised by market. With management being entrusted to marketing people who are generalists, the specialists have the feeling that they are being judged twice over by incompetents: both internally and externally. The feeling of dissatisfaction which ensues, combined with their being scattered around the business because of the new structure, causes a lowering of their motivation and, very soon, in the technical competence of the business. As in the case where the scientific organisation of work was called into question, the symptoms of rejection and resistance on the part of employees can be extremely strong. It is not easy to lose or dilute the fundamental values which underpin one's thoughts and actions, and they rarely disappear completely, even when overshadowed by the new values which gradually take their place.

Headcount Reductions

Staff cuts provoke strong resistance which must be anticipated. This resistance comes not only from the employees affected by redundancy, but also from those who stay in the business and are called on to carry out the changes. Any job cuts increase the feeling of insecurity already aroused by change. Identification with the business and with its purpose is weakened or destroyed. Some employees can become detached from the business and now consider it as merely a way of earning their living. The risk is that they will not make the effort needed for change to succeed. Attitudes of concealed withdrawal then frequently develop.

Stage 3: Dealing with Resistance and Mental Blockages

In dealing with resistance and mental blockages, there are various methods, techniques and tools available:

- earliest possible involvement in the process of the employees concerned;
- endorsement of their efforts and of the results they obtain;
- continual reaffirmation of the will of management to carry the changes through successfully;
- training and coaching;
- active communication on how changes are progressing.

These points are dealt with largely in the chapters on other keys: 'Obtaining Participation', 'Training and Coaching' and 'Communicating Actively', so we need only touch on them briefly here.

Drawing in those involved in the change process as early as possible helps to reduce resistance and, to a lesser extent, mental blockages. The decision to change and the vision are always imposed on the employees of the business, even if they have made a major contribution to them. They must be induced to participate in the many decisions which will have to be taken before the change process reaches completion. We have already seen that involving employees at the decision-making level is necessary for the process to seem real and to enhance it. This also helps changes to be more readily accepted and speeds up their implementation. It has in fact been proved that a decision's acceptance and implementation are improved if the people who have to apply it are genuinely involved in working it out, because they feel more responsible. It has also been shown that implementation succeeds more fully if the people affected are fully acquainted with the reasons for which the decision was taken, as well as with the objectives.

The level of participation in decision-making varies according to the types of decision to be taken, the categories of employees and the role expected of them in relation to the change process, but they must always be consulted. Consulting someone does not mean that his opinion will prevail, but it does mean that it will be taken into account and that the person concerned will be informed of the decisions taken. These last two points are essential, for the consultation procedure must not be just a sham designed to appease employees' concerns. Nobody would be fooled for long and the consequences would be extremely negative. Employees would be distrustful; they would consider themselves deceived and their resistance would increase instead of decreasing. Participation in decision-making must therefore be genuine. Everyone must be kept informed and have the opportunity to express himself and to be heard, with internal channels of opinion having a decisive part to play in getting all the participants properly involved in the decisions affecting them. Full involvement enables employees to understand the objectives of change better, to express their reservations, their fears and their opposition, but also to feel that they have the power to influence their own future and to strengthen their sense of belonging to a group. These last two factors are at once validating and reassuring, because they reflect the importance of the individual and affirm his existence and his power.

Endorsing their efforts and the results they obtain shows individuals that the efforts they make are appreciated and that the irritations they may be experiencing are known. This endorsement encourages employees to continue and redouble their efforts at personal transformation as well as their participation in the process (see Key 6: *Obtaining Participation*). Group dynamics play an essential role here, not only because they enable the effect of endorsement to be reinforced by communication with other employees, but also because they stimulate those opposed to change by showing them the results achieved by their colleagues (these points are developed in Key 10: *Communicating Actively*).

Reaffirmation of the will of management to carry the project through successfully is essential for success. It stimulates everyone's energy for implementing change, the success of which is seen to be important. People then feel that they are doing something useful for the business, and this motivates them and further strengthens support. This continual reaffirmation by managers is needed most of all during periods of doubt, when employees are tempted to give up. How it is done is discussed in Key 10: *Communicating Actively*.

Tackling resistance and mental blockages also requires the utilisation of specialised techniques and tools which the change facilitation team must have at its disposal and make available. There are many techniques and tools for handling the emotional dimension of change: repositioning the solution by modifying the system through a type 2 change, reformulating the problem to transform it into a positive factor, training for action, etc. We shall describe two of these which we know to be effective. They focus principally on identifying what needs to change and on how this change is implemented; they ignore backward-looking causal research into why change is necessary. The use of these techniques presupposes a positive and proactive attitude on the part of the facilitators. This requires emphasising the benefits at the expense of the negative aspects (without necessarily denying these) and, finally, it entails talking about problems rather than people, except where the latter specifically ask to be considered.

Active Forces Analysis (AFA)

The objective of Active Forces Analysis is to identify the positive and negative forces acting on the implementation of a decision and to redirect them so that the decision can be carried out. This analysis can be made at the individual or group level. It is made with the help of a member of the change facilitation team trained in this technique (or by another employee trained by the change facilitation team in the use of AFA), who plays the role of animator and champion of change.

AFA first identifies the forces at work for or against implementing the decision. It then tries to understand the sources of these forces: what the group (or individual) perceives as positive and negative factors for itself (himself), for its colleagues or for the business. Then it aims to redirect the negative forces by responding to objections point by point. The facilitator's argument is designed to convince the others of the validity of the decision and their interest in implementing it.

AFA can be used several times during a change process to tackle different problems. The example of how production unit operatives in a business manufacturing mass consumer goods resisted change illustrates the efficiency of the technique. The vision was to reinforce the position of the business using, among other measures, greater flexibility. The manufacturing directors had decided to replace each large-capacity production line with three smaller lines, each having a theoretical capacity of slightly less than a third of the theoretical capacity of the current production system. This change was meant to allow the whole unit to become more flexible and to increase actual output by reducing idle time caused by incidents on the line. The operatives' work should become more interesting, because they, together with one or two other colleagues, would be in charge of the whole production process and would be able to structure their work more independently.

Those in charge had therefore thought that this change could be made without too much difficulty; yet the operatives resisted strongly at first. AFA was applied once the three groups of operatives had been set up. It was apparent that the benefits had been identified accurately, leading to greater autonomy, greater responsibility, lower rates of production permitting better working conditions, and so on. It also revealed that many negative forces were present, leading the operatives to resist despite the positive factors: the fear of not having the skills demanded by the new level of autonomy and responsibility, these included the fear of a major modification of the planned work rate, the fear of having more restrictive working hours imposed, the fear of job cuts, and so on.

The first meeting enabled the positive and negative factors to be identified, while the second was devoted to demonstrating that the operatives' fears were unfounded, leading to solving the real under-lying problems and to drawing up training and coaching programmes for the operatives. The third was used to turn the negative forces into positive ones, by specifying improvements which would make the installation of the new lines more effective; finally, the fourth meeting served to check that the problem had really been solved and also to confirm the actions to be taken.

Group Problem-solving

This technique aims to solve the problems which can arise as change proceeds and for which a solution has not yet been found. The only constraint imposed is that the solution should be consistent with the vision and the means available to implement it. Unlike AFA, this is not a matter of winning people over to an idea, but of people working together to find a realistic solution to the problem confronting them. Thus the aim of the facilitator, a member of the change facilitation team or another specially trained employee, is to help people to work out this solution by structuring the problem-solving process.

To create good group dynamics, the group usually comprises between six and ten participants. Chosen for their skills and their perspective on the problem, they may therefore belong to the same division or department, or come from different backgrounds. The composition of the group is critical to the success of this undertaking, since success often results from bringing together people whom the structure of the business usually keeps separate and prevents from communicating with each other. This is because the problems encountered often cannot be genuinely solved without a cross-functional perspective. In certain cases, individuals can participate selectively in one or two meetings to contribute their particular skill or expertise.

Group problem-solving involves a series of meetings structured so as to work towards a solution to the problem. All participants must prepare for each meeting. Unless this preparatory work is done between meetings, they will lose most of their effectiveness and the problem will not be solved. Each meeting generally follows the same pattern:

- a statement of what each participant expects from the meeting;
- a progress report on solving the problem and implementation of the solution, including points resolved, and questions or matters still to be dealt with;
- brainstorming to resolve the questions tackled during the meeting;
- selection of ideas according to their potential for answering the questions effectively;
- tackling the negative aspects of the ideas adopted;
- identification of the matters still needing to be dealt with in order to find the desired solution;
- allocation of the tasks to be accomplished by the time of the next meeting.

These meetings last two or three hours, as is normal for group meetings. How many there are depends on the complexity of the problem to be solved. If there is considerable resistance originating from deeply ingrained ways of thinking, some ten meetings, or more, may be needed. What is more, the early meetings are often not very efficient, because the participants have not fully mastered the technique. They tend to focus on negative factors, on obstacles and on individuals. These early meetings therefore function as training sessions in group problem-solving techniques: positive thinking, contributing to each other's suggestions, focusing on the problem, and so on.

The technique of group problem-solving was used, for example, to solve the problems encountered by the managers of a service business when improving relationships with their 'big account' customers, as part of a transformation of the business, which was to move from an organisational structure emphasising different jobs and products to one that was market-oriented. The problem of coordinating sales effort on the 'big accounts' could not be solved. A group was formed, comprising representatives from different job and product categories, a representative from management, a person from the administration and financial department and another from the IT department. Other people intervened selectively according to their skills to help in discussions: technical sales people, product managers and area managers.

The early meetings made the participants aware of the difficulties created by having people in each job category searching separately for a solution, and the benefit of taking into account the interactions between these categories, and therefore between members of the group. One of the other crucial advantages of using this technique was the understanding it gave of the need to move to a higher level (that of the business rather than that of the job or product category) to devise the right solutions, to make a type 2 change, which nobody had in fact done until then. After about ten meetings, thanks to understanding the interactions between individuals and the necessity of locating the solution in the system constituted by the business itself, the answer to the problem had been worked out and could be delivered. The problems of sales coordination, account development, relationships between administration and finance, of measuring the profitability of an account, of a system for assessing the performance of different job and product categories on each account were all tackled by this means.

It can be seen that the solution of the nine-dot problem involves

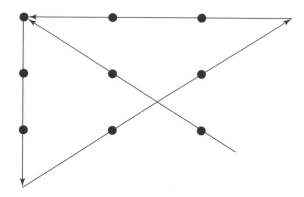

The requirement is to draw four straight lines without leaving the paper and cover all of the dots.

Figure 10.5   Solution of the Nine-dot Problem

going outside the frame formed by the nine dots, which one automatically tends to limit oneself to. This is what often happens when a problem needs to be solved in a context which is well known or reminds one of a familiar context. Without enlarging the frame, the problem cannot be solved correctly.

CASE STUDY ON MANAGING EMOTIONAL BARRIERS TO CHANGE: THE LEICESTER ROYAL INFIRMARY NHS TRUST

The Leicester Royal Infirmary, an NHS Trust, is one of the largest UK teaching hospitals. It treats over 400 000 out-patients, handles 120 000 emergency attendances and more than 100 000 in-patients and day care patients each year. The staff comprises 4000 employees.

The Leicester Royal Infirmary Change Process

The Leicester Royal Infirmary was chosen as one of two National Health Service pilot sites for whole-hospital re-engineering in 1994. Peter Homa, Chief Executive, explains: 'We wanted significantly to improve the quality of patient care and the working environment for staff. We wanted to do more with the same or slightly less amount of resources.' The re-engineering programme was also a key milestone for the Leicester Royal Infirmary mission, defined as follows :

'We, at the Leicester Royal Infirmary NHS Trust, will work together to

Table 10.2   Patient Visit Process Performance Improvement

Measures	Baseline Sep 1994	February 1995	June 1996
Out-patients benefiting from patient visit re-engineering (%)	0	11	95
General practitioners benefiting from patient visit re-engineering (%)	0	12	100
Number of 'hand-offs' in referral process	7	1	1
Mean time between referral letter received and appointment made (days)	14	2	2
Mean clerical time per visit (mins)	34	18	18

become the best hospital in the country, with an outstanding local and national reputation for our treatment, research and teaching. We will give to each patient the same care and consideration we would to our own family.'

The Results

Results achieved have been dramatic in terms of quality of service to patients and processes efficiency. In fact, a 'new' hospital has been constructed in terms of the nature of work undertaken. The redesign of the patient visits (out-patients) process and the diagnostics test centre are two examples of breakthrough improvements realised. The redesigned patient visit process allowed 95% of out-patients to be received within 30 minutes. Over a period of 12 months, it represents a saving of more than 50 years of patient waiting time. Service quality has been enhanced and the total visit process cost reduction amounted to £360 000 per annum, (see Table 10.2).

An integrated multiskilled staff diagnostic test centre was set up. Patients said that they wished to obtain the necessary diagnostic test in one location and on the same occasion as their medical consultation. This facility, carrying out 80% of out-patients' tests, combines high volume phlebotomy, ECG, pathology and radiography in a single centre next to the out-patient clinics. The results achieved were highly satisfactory as shown in Table 10.3 (Test centre performance).

Such results have been achieved through major changes within the organisation as illustrated in Figure 10.6.

Table 10.3   Test centre performances

Measures	Baseline Nov 94	Jan 95	Sept 97
Time between test request to receipt of results	79 hours	34 min	34 min
Number of 'hand-offs' of test information	16	5	5
Distance patient must travel for tests (paces)	650	90	90
Patient waiting time for tests (mins)	90	8	8
Patient second visit eliminated (%)	0	8	15

Emotional Resistance to Change

Emotional barriers to change are typically huge in hospitals for the following reasons:

- the organisation is usually fragmented, functional and isolationist with various groups of stakeholders including doctors, nurses, operational staff, administration staff and management;
- the pace of change has been traditionally very slow in hospitals. Dr. Paul Millac, today a retired consultant neurologist and one of the leaders of the change programme, explains: 'It is an anathema: in hospitals doctors are always pushing back to old management rules. If a doctor who used to consult 150 years ago came back, he would not find a lot of changes nowadays.'
- the nature of the healthcare process fosters individuality: every patient group, even every patient is different. As Helen Bevan, Reengineering Programme Leader explains: 'You cannot assume the level of generalising you find in industry.' Thus acceptance of change and ownership of any solution is extremely difficult to create but must be on a very individual basis.
- Finally, as stated by Helen, 'The culture, the history, the context of a hospital limit what you can do.'

Managing Emotional Resistance

Several tactics were used by the programme leadership team to overcome emotional barriers to change.

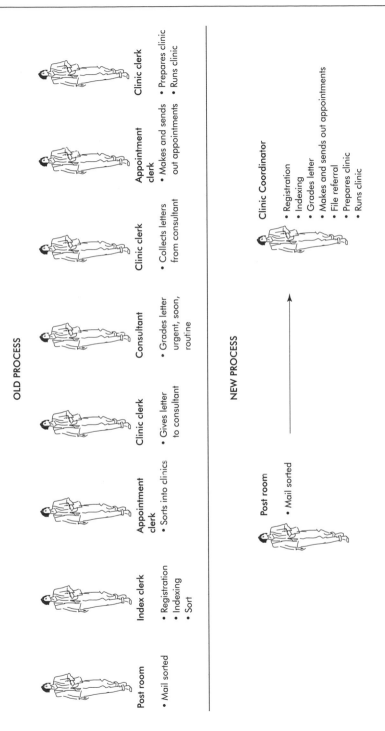

Figure 10.6 Patient Referral Process

- Communication was heavily used to explain the reason of change: better patient care and a better environment for staff. As stated by Helen Bevan, 'if you want to make change happen, people have to understand the problem before you sell the solution.' Peter Homa explains: 'We managed to create a lot of discussions during the programme. We brought together some of the most powerful doctors, opinion leaders and university representatives. We spent a lot of time talking to others.' These discussions were key to obtaining information in order to create awareness and acceptance for change among the various groups in an environment traditionally opposed to change.

- The specificity of each clinic and consultant was acknowledged, and a dedicated project was set up for each of them. Helen Bevan says: '100 separate projects were running at the same time. It was a nightmare in project management terms, but it was the only way to do it.'

- The impact of fear of change was lowered by stating upfront the objectives of the programme.

- In order to demonstrate the feasibility of the change process and create acceptance of the solution, 'as-is' analysis and visioning phases were kept to a minimum while implementation was where most of the effort was concentrated.

- Heavy participation was also organised throughout the Hospital to overcome emotional barriers to change. Participation accelerated the programme objectives and acceptance of solutions. Three full-time programme teams with approximately 40 people (doctors, nurses, managers, administration staff) were appointed and populated with the 'brightest and best' people while up to 450 staff were significantly involved part time.

- Quick wins played a major role in capturing energy, attention and enthusiasm. Most probably, failure to achieve early demonstrable results would have caused the programme to end through dissolution of support from internal and external stakeholders.

Chapter 11

Key 8: Handling the Power Issues

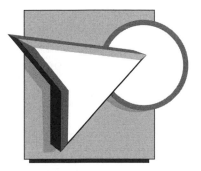

THE POWER ISSUES OF CHANGE

Power plays an extremely important role in the workings of a business, through its effect on the ways employees relate to each other and to the rules. Since a business is the seat of many and complex forms of power, any change will alter or even overturn existing power relations, so the success of business transformation depends in part on the ability of change managers to handle the power issues in such a way that they are favourable to delivery of the vision.

Handling the power issues is complex, because power itself is complex. It is neither an institution nor a structure, but something entirely different: 'it is the name given to a complex strategic situation within a given society'. Identifying the principal mechanisms of power is a prerequisite to understanding the issues associated with change in this field. The following are the five issues which seem to us to be the most significant.

1. Power has many sources and is exerted through an interplay of unequal and fluid relationships.
2. Power comes from every direction and does not just trickle down

from the top. It is not exclusively hierarchical, but is exercised through the interactions of multiple forces, which themselves arise in small domains, crossing structural boundaries and tending to support one another.

3. Power relations are intentional and not subjective. Power is never exerted at random; it is always driven by a series of goals and objectives, but there is no point in looking for an individual or a group of individuals behind it, governing its logic. The ownership of the great power strategies in business is difficult to discern. Such strategies reflect very specific tactical moves at their level, which spread and reinforce each other to form a whole that is not the property or conception of any single individual.

4. Power relations are not a superstructure foisted on the business with the sole function of issuing commands and prohibitions. Power-based activities come into play in response to other initiatives and are precipitated as soon as any inequality or imbalance is perceived to arise.

5. The inevitable corollary of power is resistance. Resistance, which is the other term in power relations, is therefore distributed throughout the business, like power, in an irregular way. Resistance is scattered all around the business, and cuts across all structures, just like power relations themselves.

The relationships and interactions between employees at every level are a decisive factor in the smooth running of the business, as we saw in Chapter 2. Since power is in turn an essential factor in these relationships and interactions, the types of relations which underlie contacts between employees are one of their main preoccupations. These relations might be trust, dependence, respect, liking, fear, etc., but in many cases power factors are at work here too, penetrating, influencing and transforming them. The topic of power is an extremely sensitive area, which goes to the heart of individual identity and self-perception. This is all the more difficult to handle because every individual analyses the manifestations of power in terms of his or her own frame of reference, which is different from the logic of the economics that governs business. This difference makes it a tricky matter to bring them together. One of the major issues for the success of change is to make allowance for this diversity and to direct everyone's interests towards the ultimate objective, that is to say towards the implementation of the vision.

The decision to change and the vision are always, to a greater or lesser extent, imposed on staff, who experience the necessity of change as an effect of the power relationship which exists between them and the managers and owners of the business. Support for change is encouraged if the business has an overall purpose with which everyone can identify and of which the change is an integral part. Staff can then be involved in change without feeling that they are simply submitting to management power. 'Improving the service given to customers', 'improving working conditions', 'strengthening/ supporting the national economy'—these are aims towards which anyone would be proud to contribute. On the other hand, if the only aim is 'to be more productive', 'to capture new market share' or 'to increase profitability', there are many who will refuse to identify with it. Such aims are not universal: they reflect personal interests (those of managers, shareholders, etc.) which the employees concerned will serve only if forced to do so. In this case, change is imposed on those who see it as first and foremost reinforcing the power of certain people who want to promote their own interests. The way the vision is communicated and explained must therefore take into account this need to associate it with an overall purpose acceptable to all. The nature of employees' participation in change will depend partly on the nature of the power relationship which they associate with their participation.

The operation of the business is governed by rules, which are one of the expressions of power. Wherever there are rules, there is power, for rules are only the expression of the inherent strengths in the business. The whole formal side of the running of the business is therefore based on power relations, which gives them an extremely important role. The informal side also gives a major role to power relations, but this sort of power is more shifting and has more complex origins, in skills, expertise, information, relationships and networks.

The informal relationships between employees do not necessarily depend on power themselves, but they often give rise to power relations with others. The informal relationship which can exist between a salesperson and an engineer, thanks to personal affinity or shared tastes, for example, does not create a power relation between these two people, but can create one between them and their superiors, other salespeople or other engineers, because they may be the only ones in possession of certain information, or because they can develop skills together.

The changes sought by businesses tend to create more complex power relations. New organisational structures are set up which increasingly favour multicellular or network models over the traditional pyramid models. This means that power relations are less uniform and simple, but manifold and complex. Superiors share power among themselves and their subordinates have to cope with reporting to several people. Here, too, power is asserted and exerted rather than delegated. The ability to handle complexity and ambiguity becomes an even greater source of power. The traditional roles of communicator and receiver of information are merged: everyone both sends and receives messages. The rules of the game have changed: it is no longer a matter of changing the old rules, but of introducing new rules, along with the completely different power relations that they generate. The official power map is deliberately blurred, as it reflects the multiplicity and complexity of power.

Power always looks to be strengthened, never weakened. Few people in business willingly use their position and their power to initiate changes, whatever their status. The holders of power only question the *status quo* if they think they can profit by doing so or are forced to do it. This is illustrated by the fact that the elements which change the most in businesses are those directly associated with the factors impelling change: products, distribution, technology, etc., while certain other factors such as social relationships and shared values, which ought to be modified to optimise the effectiveness of change, generally remain unchanged despite the dysfunctions which this causes.

Change requiring a complete break with the *status quo* (in accordance with the principle of dislocation) destabilises power relations. Some people will benefit from this destabilisation while others will suffer from it, but it is difficult to make precise forecasts on this point. The existing power situation in the business being the result of fragile balances, complex configurations and the interweaving of the official and unofficial at every level, any questioning of the power relations that have been established at such cost is opposed by almost every employee. Even those who appear the least well placed in these relations generally do not want to see them change drastically, through fear of the unknown.

Opposition to change is all the stronger since it tends generally to reduce the power which individuals enjoy. Within businesses, the desire for improvement which underpins change is almost always synonymous with increasing rationality of behaviour and thereby reducing sources of uncertainty for managers. Those who promote the change process want to organise business systems better by increasing the capacity to forecast their effects. Responsibility may be decentralised and autonomy increased, but all this is shaped, rationalised and ordered. In the end, employees will have less room to manoeuvre, and therefore less power at first, since their power is limited to that officially linked to their position. Subsequently, delegated power (associated with title, job description, etc.) or structural power, which can only have the appearance of power, will be supplanted by exerted power, which may be a more or less faithful copy of the original.

The power that *is* exerted, in other words the real power, will be the result of delegated power and of the informal power arising out of individual interests and knowledge, whether technical, interpersonal or informational. Once the changes are complete, everyone will re-construct their power relations within the new structure, which they will avoid and bypass in order to promote their own interests. To regain a power level comparable to one's position before the changes will require time—several weeks or several months depending on the nature of the changes. This phase of reconstructing power relations is generally very noticeable after a restructuring, which redraws the business's official power map. As nobody is really at ease with his or her new role, everyone must 'find their spot' again. During this phase it seems as though the holders of formal power are playing a role, observed for a short while by the rest of the staff.

The power issues need to be carefully handled by change man-agers, who must make allowance for the principal characteristics of power: the importance of power relations to employees; the presence of power relations throughout the business, even if its managers generally exercise stronger and more visible power; the opposition that exists between power and change; and the key role the current holders of power play in the workings of the business. Monitoring the development of the power situation during the change process is one of the principal tasks of the change facilitation team, who ensure that the power relations are consistent with the objectives in view. It is impossible to predict in advance exactly how power relations will develop. It will therefore be necessary to monitor and guide these developments. Allowing power relations to develop in this way is essential to ensuring the participation and motivation of staff, because it gives them a sense of autonomy and responsibility encouraging them to act and take the initiative.

Changing successfully very often requires redirecting power within the business, because the key people in the current situation will not necessarily play the same role in the target situation. A two-way change is therefore needed, aimed at weakening some of the current key people and strengthening the new ones. It is a difficult exercise, because those who at the moment enjoy most power are generally important influences on the smooth running of the business. Their active participation would facilitate change, whereas their fierce opposition would reduce or even eliminate its chances of success. At the same time, the people who will be strong in the target situation will have only limited power at the moment. Out of step with the business's current power relations, they are power holders in waiting. Their manager delegates authority to them which they have yet to acquire in their own right.

The redirection of power at the level of senior management and key employees is the most spectacular aspect of redirecting power, but not the only one. We have seen that power permeates the business through complex and fluid relationships, official or otherwise. Change managers must ensure that these relationships develop in line with the ultimate objective and that they do nothing to impede the transformation of the business. This is particularly important in the case of the decisions which are constantly being made during the process and which must be made in accordance with the purpose of change and not in pursuit of individual interests. Power relations are frequent and significant causes of resistance and obstruction to change, so their obstructive nature must be recognised as early as possible. The techniques and tools described in the preceding chapter on handling the emotional dimension come into play again here.

Challenging current power relations, whether official or unofficial, must be undertaken with extreme caution. Some changes cause profound upheavals in the balance of power, alterations that are significant in any terms and may affect every level of the business. The power gains, generally easier to handle than the losses, must however be given special attention to avoid excessively authoritarian behaviour, which would arouse symptoms of rejection among staff. Managers who go beyond what is expected of them—in contradiction to corporate culture—could obstruct the change process or distort it.

The wish to assert a newly acquired power often provokes this type of reaction.

The power losses pose the most severe problems in human terms. The people who will suffer such a loss must therefore be carefully identified and the nature of their loss appreciated. The effect of modifications in the structure is quite easy to detect and assess. The territorial manager who used to report directly to senior management and is now responsible to an area manager, or the director of a subsidiary who now comes under the authority of a business area head, are easy cases to pick up. On the other hand, the detrimental effect on a branch manager whose branch loses its strategic position during territorial reorganisation, or that on a product manager whose product portfolio is restructured, are more difficult to assess. These situations can be extremely hard to cope with for the people concerned, who may indeed have an important role to play in running the business in future, although they are in a disadvantaged position at the moment. If one wants to keep these people and see them participate actively in the change process, one must provide support for them. This is particularly important where entire categories of employees are affected.

This is often the case among executives, where line managers find their role and the system of authority which supported it being called into question. The issuing of commands is on the decline, while the giving of assistance, advice, training, information and coaching should be on the increase. Executives no longer exercise the power conferred on them directly, through decision-making and control, but indirectly, by exploiting skill, information and interpersonal relationships.

REDIRECTING POWER TOWARDS THE NEW OBJECTIVES

Redirecting power in line with the new objectives makes a decisive contribution to the success of change. It demands a high level of involvement on the part of the chief executive, because it can only be partially delegated to colleagues. Drawing up a new organisational structure, defining managers' responsibilities and deciding who will occupy key posts: these tasks, among others, are incumbent on the chief executive.

The approach to handling and redirecting power can be subdivided into three stages:

1. defining the planned balance of power
2. handling the power issues
3. using new systems and procedures to redirect power.

Phase 1: Defining the Planned Balance of Power

The power issues should be identified very early on: when defining the vision in the case of top executives, during the mobilising stage for other salaried staff. Power factors can therefore influence both vision and mobilising, making some components of change unrealistic, extremely unpredictable or very expensive. In extreme cases, the change process may need to be delayed or cancelled.

This is what happened in the case of a service business whose chief executive wanted to restructure it to strengthen its position in the market. The business was organised by customer sectors and changes in the market had made the existing structure obsolete. One problem was that there were two sections of the business whose separate existence could no longer be justified. The section that was originally larger had seen its business level off, while the second section had expanded considerably and had now overtaken the first, many of whose customers it shared. The increasing overlap between activities of these two sections made it sensible to merge them under the control of the head of the second, busier section. The chief executive gave up the idea of restructuring because he thought that the head of the first section would never accept the loss of his authority and would go over to the competition, and his expertise was of considerable value to the business. At the same time, it was impossible to make the head of the second section the number two or transfer him to another section without damaging the morale and confidence of other managers. The chief executive therefore decided not to go ahead with the change for the time being, thereby slowing down the development of the more dynamic section of the business.

Defining the planned balance of power requires assessing the significance of power that is exerted, first by the key people and then by the various categories of staff affected by change (regional managers, sales executives, salespeople, production engineers, main-

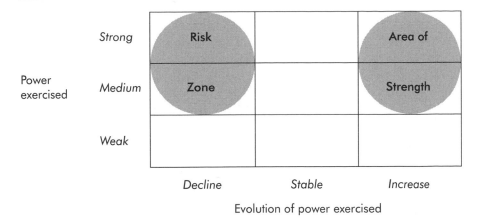

Figure 11.1   Mapping the Evolution of the Power Structure

tenance engineers, those in charge of new product development, etc.), and especially by those employees who have unusual skills. It is essential to consider all the major categories of staff, whether the power they exert is formal or informal. Once the level of importance of each person in power has been assessed, the mapping of Figure 11.1 can be made against the changes planned, taking into account people's changes in level in comparison to internal rivals and other similar categories of staff.

This analysis of changes in the power exerted identifies the areas of strength and areas at risk. The information is sufficiently detailed to define the distribution of power in the target situation, because it gives change managers the opportunity to assess the risks associated with the various possible configurations and to make a choice, which will then have to be implemented as described in the later stages below.

Defining the target situation is particularly important for the key new positions in the business, which must be settled as soon as the vision is defined, so that they can be announced in the context of communicating the vision, or alternatively at the conclusion of mobilising, depending on circumstances. The case of the human resources director of a large manufacturing group is a good illustration of the importance of this initial analysis of the change process. This group had a large number of foreign employees, who had been recruited in their country of origin during the 1960s. Because of its economic and financial position, the group found itself forced to make staff cuts, which would particularly affect these foreign employees, as part of a thorough transformation of the group. It seemed that the human resource director would have to play a decisive role in implementing this transformation, but this was not in fact what happened. Analysis showed that he had begun his career with the group by personally recruiting these employees on the spot, and that he had subsequently been responsible for managing them, a role which had taken him into human resource management. What was more, he was identified as 'their man'; he showed a strong attachment to them and felt responsible for them, and this was at the root of his success.

The group chief executive realised that this person, who exerted very strong power, was going to see his power decline in proportion to his success in implementing the vision. The human resource director was liable to resist change, at least in a covert way, because of his attachment to 'his' employees. He was therefore offered a post as adviser to the chairman on human relations issues and a new director appointed. At first sight it seemed obvious that the human resources director should have been retained in a highly responsible role, but analysis showed that this would have severely disrupted the change process. The power situation planned in the change process was therefore modified.

Decisions made as a result of such analysis must be consistent with the vision and must not be reassessed, except in a case of *force majeure*. This is often a difficult and delicate task for a chief executive who has been working alongside the staff concerned for a long time. The emotional dimension must not, however, be allowed to prevail over the success of change, which requires the rebalancing of power in favour of those whose skills and behavioural patterns accord best with the new objectives. The setting up of intermediate solutions such keeping some managers in post temporarily or forming joint teams of 'former key person and new key person' weakens the process by reducing the essential initial effect of dislocation and by complicating the whole process of change.

Phase 2: Handling the Power Issues

The aim of handling the power issues is to gain the support of those who wield power in the business for the change process. This phase relies on assessing and monitoring the attitude of these people to the change as the process progresses. From this point we distinguish the key people, including those who occupy the top management positions, who must be given individual and personal attention by the change facilitation team, from other employees, who can be treated category by category as discussed in the preceding section.

Handling the power issues begins with an assessment of the level of support for change, using personal interviews not only with each key person but also with representatives of the various staff categories. These interviews are carried out and analysed by members of the change facilitation team. At the same time, the significance of the key personnel and of each staff category for successful change is assessed. The combined result of this assessment is shown in a table such as Figure 11.2.

This diagram identifies the most significant issues for successful change; the ones which the change facilitation team must particularly act upon. At the outset, since those we refer to as champions of change are rare, it is important to take advantage of their support by drawing attention to them, to reinforce support for change among the rest of the staff, especially with key personnel. On the other hand, there are often many opponents, and they must be handled very carefully by the change facilitation team, especially if they are destined to have a major role in the success of the transformation. Developments in the attitudes of the key people and various categories of staff are then monitored with the help of Table 7.1 in Key 4: *Steering*, which uses the same classification of the level of support for change.

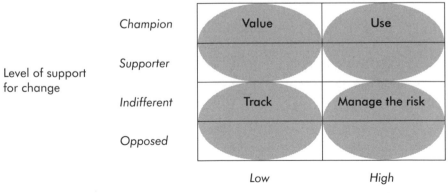

Figure 11.2   Analysis of Readiness for Change, and the Importance to Success

Members of the change facilitation team can often create a supportive attitude by using the techniques and tools for handling the emotional dimension (Key 7) and by setting up appropriate communication systems (Key 10), as well as providing effective coaching (Key 9). They can also take more specific measures, such as organising regular one- or two-day meetings with the key people in the business throughout the change process. These meetings take place off-site, to distance the participants from their everyday concerns and pressures, and to enable them to work as a group on progressing change.

The aim is to ensure that all these people understand the vision and the change process, share their ideas and take part in important decisions, all these elements being ways of obtaining or strengthening their support. These seminars are organised and led by the change facilitation team, their content and the way they are organised having been approved by senior management. They follow the same pattern as the group problem-solving techniques described in Key 7: *Handling the Emotional Dimension*. The seminars are held at points when important decisions have to be made, i.e. generally in the closing phase of defining the vision, after mobilising, at the end of the design or testing stage, and then every two months during the rest of the delivery phase. The timing of these seminars must be coordinated with the taking of major decisions to have a positive impact on participants' level of support.

Some people's resistance to the challenging of their power position may be extremely strong, and it is absolutely necessary to break down this resistance. This can be done by intensive efforts of persuasion, especially aimed at people whose support is needed, but also by moving implacable opponents to less influential positions or even by placing them under the authority of a strong person who is committed to change. Sometimes, however, the only way of overcoming certain people's resistance is to let them go.

As soon as the planned power situation has been settled on, managers have a decisive role to play in redirecting power effectively to promote change. This applies to the chief executive in relation to key personnel, but it is also the case lower down the business, where those in charge (divisional director, sales manager, factory manager, regional manager, etc.) must play an active role in redirecting power. Their performance in this role is a good indicator of their level of support for and participation in change.

Managers must establish a very clear link between the redirection of power in the business and the objectives of the vision; this link is essential if the new key people are to be identified and prove their importance. Managers must bring forward regularly the colleagues on whom they are counting to deliver the vision. This is usually done by physical proximity (private discussions, where they are seated in meetings, etc.), by mentioning their achievements in talks to staff, by displaying the results they have obtained and by actively supporting their actions. Managers must also adjust their management style to support change. We saw in Chapter 2 that management style has a strong influence on the way colleagues behave.

Once persuaded of the new distribution of power that needs to be achieved within the business, managers use all their own power to put it into effect. They make use of consultation and authority in varying proportions according to circumstances. If consultation leads to genuine agreement with the new situation, the change process will be reinforced, but in most cases consultation alone is not enough. The new situation is not accepted and people try to modify it to their advantage. This rejection is prompted by a refusal to see one's power reduced or by being disappointed in one's hope of seeing it increased further, or even by seeing the power balance modified to one's own disadvantage. A certain flexibility is necessary in the face of such situations, but it must be emphasised that this flexibility must not cast doubt on the objective or the success of change.

Experience shows that accepting a compromise, far from making change easier to achieve, actually jeopardises it, without solving the individuals' problems. Conflicts may arise and resignations may occur, so it is necessary to foresee them and know how to tackle them (this is one of the aims of the analysis carried out earlier). The wish to avoid conflicts at this stage does not prevent them, but only post-pones them and is liable to spread them by creating a chain reaction. The technique of compromise must not, however, inhibit discussion, nor must the wish to avoid conflict replace the consideration of everyone's interests, because this would only widen the conflict. If the objective of transformation is not imposed on all, including the key people, then managers will constantly have to intervene and broker compromises in response to conflicts. It is essential that managers refuse to do this from the outset and impose an overall purpose (the ultimate objective) which overrides personal interests.

The managers of an international manufacturing company had this experience when they decided to move from a structure organised by geography to one organised in worldwide product divisions. They intended the new divisions to form the top decision-making level, with commitments to results and the management of resources. The geographical areas would disappear and at the country level there would only be an office to coordinate the divisions within each country. The area and country managers strongly opposed the project, basing their argument on the special features of each country, the organisational structures which had been established, and the results that had been achieved. The group directors had certainly anticipated these reactions but, faced with such violent opposition and conscious of the role of these people in producing the group's results, they decided to let them retain significant power by setting up a division-by-country matrix structure.

Some weeks after this reorganisation had been effected, the first significant conflict arose, with a divisional head and a country head clashing over how to respond to an invitation to tender issued by one of their large international customers. The group directors had to find a compromise, which only further complicated the situation which was next taken up by the heads of the other divisions and countries. Then another conflict arose, followed by still others. The group directors had to spend considerable time resolving them, while performance in the countries concerned worsened because of the amount of energy that managers were now devoting to these conflicts and the dysfunctions which resulted. A more radical decision was made a year later, by which time the situation had become even more difficult and full of conflict.

Phase 3: Using Systems and Procedures to Redirect Power

Redirection of power is realised by modifying the business structure. The new key personnel are in fact appointed on the basis of a new structure and the new roles which follow from it. The evolution of corporate culture can also help to redirect power, but this evolution is always slow, and serves to sustain the new situation rather than helping to create it. Systems and procedures, on the other hand, offer useful opportunities to put the new power situation into effect quickly. The systems involved here are essentially those for reporting, performance appraisal and remuneration. These three systems must often be modified as part of the change process to ensure their consistency with the global objectives of the vision, but modifications can also be made to further the redirection of power.

The reporting system reflects the control structure of the business. It specifies the person or persons to whom one reports on one's activities, the decisions one wants to take and the results obtained. The reporting system is therefore almost always modified during a change process, some of these modifications being self-evident and occurring naturally. For example, superimposing geographical areas on a country-by-country structure means that country managers must now report to the new area managers and not directly to senior management. But in addition to these necessary adjustments, the way the reporting system operates can also be used to change power relations so that they support the change process. When these relations are not obvious, the new system must reinforce the power of the new key personnel and weaken that of the old. In the previous example, the wish to assert the prerogatives of the divisional heads might lead to the country-level managers of some functions (marketing, management control, etc.) reporting directly to divisional level and not to the area or country manager.

The performance appraisal system must also be modified as soon as the consolidation phase of the change process reaches general application. It is important to measure performance by the new criteria as soon as possible. This enables everyone to understand the new objectives, grasp their significance and work out their own position in relation to them. Adjustments in ways of behaving, thinking and acting become easier and quicker. The nature of the appraisal system must highlight those aspects which are in sympathy with the new objectives, and thus with the new key people. The importance given to these new aspects of behaviour, etc., can be temporarily or permanently exaggerated to reflect their priority. Thus a business setting itself the objective of reducing the time between taking an order and delivery to the customer will give priority to time-related criteria such as order processing time, production time and quality failures (meaning that a task has to be repeated). Other appraisal criteria, such as productivity and cost, will naturally be retained, but the emphasis will be on time-based management. The people who have an influence on this variable will be strengthened in their position by the vital importance attached to the time factor by the overall appraisal system. Similarly, the divisional directors cited in the earlier example will see their power increased by a new emphasis on divisional performance criteria at the expense of the geographical reporting which formerly took precedence.

The remuneration system, in its turn, clearly and straightforwardly reflects the new regime by making the variable portion of income dependent on participation in the new objectives and by making the new key personnel responsible for deciding on remuneration levels. Using the remuneration system to redirect power in line with the new objectives is usually most effective at the higher levels of management, if these people have a high proportion of variable income. Often, therefore, this is an efficient way of ensuring their active participation in change.

By acting on any of these systems, power relations can be shifted effectively, but the goal must be to act on all three systems simultaneously, because a combined change in all of them has a very much greater impact than the simple sum of separate actions on each system.

CASE STUDY ON MANAGING POWER RELATIONS: LEICESTER ROYAL INFIRMARY NHS TRUST

As explained in the previous chapter, major and spectacular changes have been achieved within the Leicester Royal Infirmary NHS Trust in an environment where emotional barriers to change are difficult to overcome. In addition, strong political barriers had to be surmounted in order to gain support from the various groups (including doctors, nurses, managers and operations staff).

Political Resistance to Change

Power plays and political resistance to change are particularly challenging in a healthcare environment:

- As a group, doctors are the most powerful people in a hospital. There are no or very few hierarchical levers to influence them:
  - the management has little influence on their salary
  - terms and conditions are subject to national agreement.
- Individually, doctors' possess significant power. It is a system of 'micropower' at the level of individual doctors. Re-engineering Programme Leader, Helen Bevan, explains: 'If a consultant vetoes your proposal, you simply cannot do it.'

- Management and doctors may pursue conflicting objectives. The former are accountable for the management and the integration of three dimensions at hospital level: quality of patient care, cost effectiveness, and utilisation of equipment, bedrooms and premises. On the other hand, doctors have accountability to provide the best and most appropriate care to each individual patient. Doctor Millan explains, 'There is a key difference between managers and doctors: the doctor minds only the one patient he or she takes care of at a given point in time. The manager's job is to go as far as possible for most of the individuals.'
- There are many other professional groups (nurses, radiologists, therapists, etc.), each with their own objectives and each individually powerful.
- The primary decision-making processes are therefore based on negotiation and consensus building.

Managing Political Resistance

'We learned several lessons on managing political resistance', explains Helen Bevan:

1. 'Do not try to sell concepts to doctors. You can do all the mobilising you want, at a conceptual level, but . . .
2. 'Work with visionary and pioneering doctors and create change with two or three of them.'
3. 'Go by peer pressure: you go from one to the other, one by one.'
4. 'Never use a "push-strategy". If you think of a change to be conducted in a speciality, make a pilot with the one who volunteers. He or she would then demonstrate it to the sceptics.'
5. 'Asking questions is better than giving answers.'

Nick Naphtalin, Medical Director and a leading member of the programme, insists on the difficulty of rolling out ideas to other people: 'Consultants are individual powers and powerful as a group. The only way to convince them was to find a critical mass of innovative first class clinical leaders. They would influence most of the others, the grey area, while a small number would never change.'

In addition, appropriate power and political management proved to be critical to the success of organisational change in two particular areas: management of benefits and anticipation of stakeholders' (doctors, nurses, management, staff) reactions.

Benefits originated in various areas including quality improvement (e.g. patient satisfaction, turnaround times, continuity of care), cost reduction (administration streamlining, staff reduction, purchasing stock reduction)

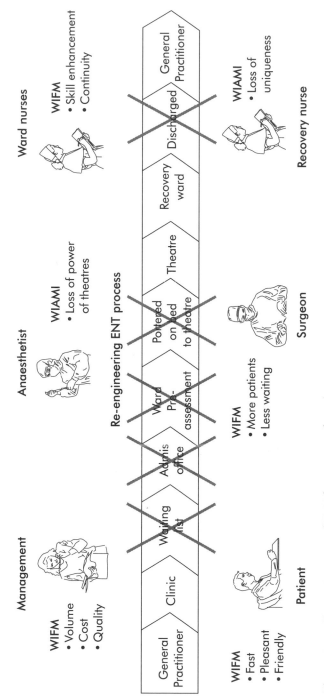

Figure 11.3   Re-engineering of ENT (Ear–Nose–Throat) Process

and purchaser value (potential volume increases through: increased theatre throughput, bed utilisation improvement, waiting list reduction, reduction in length of stay). These benefits obviously necessitated trade-offs. Improved processes (patient visit process, patient staff process) could be translated either into cost reductions (fewer staff, fewer facilities) or an increased number of patients treated ('purchaser value') while bringing better client satisfaction (quality improvement) in both cases. Yet these trade-offs often appeared excessively sensitive and difficult to deal with. If cost reductions were to be perceived as the primary objective of the programme, then acceptance of change as well as support and leadership from clinical staff could not have been achieved. On the other hand, cost reduction was critical to recover the programme investment as well as to comply more broadly with cost control and reduction objectives in the healthcare sector. In conclusion, if not handled carefully, benefits management would have critically damaged the overall success of the programme.

Careful management of each stakeholder's interest meant understanding and anticipating the impact of change on each group. Figure 11.3 shows how stakes were analysed using a WIFM/WIAMI (What is in it for me/What is against my interest?) approach. In this case, careful communication and piloting of the redesigned process helped reassure staff and nurses who felt threatened by the new process. Supportive patients' feedback reinforced the value of the approach to all stakeholders and contributed to overcoming political barriers.

The Leicester Royal Infirmary change project has won national and international recognition of success. It won the 1995 'Association in Quality in Healthcare' Silver Prize for quality innovation and the 1996 UK Hewlett-Packard Golden Helix Award. It receives 30 requests a week for site visits or speakers. The Leicester Royal Infirmary change initiative continues to achieve excellent results. As Peter Homa explains: 'We are moving now to a time of continuous improvement. The mind-set to change is moving from "change is bad" to "change is an opportunity".'

Chapter 12

Key 9: Training and Coaching

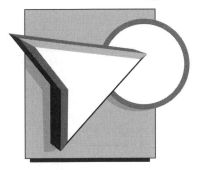

Change demands an upgrading of employees' knowledge and skills in two respects. On the one hand, the nature of their activities and responsibilities may change drastically, making it necessary for them to acquire new expertise in the way they actually fulfil their role or do their job. On the other hand, these same employees will also be in the front line of the change process, so if they are to contribute to change as effectively as possible, they will need to know how to carry out change. The aim of training is to help the workforce rapidly acquire these two types of skill.

But change also requires alterations in the way people behave, and training alone cannot achieve this. Moreover, the approaches suggested under Key 5: *Delivering*, to encourage changes in behaviour (listening to what the customer has to say, opening up to the outside world or being placed in the position of exercising the new roles and responsibilities), can also turn out to be unsatisfactory or take up too much time. The obstacles are such that it proves necessary to give some key people in the business (especially managers) one-to-one support to help them accept change and transform their methods and behaviour in line with the objectives defined in the vision. This type of support is known as coaching.

ASSESSING TRAINING AND COACHING NEEDS

What are the training needs? What are the coaching needs? Who needs to be trained or coached? The matrix shown in Figure 12.1 can be used to analyse the need and answer these questions, by deciding where all the employees involved in change fit in the needs analysis.

On the vertical axis of this matrix, the job skills include all forms of expertise related to fulfilling a role or doing a job. Change may require drastic development: for example, mastering a new software application, acquiring greater management skills or expanding one's customer relations role, where in the past the job was purely technical (such as maintenance or technical support). The change-related skills will allow employees to contribute to the change process as effectively as possible (by understanding the dynamic for change, handling resistance to change, group problem-solving, project working, etc.). While the skill needs will differ according to employees' status and their role in the business, almost all of the change skills are directed towards improving the quality and effectiveness of interpersonal relations. They will be discussed in detail later in the chapter. Most change-related skills also have a part to play in helping employees to master their everyday duties. For example, whether a cross-functional

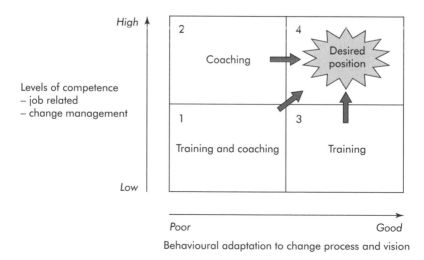

Figure 12.1   Matrix for Evaluating the Need for Training and Coaching

project structure for new product design and development, which involves creating multifunctional working groups (for research, design engineering, purchasing, manufacture, quality and costing) can be made to work depends on the employees' ability to work in teams or in networks and to solve problems or look for solutions as a group. These are precisely the skills which are developed in the course of the change process itself.

The horizontal axis of the matrix represents how appropriate employee behaviour is, both to the process of change and to the way the target organisation is intended to work, as defined in the vision. Behaviour related to change may be a matter of accepting change and being willing to take part in it. Behaviour related to the target organisation may mean greater readiness to delegate, more self-confidence *ab initio*, or a more positive attitude to risk.

Square 1 of the Matrix: Inadequate Skills/Inappropriate Behaviour

Employees in this situation do not have the necessary technical skills to take on board their new responsibilities. Shortcomings of this kind are generally easy to identify, and it is the job of human resource management in collaboration with line managers to assess them accurately and draw up an appropriate training plan.

In many cases, employees also lack the interpersonal skills so vital to the change process, such as the ability to work as a group or form a project team. To ensure that change is carried through effectively, a portfolio of methods must be made generally available throughout the business to facilitate communication and cooperation among the people who find themselves thrown together by the change process. Mobil Oil's European operation, for example, launched a Europe-wide project at the start of the 1990s aimed at transforming itself into a pan-European organisation based on common processes across all the various different countries (France, the United Kingdom, Germany, etc.). Several thousand people were involved, and from the outset, the training department undertook to train them all in the use of three tools, to optimise the course of the change process: running effect-ive meetings, group problem-solving and analysing the roles and responsibilities of contributors to a process.

Rank Xerox, faced with the worst crisis in its history some years ago, set its transformation programme in motion by training all its employees in the use of a few tools: running effective meetings, decision-making and group problem-solving.

Because of the many and complex communications the change process generates, the drive for efficiency means that a common base of expertise in carrying out change must be established throughout the business. All the employees involved in implementing change will therefore require this type of training, unless such a body of common techniques already exists, as it may, for example, if it was introduced during a recent process of change. In our experience, however, this is still all too rarely the case. Besides this general training programme, specialist training can be provided for key people in the organisation. Line managers, for example, would be trained in mobilising their subordinates.

The behaviour of employees in this square of the matrix is also inappropriate to the change process or incompatible with the objectives in view. If their position in the business (e.g. manager or opinion leader) is such that they could slow down or even obstruct the change process, it is advisable to combine their training with individual coaching. As this chapter makes clear, this form of coaching is time-consuming and must therefore be limited to a small number of people. Even coaching is not sufficient to overcome some people's obstructive effect and these people must be relieved of their duties.

On the other hand, where employees are not in a position to be obstructive, the more informal type of coaching provided by feedback from the facilitators, or from their peers or line managers, will speed up their behavioural development. These techniques will be examined later in the chapter.

We have found that behaviour which is at odds with the course of the change process or with the sought-after objectives is often linked to employees' anxiety about not being up to their new responsibilities or to their fear of losing status. Training reassures them, restores their confidence and thus itself acts as a trigger for behavioural development.

Square 2 of the Matrix: Adequate Skills/Inappropriate Behaviour

Employees in this situation have the necessary skills for self-development but their behaviour is either opposed to the change process or incompatible with the objectives defined in the vision. In other words, the skills base for change is there, but they either refuse to change or have simply not understood that the vision requires a significant change in their behaviour or attitudes. The aim of coaching will be to help these employees to become aware of their behaviour and attitudes, to analyse them and to change them. Depending on their position in the business, coaching may take the form of formal one-to-one support, or it may be less intensive and more informal.

Square 3 of the Matrix: Inadequate Skills/Appropriate Behaviour

These employees are motivated by the vision and enthusiastic about the current change process. They want to take part in it and their behaviour is consistent with the changes brought about by the vision, but their skills are inadequate. Here the task is to identify the new skills which they need to acquire and to offer them suitable training.

Square 4 of the Matrix: Adequate Skills/Appropriate Behaviour

These employees have the necessary skills and have adopted the appropriate behaviour. They are already motivated by the changes taking place, but they could be encouraged to give more of themselves. They could also be invited to play a leadership role in running the change process, or be trained as a trainer or a coach for their colleagues.

These employees play a leading role in delivery. They are the role models their colleagues can look to for an understanding of the ways of working and behaviour expected of them.

TRAINING

We have defined two types of training: one relating to job development and the other to development of the interpersonal skills necessary for the change process to succeed. In fact, the more ambitious the objectives of change and the greater the dislocation they represent in relation to the *status quo*, the more critical the dissemination of change-related skills becomes for the success of the change process. We shall illustrate this point by looking at three examples of increasingly profound change and describing the skills required in each case.

The first type of change is adapting the business to new circumstances. Typically, adaptation of this kind can be triggered by introducing a new technique or new technology into the business; for example, installing an integrated software package, such as SAP, Oracle or Baan, or computer-aided production control. The declared objective of management is of course to make a success of installing this new technology by combining it with changes in working practices or essential organisational changes. However, management has not decided to take advantage of the potential dislocation caused by the introduction of this new technology to achieve significant advances (e.g. reducing costs and service cycles) or to develop management methods (e.g. introducing closer guidance or more delegation) and behavioural patterns (e.g. reinforcing the economic and management culture, improving cross-functional links). These advances may be looked for at a later stage. In the case of this type of change, the change-related skills needed are limited and the training required is mainly technical. Given the number of people involved, it may be worth making sure that employees' skills in running meetings and group problem-solving are well developed. Because of the risk of rejection of the solution (due to fear of new technology, etc.), the project team must in addition be capable of understanding and handling resistance to change.

The second case we shall consider involves a more profound change in the business. Unlike management in the example described above, the managers in this situation decide to use the installation of new technology to call into question the way the organisation works and thereby make advances which create dislocation: to professionalise management methods and to make some behavioural changes. Training, communication and the management's powers of persuasion are not enough to achieve these much more ambitious aims. In many cases it will be necessary to convince staff of the necessity (or even urgency) of change, to involve the employees concerned and to get them to participate in analysing the *status quo* and searching for new solutions. Cross-functional working groups (expert teams) will be created. It can be seen, then, that the command of a portfolio of change-related skills is necessary for success in:

- structuring a change project (which has far more elements and far greater social implications than a project of a purely technical nature);
- guiding a change project;
- mobilising the employees concerned;
- making a collaborative critical analysis of the *status quo* (see Key 5: *Delivering*);
- understanding group dynamics;
- facilitating;
- analysing and removing resistance to change;
- communicating;
- group problem-solving, running effective meetings.

The third and last case is an example of still more profound change, involving the complete transformation of a business or of one of its divisions. Concrete advances at odds with the *status quo* are sought, both in terms of cost reduction (e.g. re-engineering or restructuring) and growth (e.g. focusing better on customers, speeding up the introduction of new products). Less tangible advances are also sought, such as creating a new shared vision and changing business values. Without a perfect command of change management, a procedure of this kind would probably be doomed to failure. In addition to the skills listed above, the business will also need to master the following:

- working out a shared vision;
- constructing a change process for a whole business or division (transformation plan);
- mobilising the entire workforce of a business or division;
- steering a complex process of change;
- organising management seminars for senior management;
- coaching managers;
- controlling the levers for behavioural changes.

These three cases show how the content of training in change management must therefore be devised to suit the nature of the change process, and particularly how intense it is. Moreover, which modules of the training programme are made available will depend on the level of responsibility of the people and their role in the business as shown schematically in Table 12.1.

Table 12.1 Training in Change Management and Level in the Organisation (example for profound change)

Position	Change management skills required
Business leaders	– Develop a vision for the business – Manage change: construct a change programme, initiate change, understand the levers for change and the obstacles – Set up a system for communicating change – Mobilise an organisation – Recognise and handle resistance to change – Steer change – Work in groups, etc.
Departmental managers (administrative and operational)	– Articulate the business vision at their unit – Manage change: construct a change programme – Recognise and handle resistance to change – Mobilise their organisation – Solve problems in groups – Set up a system for communicating change – Lead group analysis of the *status quo* (processes practices, etc.) – Draw up a target organisation or structure, etc.
Supervisors	– Recognise and handle resistance to change – Lead an Active Forces Analysis – Build a team – Run effective meetings – Solve problems in groups – Lead group analysis of the *status quo*
Employees, white-collar and blue-collar staff	– Solve problems in groups – Run effective meetings – Analyse a process or sub-process

As shown in the table, group problem-solving methods concern everyone involved in the business, while procedures for developing a vision or a target for divisional or general business development concerns only a small circle of decision makers. Thus a proper training plan must be drawn up on completion of mobilising, as soon as the objectives of change have been defined. The plan should cover both technical, job-related, and change-related training. It will generally be refined on completion of setting the objectives, which forms part of the delivery phase of the change process (see Key 5), because it is at this point that the detailed choices are made about how the organisation will develop, making it possible to identify training requirements with accuracy. The training plan is drawn up by the training division, working closely with the change facilitation team. Change-related training is first offered to the expert teams, as soon as delivery is launched, then made available to all those involved in changing the business. Technical training is given during the general application stage to all those involved in the changes.

By way of example, here is what one of the people in charge of Mobil's European change programme, which aimed to move from organisation by country to pan-European organisation, wrote in the in-house journal about change management skills:

"Our functional reorganisation programme, 'Méta', is not just the 'heavy-weight' project that we have already described. At the same time as optim-ising our management processes, 'Méta' also aims at creating a common pro-fessional culture among our European associates, to make it easier to adapt to change and speed up change. The change division and the training depart-ment have identified many skills which enable us to anticipate changes better and facilitate them. These skills consist of new ways of approaching problems and working in groups and new habits in communicating. To help us acquire these new skills, management has initiated the development of simple teaching tools which make it easier for all of us to assimilate them: cue cards describing the 'what' and the 'how' of the proposed new 'ways of doing things' will be distributed to every employee, covering for example:

- managing an effective meeting
- analysing the roles and responsibilities of a group of people
- team problem-solving
- process analysis.

These tools will be explained and their use discussed in short workshops for all personnel."

COACHING

Coaching Managers

Coaching consists of giving one-to-one support to managers to help them cope with exceptional or novel circumstances, while capitalising on their own potential and accelerating their self-development. The term is borrowed from sport, where the champion (in tennis, for example) or the champion team (in basketball, soccer, etc.) has a coach who helps them to optimise their performance and excel. Outside the realm of sport, coaching is an increasingly common technique in business today and has been the subject of many books and articles. François Mingotaud's definition of a coach seems to us to give an explanation of coaching that is particularly relevant to the context of change:

"The function of the coach (or trainer) is to advise and support the manager and his team in taking control of the structural changes which are imposed on them (business transformation, new responsibilities, management of a strategic project, etc.). He enables each person's potential to unfold and blossom, letting them all share in the aims of the business. ... In the face of the disruptions and uncertainties which complex circumstances bring, the coach is a 'mirror' who must facilitate reflection and the taking of decisions. The coach goes to work on changes, preoccupations, issues, obstructions and conflicts."

In the context of a change programme, the aim of coaching is to give one-to-one support to the managers or decision-makers who, because of their role in the business or the responsibilities they exercise, play a key part in making change successful. Coaching helps them to reinforce the aspects of their behaviour which promote the smooth running of the change process and the attainment of its goals, and on the other hand to correct or abandon those which obstruct or hinder change. The aspects of behaviour (or practices or attitudes) which coaching is concerned with include:

- the capacity to cope with the ambiguity and complexity inherent in any change process;
- enhanced expertise and a stronger command of oneself in the resolution of conflicts;
- an intrinsically confident attitude;
- a stronger inclination to accept and take the necessary risks involved in change or more generally in any new situation;
- a greater capacity to trust people, delegate to them and make them accountable;
- a greater capacity for listening;
- more efficient time management;
- the ability to overcome the fear of change, including loss of one's bearings, and perceived loss of power.

Coaching takes the form of a series of joint sessions including the coach and the manager being coached. These sessions concentrate on analysing the situations the manager has encountered, on exchanging views and on sharing experiences. The coach has the role of a catalyst or accelerator in helping the manager to recognise both his strengths and his weaknesses and then to find solutions appropriate to his particular circumstances. This approach is based on the principle that people do not learn new attitudes and ways of behaving by being given advice or having ready-made solutions imposed on them, but by analysing their own experiences, by drawing lessons from the root causes of their successes or failures, and by looking for their own solutions on the basis of their own analysis. The coach, by helping in an objective way with the analysis, speeds up this learning process. He asks questions, points out contradictions, prompts a greater depth of analysis, aids consideration and gives a neutral interpretation of past actions or events. Outside these working sessions, the coach can be present (as an observer only) during the manager's day-to-day activities, in order to improve the way in which he subsequently questions, challenges or interprets the manager's experiences. The working sessions are in fact part of a multi-stage process:

1. The coach and the manager being coached agree on the aims of the process, for example, to prepare for potentially difficult conflicts arising out of the current changes, to learn to delegate more, or quite simply to prepare oneself for overcoming fear of change. This first step relies on a factor which is essential to the success of the coaching procedure: the manager is being coached voluntarily. The coach and the coached agree on their respective roles and responsibilities: length of involvement, availability, methods employed (working sessions, observation sessions, etc.). Experienced coaches recommend that stage 1 ends in a contract between coach and coached, formalising the aims of coaching and the methods to be employed.
2. Coach and coached draw up an action plan: the number of sessions, the situations to be observed by the coach, the timetable, etc.
3. The action plan is put into effect, generally requiring six working sessions and several observation sessions over a period of two to four months.
4. The results are assessed by analysing the manager's actions, most recent experiences and day-to-day routine.
5. A plan is drawn up to ensure that the progress achieved is lasting.

At this point it is quite legitimate to ask: What about the coach himself? Who is in a position to coach the managers of the business? The literature on the subject generally suggests the following options, most of which have been tried out by different businesses:

- the immediate superior of the manager being coached
- a peer of the manager being coached
- an internal consultant
- an external consultant.

For one-to-one coaching of managers, we recommend that a coach should be found outside the business (generally an external consultant), because of the independence of mind and objectivity he can bring to bear on the business's internal issues (power, recognition, status, etc.), the more so in the context of managing change, where the power issues and emotional reactions can be particularly heightened.

Feedback or 'The Mirror Effect'

Given the financial and human resources which it requires, feedback must be limited to supporting the few managers who are the initiators of change and in charge of its implementation, as well as a few other key participants. But the other managers, and more generally all employees involved in the process of change, would also benefit from a process designed to help them make progress and develop their potential. Feedback or 'the mirror effect' is a less intensive form of coaching (see Figure 12.2). It aims to speed up the development of employee potential by encouraging them and supporting them in analysing their performance and behaviour after taking part in activities, projects or meetings. The coach, in this case, can be one of their peers or line managers, or a member of the change facilitation team who was present at the event and can give feedback.

Feedback is not a natural process and it can seem all the more threatening and lacking in objectivity when carried out by someone within the business. This is why it must be explained carefully and introduced methodically by the change facilitation team, and applied generally only when it can be a success. We shall see later how feedback can be extended to the whole business, but first, here is an example of a feedback sequence.

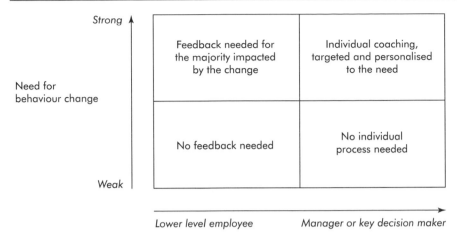

Figure 12.2   Choosing Between Coaching and Feedback

Before the Feedback Session

The person responsible for giving feedback—a member of the change facilitation team—prepares for the meeting with the employee. There is no room for improvisation, so the following points are carefully prepared for:

- What aspects of the employee's behaviour should be reinforced, modified or even dropped?
- What are the most recent specific examples of these?
- What sort of cause underlies the behaviour to be changed or dropped (e.g. fear of the unknown, lack of understanding)?
- What plan of action might be drawn up together with the employee to help him overcome the difficulties he is having?

During the Feedback Session

The coach begins the session by explaining its aims and outlining the way the discussion will develop. A good way of taking the tension out of the session is to encourage the employee to begin by stating what he sees as his own strengths. The person giving the feedback underlines the employee's view by emphasising the ways of working, behaving and doing things that he himself has identified as strengths, at the same time asking for an explanation of the things he does not understand. He may draw attention to other strengths that the employee has not mentioned, always justifying and clarifying his remarks by referring to specific and concrete examples from the employee's experience.

The employee is then invited to identify his weaknesses, with the aim of agreeing on the ways of working and behaving which he must give attention to improving. The person giving the feedback under-lines the employee's view of the weaknesses that he has also identified, asks questions about the ones he has not noticed or has not understood and describes any other opportunities for improvement which he may have noticed. Here again, he must be as practical as possible and illustrate his remarks by referring to specific recent situations. The employee is never personally challenged in the discussion, but facts and attitudes may be questioned or judged. The employee must never feel himself to be under personal attack.

For this exchange to be effective—that is, for the employee to take it on board—it must, in short, be:

- factually based
- descriptive and not judgemental
- based on a relationship between equals
- held at the right time, that is to say soon after the events which provided an opportunity to note the employee's strengths and weaknesses
- targeted on behaviour, attitudes and actions and never on the employee personally.

To conclude the feedback session, a progress plan is drawn up to help the employee to reinforce his strong points and improve on his weaknesses. This plan must include:

- a list of strengths, and recommended action for maintaining or reinforcing these strengths;
- a list of the aspects of behaviour, attitudes and ways of working that need changing;
- recommended action (e.g. training, exposure to new situations or responsibilities, specific measures) for achieving this;
- a date for a further feedback session to assess the employee's progress and to analyse and deal with any problems.

Feedback has a particular bearing on the following attitudes or behaviour:

- aptitude for group work;
- ability to listen to and understand others' ideas, discern their strengths and devise ways of improving their weakest points;
- ability to motivate others;
- capacity to grasp the positive implications of events first, and then tackle the potential problems;
- willingness to accept novelty without rejecting it out of hand;
- constructive approach to meetings;
- willingness always to help colleagues to succeed;
- capacity to recognise and reward effort;
- ability to communicate, explain and persuade.

Feedback is particularly good at accelerating behavioural changes if it is given systematically and thoroughly to the majority of the workforce. It must never be just a series of isolated events, and because there must be a limit on their workload, members of the change facilitation team cannot conceivably carry out this task on their own. In fact, the most efficient and viable long-term solution is to set up a feedback network, in which each employee gives feedback to a second employee and receives feedback in turn from a third. Once this is established, any event or initiative (meetings, projects, initiatives, etc.) can occasion an individual feedback session, which means of course that all employees must first have been trained in the technique. In addition, this procedure can make up for the infrequency of appraisal interviews, which take place only twice yearly or even annually in most businesses. However, feedback cannot, of course, be a substitute for these.

Coaching and feedback therefore constitute major levers for behavioural changes and development of potential in both the managers and the employees responsible for managing and implementing change. In addition, these techniques can help to create or reinforce a true dynamic for self-development.

THE SELF-DEVELOPMENT DYNAMIC

The process of change represents a unique opportunity for staff to learn and progress. Because of the scale of change a large number of employees at various levels and in different divisions or departments are affected.

Moreover, change must become more and more of a continuous improvement process in order to guarantee the business's long-term success. Sooner or later after its implementation, the solution adopted is called into question for various reasons (such as the appearance of cheaper or alternative products, a development in the competitive situation or a change in regulations), and the business is once again forced to embark on renewed development or change to respond to the new competitive situation, as shown schematically in Figure 12.3.

A striking example of the need for continual progress is given by one of the big European automobile manufacturers, which embarked on a huge programme to improve production-line productivity during the 1980s. The productivity gains achieved after five years, considered spectacular at the time, were of the order of 40% (measured by growth in value added per employee). To meet Japanese competition, which it anticipated would increase following the gradual removal of European customs barriers from 1992, the same manufacturer decided to launch a second productivity im-provement programme at the beginning of the nineties. The aim was to make another great leap forward in production-line productivity: a further 40% gain in the four years from 1990 to 1994. The hypothesis was that despite the spectacular progress generated in the first programme, it was both essential and possible to launch a second plan capable of generating comparable or even better results in an even shorter timescale.

Consequently, one of the major issues in the change process is the

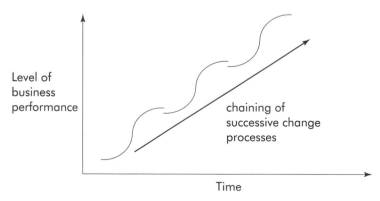

Figure 12.3   Chaining of Change Processes

need to ensure that every employee profits from the experience of change in terms of personal growth and development so that the learning curve for all employees can subsequently be steepened. Unfortunately, both the training department and the change facilitation team have limited resources, so it is unrealistic to expect that a personal trainer can be allocated to each employee to help him make the most of the opportunities provided by the process for acquiring knowledge and developing skills. The challenge is therefore to devise and put in place a self-development process which can enable employees to train themselves and to achieve greater progress than training, coaching or feedback alone could produce. In other words, the business must learn from its own experiences in order to become a learning business.

One way of doing this is by activating a virtuous circle of self-development (Figure 12.4). This takes advantage of the catalysing organisation set up to accelerate change development (see Key 5: *Catalysing*) and of the drive for participation created by Key 6: *Obtaining Participation*.

Let us take consideration as the starting point. The dynamic created by the change process gives employees the opportunity to reflect on the improvements being made, for example in the work of the expert teams. This makes them more inclined to think of ideas and put them forward, and this is made easier by having team-working and problem-solving tools at their disposal which they have been trained to use.

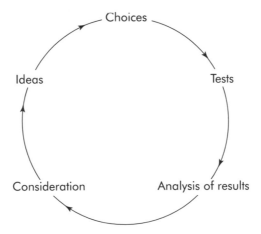

Figure 12.4   The Virtuous Circle of Self-development

Still working with the expert teams, which are responsible for finding and recommending progress targets (see Key 5: *Delivering*), employees can take part in researching and selecting the recommendations which will eventually be endorsed by those guiding the change process (the management committee or change committee). Once they have been endorsed, the employees themselves will be able to test and confirm the relevance of their ideas and recommendations during the implementation of short-term improvements or during the phases of pilot testing and general application.

When monitoring indicators are set up by the expert teams or the financial results support team, employees can monitor and assess the impact of the measures they have implemented, enabling them to see and measure the strengths and weaknesses of their ideas and the choices they have made.

Returning to the consideration stage, employees can put forward even more effective ideas than before, because of the experience they have now accumulated. Things have come full circle and employees find themselves engaged in a self-development process for which they are the prime movers.

Self-development is facilitated and reinforced by several of the characteristics of the change process:

- *Feedback and coaching*:   These activities help employees to assess their strong and weak points systematically and to devise a personal plan for improvement.
- *Delegation:*   Employees are given sufficient autonomy to allow them to act freely, without too heavy a burden of control, which would block most of the ideas, actions and initiatives that are the instigators of change and progress. Interpersonal skills training programmes include a module on awareness of the need to delegate and how it is done, especially for middle managers and supervisors, who are very often inclined to see any increase in their subordinates' autonomy as a loss of power or a threat to themselves.
- *Groupworking*:   This helps employees to think, to listen to different points of view and to acquire new concepts and methods of working together.

Training and coaching thus constitute one of the keys to change. The effectiveness and efficiency of such actions are enhanced by the work of the other keys, including catalysing, delivering, and obtaining participation. These lay the foundations for training and coaching and creating the conditions in which all employees can derive maximum benefit.

CASE STUDY ON TRAINING AND COACHING: FRANCE TELECOM

France Telecom appreciated the need to boost the performance of its organisation and processes in order to be able to face the upcoming new competition following the 1998 deregulation.

Three areas of improvement were retained as a priority; increase client focus, enhance reactivity and boost operational performance. Therefore France Telecom created a task force composed of five top managers headed by Denis Varloot and reporting directly to the CEO. Their mission was to create the France Telecom business transformation strategy and change process (the PAC). After a few months, the PAC task force had designed the transformation strategy and buy-in was obtained from the company executives. Yet Denis Varloot quickly realised that it could not be successfully implemented unless new change management techniques and competencies were introduced or reinforced within France Telecom. They included: benchmarking, project management, quality, and facilitation.

Benchmarking

A corporate benchmarking function was created.

The first objective was to reinforce the sense of urgency among France Telecom's management regarding the need for change in order to prepare the company to face competition. The benchmarking function created the conditions so that the top 200 executives could get the opportunity to be exposed to change management experiences in the telecommunications industry outside France and in any other industry which had coped or was coping with an acceleration of the pace of change in their environment. Each of these executives was invited to attend a weekly conference where a keynote speaker from another company was to speak about his experience in change management and the key lessons learned. Speakers included top representatives from Rank Xerox, Renault, Hewlett-Packard and IBM. In addition, trips were organised in Europe, the US and Asia to allow these executives to learn in more detail about other companies' lessons learned. Visits included Bell Atlantic, Bell Canada, Motorola, Philips, Federal Express, Ricoh, and United Parcel Services.

Project Management

Enhanced project management capabilities appeared to be critical in order to increase the organisation's adaptability and reactivity by creating linkages between existing functional silos. A top executive was appointed full-time and given responsibilities to boost France Telecom's capacity to manage large multi-functional projects. Several action steps were taken:

- A charter for project management was developed and communicated within the whole organisation. It defined the high level principles and organisation of projects at France Telecom.
- 12 major projects (development of a new product, a customer charter, business process reengineering, . . .) were selected as showcases. They were monitored directly by France Telecom's Chief Executive Officer on a weekly basis so that the criticality of diffusing new project management techniques and culture was understood by everybody within the company.
- A detailed project management methodology and associated techniques were developed.
- Several hundred project managers were trained both at corporate level and within the 48 regional districts.

Total Quality

'At the end of 1992, quality problems were mainly due to a lack of contact between France Telecom's divisions. The situation was symptomatic of an incoherent technocratic management process at the expense of an integrated customer approach. The change process played a key role in the evolution towards Total Quality because it encouraged focusing organisational and management decisions around customers. As a result, quality itself made a new start within France Telecom' explains Denis Varloot.

Quality techniques were introduced through a number of means including:

- Extensive customer satisfaction surveys were conducted and regularly published within the organisation .
- Visits to best-in-class companies worldwide regarding quality management were organised and attended by a large number of France Telecom executives and operational managers.
- A quality training program was implemented for managers, supervisors and technicians so that they could all contribute to accelerating quality improvement and therefore to the France Telecom transformation.

Facilitation

Competence in facilitation rapidly became a necessity for the various change actions or initiatives launched to transform the organisation in areas such as process reengineering, management development and organisation development.

Several hundred internal consultants were trained to master facilitation and change management techniques: problem solving, meeting management, as-is analysis, to-be design, overcoming resistance to change and coaching.

The following statements from France Telecom management demonstrate the prominent role of facilitation during the change process:

- 'Facilitators played a decisive part in the mobilisation of the organisation. Apart from in meetings, they gave a boost that would not have existed without them.'
- 'Change is impossible without facilitators, or needs significantly more time for similar results.'
- 'Because of the importance of rapid changes we must develop this competence and drastically increase the number of facilitators in the organisation.'

Chapter 13

Key 10: Communicating Actively

THE AIMS OF COMMUNICATION

Communication is intrinsic to the entire change process, and we have often emphasised its importance in the preceding chapters. In fact it could be said that mobilising, obtaining participation, removing opposition and hence delivering the vision are all made possible by communication. While helping in the application of the other keys, communication is also an autonomous key in itself, with its own specific aims.

The overall objective of communication is to create a flow and then to increase that flow and channel it in the required direction until the objectives of the vision have been achieved. This means making the business more mobile, more 'fluid'. But to make that possible, it must be borne in mind that communication implies the creation of inter-personal relationships, so that a dialogue can take place in which both parties listen as well as speak. Communication is *not* just about providing information, which involves a relationship between people and facts and in which the roles of speaker and listener are quite distinct. Information is only part of communication.

The overall objective of communication can be broken down into eight components in the context of change:

1. make all employees aware of the nature of the vision;
2. provide information on the progress of change;
3. give reassurance that change is justified and that it is being properly managed;
4. assist individual development by indicating the variety of options that exists;
5. draw attention to the actions of those involved in delivering change;
6. speed up resolution of any difficulties that arise;
7. spread the new patterns of behaviour that are already beginning to reinforce change;
8. reassure all concerned parties outside the business.

The first step in communication is to make all employees aware of the nature of the vision which is to guide the process of change. This task goes far beyond merely informing them, since it marks the beginning of mobilising. It is therefore a matter of indicating the point where the break with the *status quo* (dislocation) occurs and initiating a shift among employees, if only in their attitudes at this stage. Communication impinges upon all three elements of the vision: the problem, the solution and the means of implementing it. Every employee must understand the vision, as defined in Key 1, as fully as possible. Only if they have a global and accurate view of what is at stake will it be possible to make employees themselves contribute to and assume responsibility for change and avoid excessive anxiety.

Secondly, throughout the process of change (which means continuously if a business is permanently on the move), communication will inform all participants as to how it is progressing. Every employee will therefore have a clear overall understanding of the process. Their knowledge will not be restricted to what is going on in their immediate surroundings and they will not have to rely on hearsay to find out what is happening elsewhere. They will all be able to see what ground has already been covered and what still lies ahead, understand any deviations from the intended path and relate their own position to that of the process as a whole. In this way communication will demonstrate to everyone that their importance to the success of change is recognised and will encourage their involvement.

Since all change generates anxiety, one of the most important aims of communication must be to provide reassurance. Employees must be made aware of the improvements and benefits that change will bring as and when these become apparent. The fact that the change process is a controlled and consistent one must also be communicated, and employees must be given tangible evidence to set their minds firmly at rest. This kind of communication should enable employees' perception of change to develop from a more or less negative and worrying one to something more positive and hopeful.

Employees all have their own images of the business, of change and of the role it plays. This diversity of opinion should be used to help them develop towards the target situation. By making them aware of this diversity, communication should show them how limited and questionable their view of 'the world' is and present them with new perspectives and alternative points of view. Even colleagues with whom they identify may see things differently. This is how change begins, by questioning what seems certain and obvious. The process also applies to change managers, who will have to allow for this diversity of opinions and the variety of behavioural patterns and expectations resulting from it. They will come to interpret their environment in a different way and consequently respond more appropriately to it.

Drawing attention to the achievements of individuals or groups, however modest they might appear, is another aim of communication because this publicity plays an important part in the dynamic of change. In fact it gives the process of change credibility by demonstrating that things *are* changing. It also gives participants confidence by showing them that their contributions do have an impact on the process and that their efforts are recognised without being underestimated or devalued. If it is to be effective, this type of communication must be factual and practical and not degenerate into a series of 'success stories'. It should mention the results that have been achieved, but also make clear how they were achieved, what obstacles were overcome and what solutions found.

Communication should also aim to speed up resolution of the difficulties that arise. Everyone involved in change will encounter difficulties, and communication should come to their assistance by encouraging the various skills present in the business to converge on the problem, whether these are skills that are to be applied to the new situation or skills that have been acquired through developing a solution to a similar problem in another part of the business. Communication plays a part in establishing a genuine learning environment, by encouraging the development and dissemination of skills and expertise throughout the business. The emphasis on the successes achieved in different parts of the business further contributes to the learning process by accelerating the spread of best practice.

Communication also helps to spread new patterns of behaviour which are in line with the objectives of change. It does this by exploiting the inspirational power of 'role models', who will of course be the managers of the business. Communicating actively draws attention to these role models in order to help employees identify with them and change their behavioural patterns.

Active communication must also include business partners such as shareholders, customers, suppliers, etc., who may, for various reasons, need to know about changes that are taking place. Like the business's own employees, they will have to be informed and reassured. Advising them of the objectives of change and the way they are to be achieved, as well as how their own objectives are to be taken into account and integrated into the process, will undoubtedly be good for relations, although a degree of confidentiality will be required in certain areas.

PRINCIPLES OF COMMUNICATION

In order to achieve the above aims, communication must be not only good but also plentiful. As we have said, communication is more than a tool to be used when using the other keys: it is a key in itself and is intrinsic to the change process. To guarantee successful change, the potential of communication must be fully exploited.

Communication aims to create a perfect exchange of information between individuals. It therefore creates its own flow of ideas which is largely independent of established business structures and traditional operating procedures. Whereas businesses usually have a branching structure and operate from the top down, communication is more root-like, a network spreading in all directions at once. Traditional lines of communication and established systems are not bypassed; on the contrary, they are used more than ever. However, these are not enough to meet every need and must be complemented by other methods which cut across structural boundaries or work from the bottom up.

It is essential for communication to be at once vertical, horizontal and diagonal, to work from the bottom up and as well as from the top down, to cross boundaries and to operate at a global as well as a local and individual level. This 'communication explosion' plays a vital role in stimulating and accelerating movement away from the existing situation and towards the objectives of change. We have seen in previous keys that many problems can be solved by connecting people who would not normally be in contact. This is particularly true of employees who may be working on the same basic process but have different roles in the business or work in different parts of it. Experience shows that a system of communication can be established quite easily once such an explosion has taken place, for it not only encourages individual expression, which is essential to success, but also avoids the distorting effect of relaying messages through serial channels, whether direct or indirect. The communication explosion must of course be controlled, not only to ensure that it effectively supports the change process and the objectives of the vision, but also to avoid causing a commotion and a waste of time and money.

As far as content is concerned, change managers always face the dilemma of whether to communicate what is familiar or what is unfamiliar. If the content of a communication is too far removed from the current practices and ways of thinking of the recipients, it may have little or no impact because they will not know how to interpret the message or signals it contains. On the other hand, if the content is too closely related to their existing world, they will not even hear the message because it is unfamiliarity that arouses attention and makes people listen and want to get involved. It is not only the content of communication which presents this dilemma, but also its form—form and content being so closely related.

The content of a communication must therefore strike a balance between familiarity and unfamiliarity. Where that lies will vary according to what stage the process of change has reached, which group of employees are being addressed, and how flexible and re-ceptive to change they are. Since the purpose of communication is to encourage, facilitate and accelerate change, it must be ahead of the existing situation and anticipate the changes to come. Its content will be largely governed by the ultimate purpose of change, which everyone must identify with and be proud of contributing to. Just as this purpose justifies and authorises change, so it focuses and unifies communication. To be effective, communication must first be expressed in the form of an easily comprehensible yet stimulating message. All subsequent communications will be based on the same message in order to show consistency and to play a part in consolidating that message. The message should be developed at the same time as the vision.

To provide effective support for the process of change, active communication should meet four criteria.

First, it must be properly coordinated and consistent with internal and external communication policy. Communication about change takes place within an existing framework which, in the case of profound transformations or major changes, is subject to revision, particularly as regards internal communication. In such cases communication will be one of many activities and functions which undergo change, which is why internal communication so often concentrates largely on change-related issues.

Second, the communication of change must also be based on a strict communication policy which includes clear aims (the principal aims of communication having been described above) and a plan of action. This policy will have been defined at the very beginning of the change process and will evolve gradually according to the requirements of the implementation process, if this is to take a long time. The policy should define how communication is to be organised in relation to the objectives to be achieved, the messages to be conveyed, the target audience to be reached, the media used and the resources available. The communication of change must be handled meticulously and sensitively. So many different people must be communicated with under so many different circumstances, all with their own terms of reference and powers of understanding which will vary according to so many factors such as their function (e.g. marketing, production, accounting), seniority, age, length of service, education and location (e.g. head office, subsidiary, territory), that it will be necessary to have a variety of messages conveyed with a variety of media.

Third, since communication operates at both global and local levels, and the interaction between these is an essential element in the effectiveness of its contribution to the process of change, the way these two forms of communication overlap must be particularly carefully handled. This is in fact one of the principal issues facing those in charge of communication. Global communication, in terms of both message and medium, fosters consistency of action, creates a common denominator among all participants and encourages the exploitation of the resources available to the business. This must then be taken up and reinforced at a local level, which is where the vital communication (and change) takes place. This is where people discuss, ponder and react, possibly on quite an informal basis, but we know how important that is for successful change. Formal communication at the same level will fill in the gaps between global communications and generate a stronger reaction, as well as being better able to reflect the features peculiar to each situation. Change is asynchronous in terms of both the way it spreads and the way people perceive it. This can be a positive factor, but only if it is integrated into the communication of change.

Finally, communication must reinforce the involvement and participation of supporters of change, both actual and potential, who will include the 'champions' of change we have already identified and others who are either influential in forming opinion or are positioned at a communication crossroads. Communication is in fact one way of drawing attention to these people, not only by highlighting their actions in the actual messages sent out, but also by involving them in the act of communication itself: stating their opinion, providing information, acting as important communication exchanges. This will make these people commit themselves more quickly and more fully and contribute more positively to change. Line managers, who are often profoundly affected by change, are also among those whose attitudes active communication can help to reshape. It is generally advisable to build the communication system around people who are already known and respected by their colleagues, because they will provide high-quality communication, as long as they have been given appropriate training.

THE COMMUNICATORS

Everyone involved in the change process is also involved in communication and has a part to play in it. But although all of them communicate to a certain extent, certain groups of participants are in a particularly good position to do so. These include senior management, and especially the chief executive, the change facilitation team, managers in charge of internal communication and line managers.

Senior Management

Senior management (either of the business as a whole or of the part of the business affected by change), are the principal communicators. Cautious and economical in the use of words, the words of management carry considerable weight and significance. Whether the tone is warm, enthusiastic or provocative, the value of the message must remain intact. If there is more than one contributor, there must be a consistency of approach. A management statement is an event, a building block in the process of change, and each one must be issued at a key point in the process to provide the maximum support.

Because of their importance, these statements must be planned and prepared well in advance. Impromptu statements often have disastrous consequences. It is therefore best to decide right at the start of the change process when they are to be made and what form they should take, and subsequently to make any modifications that circumstances may require. As a minimum, management statements should announce the changes it has been decided to implement, set out the vision that has been defined, reassert the importance of change and management's commitment to making it succeed, reinforce mobilisation and participation, and finally, once change has succeeded, congratulate everyone on their efforts and inspire them to take advantage of the new situation to improve performance.

But senior managers will generally also show their commitment and involvement through other, less formal types of communication, such as site visits and meetings with project leaders. Changes in behaviour and attitudes among managers can also be counted as important active communication. Finally, as part of their communicating activity, senior management must not only disseminate but also receive information.

If managers are to make the right decisions and take the right action, they need to know how the change process is actually progressing. This means taking advantage of all the methods for steering change described in Key 4. They will also benefit from regular contact with the change facilitation team as well as their normal relations with all the other managers and executives in the business who are involved in the change process. However, it is also useful for them to complement these sources of information and opportunities for dialogue by direct contact with employees of every category. This might happen in the course of meetings or business trips, when direct communication can take place, or it might be done by studying comments made by employees via internal mail, voice messaging or group systems which have been set up to enable everyone to make their opinions heard. If employees know that senior management takes a direct interest in what they say, they will be more inclined to make use of these communication systems.

The Change Facilitation Team

It is the facilitation team whose members provide the inspiration for communication. They are the ones who, with the agreement of senior management, specify and organise the flow of communication and decide what action is to be taken in relation to each of their objectives. It is they also who request statements from senior management— although management can decide to intervene at any point if it is felt to be beneficial. The facilitation team organises other people's communication and communicates actively itself. It makes communication part of daily life. Through communication, it monitors the course of change, anticipates problems and ensures that the necessary resources are put in place to solve them.

Communication is an essential part of the activity of the facilitation team, which, throughout its life cycle, is the most active communicator in terms of both sending and receiving messages. It communicates both directly and indirectly in order to inspire commitment to change in everyone, documents all opposition and provides arguments to overcome it. It is the facilitation team which detects any lessening of enthusiasm or optimism and takes action to counter it. Being the hub of communication itself, it must obviously encourage and stimulate communication. In all their activities, members of the team must be constantly listening to other employees and 'selling' change.

Managers in Charge of Internal Communication

The managers in charge of internal communication also play an important part in the process and possess communications expertise. Moreover, they will already have in place the means to communicate with every employee in the business, who ought to regard them as their natural source of information. It therefore falls on these managers, in close collaboration with the facilitation team, to set up the necessary system for communicating change. Given the importance of communication in the process of change, it is preferable, if change is on a sufficient scale, to create a combined team composed of internal communications managers and facilitation team members to take care of all aspects of communication. This is the communication support team described in Key 3: *Catalysing*.

Line Managers

Line managers are also in an important position because of their usual function as relayers of opinion and information. They are therefore ideally placed to communicate with both their superiors and their subordinates. It is essential in any kind of communication to have such intermediaries (quite apart from their importance as targets for communication in their own right). In this role they must be as faithful as possible to those above them as well as those below, transmitting the information accurately without distorting or filtering it more than necessary. These intermediaries must be constantly monitored by the communication team. Since a certain amount of distortion is inevitable, it must be recognised and reduced to an absolute minimum. Direct contact between management and workforce will help to counter the negative effect of any distortion, without altogether eliminating it. But since this sort of direct contact is the exception rather than the rule, line managers remain vital to the business in the context of the change process as well as in general terms.

Other Communicators

The unions are another group with an important role to play. Their position within the business, their own communication network and their reputation often make them well placed to participate in communication, provided that they wish to convey the same messages as the communication team. In any case, they should be as closely involved as possible.

Certain other categories of staff can have an equally important role in communication by virtue of their influence on opinion, particularly sales team leaders, maintenance technicians, quality programme leaders and in-house trainers. These people should be identified at the beginning of the change process, possibly at the same time as the emotional factors and power issues are analysed.

THE MEANS OF COMMUNICATION

Communication needs organisation and support. It goes on all the time and all around, it is self-perpetuating and crucial to the process of change. It is therefore essential to ensure that it can and does fulfil its function properly.

Communication requires the commitment of full-time staff (unless the project is too small to warrant it). How many of them there are will depend on the extent and complexity of change. In the case of large-scale projects, the communication team can comprise up to a dozen people, all of whom must be fully available if the team is to be successful, since much time will be spent listening, discussing, arguing, persuading, advising, etc. Communication team members must be proactive as well as receptive. They should both influence and be influenced.

The communication team does not attempt to contain the communication explosion, but does try to control it. This means defining procedures and putting follow-up techniques into practice, which should be done in collaboration with the leader of the change facilitation team. The procedures, which are essential to the whole process, relate to official communications and the way they are issued, the way contact is established, the people involved and what the messages convey. But they obviously cannot incorporate unofficial, informal communication, which is such an important aspect of communication as a whole. The follow-up techniques are vital tools, alerting the communication team to the overall impact of communication and enabling them to guide it in the required direction. They may simply consist of bringing together all the lessons learned by members of the communication team from their contacts with the workforce, but in the case of widespread changes involving a long-term plan, it is recommended that more rigorous and systematic follow-up techniques are put in place. Monthly surveys are particularly well suited to this kind of situation; not only is the necessary information obtained, but the dissemination and discussion of the survey results reinforces communication.

One of the biggest challenges for the communication team is to make itself the main information exchange for all employees, the place where they go automatically to find out or convey information, obtain advice, or simply comment on something they have observed. Acting as such a meeting point enables them to acquire an in-depth knowledge of how communication works and how it can be focused in the desired direction. The communication team can only achieve this if it is skilled in managing change, possesses detailed knowledge of the process in hand and has the resources which will be needed by employees if they are to be encouraged to communicate (i.e. meeting and exhibition rooms, an in-house journal, publishing facilities, voice messaging systems and so on). These resources are an important part of the process because they are often the reason employees come to the communication team in the first instance. Further integration will be achieved if the resources are managed jointly by the communication team and the facilitation team.

There are numerous resources which can be used to encourage communication. The wide range of possibilities is another factor which must be taken advantage of, to cover as many different aspects of communication as possible. It can be expensive to install these resources and the cost must be justified in relation to the change process as a whole. In the case of major changes, where the costs can be substantial, the investment is generally easy to recoup. But in the case of less extensive changes, it will need to be decided in advance which resources to install and which not to. It is usually a simple matter to evaluate how appropriate a particular resource would be to the kind of change envisaged (e.g. how long it would take to install, how flexible it is, how well it can be targeted, etc.) and how acceptable it would be to employees (e.g. how simple it is to use, or whether they are already familiar with it). Resources which already exist within the business are obviously to be preferred. In-house journals and message systems, for example, which are low-cost and easy to use, should be considered first. We describe below the principal resources the communication team can use, in conjunction with the techniques and tools used during mobilising and delivery.

Briefing Meetings

The purpose of briefing meetings is to keep everyone involved in the change process informed, on a regular and systematic basis. They ensure that everyone is given reliable and authorised information. Depending on the context, the information is supplied by a senior manager or a member of the change facilitation team or the communication team, or possibly by several of these. The meetings can be organised in accordance with the structure of the business (e.g., by department, unit, workshop), by category of employee (e.g. executives, supervisors, clerical staff), by geographical location (e.g. different offices, plants) or perhaps by core process (e.g. new product development or order fulfilment). How frequently they are held will depend on circumstances, but they must be planned well in advance so that everyone knows what sort of information they are to be given and can make themselves available. They should normally take place during working hours in order to stress the importance of the changes in hand.

Discussion Meetings

The purpose of discussion meetings is to enable employees who would not normally meet to come together and discuss the change process. They may be employees who are at different levels within the same division, such as the divisional directors and blue-collar staff, or in different departments, such as IT managers and sales managers. The aim is to let everyone speak and be heard by the others (who may never have spoken to them before). So there should not be more than a few dozen people at each meeting, which should last between one and two hours. The subjects to be covered should be specified in advance and only these discussed. They might range across the entire change process or be limited to one or two aspects of it, something fundamental perhaps or something of current interest. The discussion should be chaired by a member of the communication team, who makes sure that everyone is given an opportunity to speak and that the meeting does not turn into a lecture or degenerate into a diatribe by one or two people. If these meetings are to work properly, they must be prepared in conjunction with senior managers. In all other respects, they will be organised in the same way as briefing meetings.

Exhibition Rooms

All that is required is ordinary rooms where the work of the various groups can be displayed to all employees in a fairly informal way.

Each group should be allocated a space or a panel which can be enlarged as required. The work on display might include, for example, a flowchart for a particular process under study, a description of the competitive situation, suggested alternative organisational structures, a proposed logistics system for customer deliveries, or simply a summary of the results achieved to date. It is also important for those visiting the exhibition to be able to comment on what they see. Written comments are the simplest, but other methods can be used, such as voice messaging or some kind of call centre, especially if greater confidentiality is required. The rooms should be in an easily accessible position, if possible on a main thoroughfare, which again will help to demonstrate the importance of the change process. Rooms near the senior managers' offices will imply that they are committed to its success. It is also advisable for senior managers to visit the exhibition rooms regularly, if only to read the comments made by other visitors. There should be at least one exhibition room for each site where changes are taking place.

In-house Journals

It is unusual to start a journal just for a project involving change, unless the project is particularly large scale. More often there will already be one or more in-house journals which can be put to good use in relaying information on the progress of change. Interviews, case histories and achievements can all provide material for interesting articles in which change should be a regular topic. This sort of journal is particularly useful for communicating with employees who are not directly affected by the change process and would therefore not otherwise be aware of what was going on, since the other resources call for active involvement. The creation of a dedicated journal might be considered, however, if it was thought likely to generate sufficient interest to outlive the change process. So, for example, if a business were to be reorganised on a Europe-wide basis, it might be worth launching an in-house journal covering European issues, since these would continue to be relevant even after the changes had been completed.

Voice Messaging and Viewdata Systems

These resources are increasingly widely used by businesses nowadays for all sorts of purposes, because they make constant communication available to all. The development of voice messaging systems in particular is making communication even easier and more accessible. Their advantages are numerous and should be exploited as fully as possible. Lines should be open 24 hours a day, the recorded information updated daily and questions answered quickly and appropriately, responses generally being geared to the major issues involved. It would be very expensive and probably uneconomical to provide individual answers to every question, but this should not be ruled out and the system should allow for it. It is up to the communication group to make these message systems work and they will need promoting strongly, especially to begin with. Employees must be made to want to use them, both for obtaining information and for expressing their own points of view. But once they have been set up and everyone is used to them, they will more or less run themselves. Success breeds success.

These messaging systems are preferable to a conventional helpline, which can be extremely costly and is not without disadvantages. A helpline does, of course, put the caller in direct contact with someone who can answer a wide range of questions, but this means that those who are answering the calls must be constantly briefed and updated on the change process. The high cost of doing this is rarely justified by the results, since the answers they give cannot always be absolutely consistent with the objectives of those in charge of the change process and problems are bound to occur. Nevertheless, everyone must be readily able to contact members of the facilitation team or the communication group if they need to, and a special 'hotline' could be set up for this purpose.

Video Systems

Some businesses have a system of video screens which give out information about such things as recently signed contracts, the latest share price movements, promotions and appointments, job vacancies, etc. These screens are usually positioned in busy areas, such as entrance halls, cafeterias and cloakrooms, so that they will be seen by all employees as well as by visitors. Like in-house journals, they therefore ensure that information is widely circulated and can be used to support the communication of change. Advances in communication technology, particularly digitisation, should lead to a rapid increase in the use of multimedia for internal communication and especially for communicating change.

CASE STUDY ON COMMUNICATION: PHILIPS

Communication was one of the main issues for Philips management when, in 1990, they launched the Centurion program to rebuild the company. They were in such a crisis that they needed to react immediately and efficiently. It was therefore necessary to inform employees about the situation and take rapid action so that people could know how to participate in the recovery program. The challenge lay in doing this with the total workforce (250 000) worldwide. It was made all the more difficult because internal communications was one of the very issues that the Centurion program was designed to address. The Centurion program was supposed to initiate and support a new way of communicating both within Philips and with the wider environment outside.

Within the Centurion program, communication proliferated through various channels. This proliferation and diversity contributed to accelerating the process. During the program, five means of communication were created:

1. the Centurion cascade
2. 'town' meetings
3. customer days
4. improvement projects
5. brochures.

The Centurion Cascade

This was one of the major components of the Centurion program and of the mobilising process. The Centurion cascade made sure that the message on the necessity of change and of the rebuilding program was widely and coherently spread. The cascade was considered an essential communication tool using as a vehicle the seminars of managers from three different hierarchical levels. In Chapter 5, mobilising the cascade method is described in more detail.

Town Meetings

A town meeting gathers all employees of an entity to talk around a topic directly related to the entity. The expression 'Town Meeting' comes from an

English lord who was accustomed to gather the inhabitants of his town together and discuss problems and find solutions. At Philips the meeting was used to establish open communication between managers and other employees. The meeting lasted between half a day and a whole day, during which time managers communicated progress on the Centurion program, answered questions, and took decisions. The decision-making aspect was one of the most important features of the meeting. The actions involved all employees and created a constructive dynamic. For the managers it was an important event, difficult to manage. The necessity of implementing the actions proposed was reinforced by the managers standing at the front and being very publicly involved.

The town meetings complemented the Centurion cascade. In the cascade, the pressure comes from the managers. In the town meetings, pressure and initiative come from below. The meetings develop relationships within the entity. The hundreds of such meetings enabled employees to ask questions and obtain a direct answer. Town meetings were implemented right after the first Centurion meetings; they ensured that employees did not feel excluded from the process which was to touch everybody personally, the recreation of the company.

Customer Days

The Customer Days were intended to gather together all Philips employees, whatever product division or entity they were from. They were organised by the 'Customer First' taskforce initiated by Centurion I. It was important for the company managers to step outside operational barriers and confront the major topic for the company: the customers. The first Customer Day took place in 1992. It brought together 100 000 people in Europe connected by satellite. It was called a Customer Day because the idea was to stimulate collective working for customers, whether external buyers or internal customers. Afterwards, the name was retained. Customer Days included plenary meetings at which the 100 000 employees gathered together and small working groups working on particular customer issues.

The plenary meetings took the form of video conferences and enabled participants to speak with Jan Timmer, President of Philips, and other managers during morning sessions. This live communication between group managers and employees was one of the most important moments of the Customer Day. Every employee could hear what the President had to say and gain a good insight into the company's overall direction.

The Day also aimed at elaborating ideas to improve customer satisfaction. This was the objective of work groups at each site who explained their ideas for improvements. Results were then distilled for each site and presented via the video conferences. Decisions to implement were regularly made live. The thousands of remaining ideas were not forgotten; they were examined later and frequently implemented. In 1994 a second event took place following the same pattern. It focused again on improving client satisfaction and more broadly on the Process Way, that is to say on how Philips wanted to implement the five core values:

- customer first
- people, our greatest asset
- quality in everything
- maximum return on equity
- entrepreneurship

Improvement Projects

Thousands of improvement projects were launched within the Centurion programme, the first being the task forces dedicated to working on general aspects of the whole company. Then each Centurion meeting, town meeting and Customer Day, as well as other complementary initiatives, created improvement projects with ambitious goals. These projects were extremely efficient communication tools. They brought together people who were not used to working together. In this way managers and their teams learned to improve their daily communication. Information was better spread, teamwork was more efficient and solutions to problems emerged more rapidly.

Brochures

The Centurion program was widely mentioned in numerous specific and more general internal documents. In 1994 the 'Building the Winning Company' brochure was distributed throughout the whole organisation. It summed up the Centurion programme, the successes and what needed to be done. Jan Timmer was personally involved and met with groups of employee representatives to discuss Centurion and their reactions to it. These discussions were fully documented, making the programme concrete to each and every individual.

The main lessons to be learned from this case study are that there were two decisive elements contributing to success: (i) communication has to be strongly integrated into a global change programme, and (ii) managers themselves must be directly involved in communication actions and activities.

Conclusion

The mobilising of all the resources available to a business will be increasingly important in the future to ensure that it remains on the move, and that it carries its people along with it. We have seen that making a success of change requires exploiting all the skills and all the capacities for initiative that employees possess, and not just those that have such requirements in their job description. The success and durability of the changes made will depend on enabling all the precious ideas and initiatives of individuals to find their full expression. No business will be able to go on exploiting only half, a quarter or even less of their employees' potential by reducing them to their primary function: the operative who operates, the salesperson who sells, the manager who manages, and so on. A business on the move cannot be a compartmentalised business. Confining employees to pigeonholes restricts their capacity to act or be creative and limits the value that they can contribute to the business.

As in the change implementation process we have set out to describe in this book, one of the major issues for managers over the next few years is to succeed in releasing and fostering the individual and group initiatives which will sustain the business's purpose. The participation and commitment of all employees in implementing strategy and objectives, in improving organisation and operation, in adapting culture and management style, and more besides, will be essential to business success. Making or encouraging every individual to be accountable, autonomous and committed are vital responses to the growing complexity of the business world.

Businesses will become larger and larger, more and more fluid and therefore less and less controllable by a small managing group. Managing this complexity will only be possible if new management methods are adopted at every level of the business. Information, which permeates the business, will play an increasingly important role. This   is what will enable decisions and actions to be taken quickly and intelligently. A high level of participation by everyone in the business will be needed to ensure that information circulates quickly, that everyone has access to it, and that it is analysed and used well. Every employee will need to gather, share and use information, even though the quantity of information is growing at such a rate that no one person or group of people can fully control its production, dissemination and use. Trust in every member of the business, which we have shown to be so important, backed up by development of their skills, will therefore become crucial to business activity.

Managing this complexity and using this capability to privilege both the competitiveness of the business and the satisfaction of its employees are among the major issues faced by business leaders.

This community of interest between businesses and their employees is one of the most critical factors to be developed in the businesses of tomorrow.

Bibliography

Argyris, C. (1993) *Knowledge for Action*. CA, Jossey-Bass Publishers.

Argyris, C. (1990) *Overcoming Organization Defense*. IA, USA, Allyn and Bacon.

Beer, M., Eisenstal, R. A., Spector, B. (1990) *The Critical Path to Corporate Renewal*. Boston, Harvard Business School Press.

Bennis, W., and Nanus, B. *Leaders: Strategies for Taking Charge*

Crozier, M. and Friedberg, E. (1980) *Actors and Systems: The Politics of Collective Action*. Chicago, University of Chicago Press.

Drucker, P. F. (1991) 'The New Productivity Challenge'. Harvard, *Harvard Business Review*.

Drucker, P. F. (1992) 'The New Society of Organizations. Harvard, *Harvard Business Review*.

Foucault, M. (1982) *Archeology of Knowledge*. MD, USA, Pantheon Books.

Gleick, J. (1988) *Chaos: Making a New Science*. Penguin USA.

Hamel, G. and Prahahalad, C. (1994) *Competing for the Future*. Boston, Harvard Business School Press.

Hammer, M. and Champy, J. (1993) *Reengineering the Corporation*. London, HarperCollins.

Handy, C. (1989) *The Age of Unreason*. London, Hutchinson.

Handy, C. (1994) *The Empty Raincoat*. London, Hutchinson.

Kanter, Rosabeth Moss, Stein, B. A. and Jick, T. D. (1992) *The Challenge of Organizational Change*. New York, The Free Press.

Kotter, J. P. and Heskett, J. L. (1992) *Corporate Culture and Performance*. New York, The Free Press.

Kilmann, R. H. Covin, T. J. and associates (1989) *Corporate Transformation*. San Francisco/London, Jossey-Bass.

Lawrence, P. and Lorsch, J. (1986) *Organization and Environment: Managing Differentiation and Integration*. Boston, Harvard Business School Press.

Levi-Strauss, C. (1966) *The Savage Mind*. Chicago, University of Chicago Press.

Levi-Strauss, C. (1983) *Structural Anthropology I. & H.* Basic Books 1974, Chicago, University of Chicago Press.

McFarland, L. J., Senn, L. and Childress, J. R. (1994) *21st Century Leadership*. CA, USA, The Leadership Press.

Mintzberg, H. (1993) *The Rise and Fall of Strategic Planning*. NY, Free Press.

Mintzberg, H. (1979) *Structuring of Organizations: A Synthesis of the Research*. Englewood Cliffs, Prentice Hall.

Monod, J. (1972) *Chance and Necessity*. NY, Random House.

Nanus, B. (1992) *Visionary Leadership*. San Francisco, Jossey-Bass.

Nonaka, I. (1991) 'The Knowledge-Creating Company'. Harvard, *Harvard Business Review*.

Pascale, R. T. (1984) 'Perspective on Strategy: The Real Story behind Honda's Success.' *California Management Review*.

Pascale, R. T. (1990) *Managing on the Edge*. New York, Simon & Schuster.

Pascale, R. T., Milleman, M., Crioja, L. (Nov–Dec 1997) 'Changing the way we change'. Harvard, Harvard Business Review.

Peters, T. (1987) *Thriving on Chaos*. MD, USA, Knopf.

Peters, T. (1992) *Liberation Management*. MD, USA, Knopf.

Peters, T. J. and Waterman, R. H. (1982) *In Search of Excellence*. Warner Books.

Pettigrew, A. and Whipp, R. (1991) *Managing Change for Competitive Success*. Oxford, Blackwell.

Prahalad, C. K. and Hamel, G. (1989) 'Stategic Intent.' Harvard, *Harvard Business Review*.

Prahalad, C. K. and Hamel, G. (1980) 'The Core Competence of the Corporation.' Harvard, *Harvard Business Review*.

Prahalad, C. K. and Hamel, G. (1991) 'Corporate Imagination and Expeditionary Marketing.' Harvard, *Harvard Business Review*.

Prigogine, I. and Stengers, I. (1997) *The End of Certainty*. NY, Free Press.

Prigogine, I. and Stengers, I. (1984) *Order Out of Chaos*. NY, Random House.

Schein, E. H. (1987) *Process Consultation*. Reading (MA), reprint Addison Wesley.

Senge, P. M. (1994) *Fifth Discipline*. IL, USA, Doubleday.

Stalk, G. (1988) 'Time-The Next Source of Competitive Advantage.' Harvard, *Harvard Business Review*.

Stalk, G., Evan, P. and Shulman, L. E. (1992) 'Competing Capabilities: The New Rules of Corporate Strategy.' Harvard, *Harvard Business Review*.

Stalk, G. and Hout, T. (1980) *Competing Against Time*. NY, The Free Press.

Tichy, N. N. and Stratford, S. (1993) *Control your destiny or someone else will*. NY, The Free Press.

Watzlawick, P. and Nardone, G. (1993) *The Art of Change*. San Francisco, Jossey-Bass.

Watzlawick, P. (1978) *The Language of Change*. Basic Books, Chicago, University of Chicago Press.

Watzlawick, P. (1977) *How Real is Real?* Random House.

Index

*Index compiled by
Indexing Specialists*